THE WHO'S BUYING SERIES
BY THE NEW STRATEGIST EDITORS

DISCARD

Who's
Buying
by Race
and
Hispanic Origin

5th EDITION

New Strategist Publications, Inc.
P.O. Box 242, Ithaca, New York 14851
800/848-0842; 607/273-0913
www.newstrategist.com

ISBN 978-1-935114-33-8
ISBN 1-935114-33-6

Printed in the United States of America

Contents

About the Data in Who's Buying by Race and Hispanic Origin

The spending data in *Who's Buying by Race and Hispanic Origin* are based on the Bureau of Labor Statistics' Consumer Expenditure Survey, an ongoing, nationwide survey of household spending. The Consumer Expenditure Survey is a complete accounting of household expenditures. It includes everything from big-ticket items such as homes and cars, to small purchases like laundry detergent and videos. The survey does not include expenditures by government, business, or institutions. The lag time between data collection and dissemination is about two years. The data in this report are from the 2007 Consumer Expenditure Survey, unless otherwise noted.

To produce this report, New Strategist Publications analyzed the Consumer Expenditure Survey's household spending data by race and Hispanic origin, calculating household spending indexes, aggregate (or total) household spending, and market shares. This report presents detailed spending data by race and Hispanic origin for the 10 major product and service categories: Apparel; Entertainment; Financial Products and Services; Food and Alcoholic Beverages; Gifts for People in Other Households; Health Care; Housing: Household Operations; Housing: Shelter; Personal Care, Reading, Education, and Tobacco; and Transportation.

Race and Hispanic origin definitions

When examining the data in *Who's Buying by Race and Hispanic Origin*, keep in mind the definitions of the race and Hispanic origin categories used in the Consumer Expenditure Survey. Asians include both Hispanics and non-Hispanics who identify themselves as being Asian alone and no other race. Blacks include both Hispanics and non-Hispanics who identify themselves as being black alone and no other race. Hispanics include people of any race (they could be Asian, black, or white) who identify themselves as Hispanic. The Non-Hispanic white and other group includes people who identify themselves as non-Hispanic *and* white and/or any other race except black. Thus, the non-Hispanic white and other group includes Alaska Natives, American Indians, Asians (who are also counted in the Asian column), Native Hawaiians and other Pacific Islanders, and the multiracial. Because of these overlapping definitions, numbers by race and Hispanic origin do not sum to the total in the Total Spending and Market Share tables of this report. Asians are counted twice (in the Asian group and in the Non-Hispanic white and other group). Hispanic blacks are counted twice (in the Black group and in the Hispanic group). Hispanic Asians are counted twice (in the Asian group and in the Hispanic group). Despite these overlaps, the Consumer Expenditure Survey's race and Hispanic origin categories succeed in revealing the unique spending patterns of Asians, blacks, Hispanics, and non-Hispanic whites.

How to use the tables in this report

The starting point for all calculations in this report are the unpublished, detailed average household spending data collected by the Consumer Expenditure Survey. (Note: The Consumer Expenditure Survey uses the consumer unit rather than the household as the sampling unit. This report uses household interchangeably with consumer unit for convenience, although they are not exactly the same. For the definitions, see Appendix A.) The Consumer Expenditure Survey's average spending data are shown in this report's average spending tables. New Strategist's editors calculated the figures in the other tables of this report based on the average figures. The indexed spending tables reveal whether households in a given segment spend more or less than the average household and by how much. The total (or aggregate) spending tables show the overall size of the household market. The market share tables reveal how much spending each household segment controls. These analyses are described in detail below.

• **Average Spending** The average spending figures show the average annual spending of households in 2007. The Consumer Expenditure Survey produces average spending data for all households in a segment, e.g., all households with a black householder, not just for those that purchased an item. When examining spending data, it is important to remember that by including both purchasers and nonpurchasers in the calculation, the average is less than the amount spent on the item by buyers. (See Appendix C for the percentage of households spending on products and services in 2007 and how much purchasers spent.)

Because average spending figures include both buyers and nonbuyers, they reveal spending patterns by demographic characteristic. By knowing who is most likely to spend on an item, marketers can target their advertising and promotions more efficiently, and businesses can determine the market potential of a product or service in a city or neighborhood. By multiplying the average amount Hispanics spend on groceries by the number of Hispanic households in a local area, for example, a supermarket chain can determine the importance of Hispanics to its market and how much to emphasize the foods preferred by Hispanics in its advertising.

• **Indexed Spending (Best Customers)** The indexed spending figures compare the spending of each household segment with that of the average household. To compute the indexes, New Strategist divides the average amount each household segment spends on an item by average household spending and multiplies the resulting figure by 100.

An index of 100 is the average for all households. An index of 125 means the spending of a household segment is 25 percent above average (100 plus 25). An index of 75 indicates spending that is 25 percent below the average for all households (100 minus 25). Indexed spending figures identify the best customers for a product or service. Asian households spend 26 percent more than the average household on full-service restaurant lunches (with an index of 126), for example, indicating their status as a strong market for this service. In contrast, black households spend 48 percent less than average on full-service restaurant lunches (with an index of 52), indicating their status as a weak or underserved market.

Spending indexes can reveal hidden markets—household segments with a high propensity to buy a particular product or service but which are overshadowed by other segments that account for a larger share of the market. Indexes are a particularly important tool when examining minority markets. Because Asians, blacks, and Hispanics account for a relatively small proportion of the U.S. population, the non-Hispanic white share of the market will almost always surpass the minority share. Spending indexes overcome this problem by revealing the household segments with a high propensity to buy a product or service. Black households, for example, control 20 percent of the girls' footwear market, although the black population accounts for just 12 percent of the nation's households. Consequently the spending index shows that blacks are more likely to spend on girls' footwear than any other racial or ethnic group. The average black household devotes 71 percent more than the average household to shoes for girls. This kind of information should be of vital importance to the footwear industry, keeping it focused not just on its biggest customers but also its best customers.

Note that because of sampling errors, small differences in index values may be insignificant. But the broader patterns revealed by indexes can guide marketers to the best customers.

• **Total (Aggregate) Spending** To produce the total (aggregate) spending figures, New Strategist multiplies average spending by the number of households in a segment. The result is the dollar size of the total household market and of each market segment. All totals are shown in thousands of dollars. To convert the numbers in the total spending tables to dollars, you must append 000 to the number. For example, households headed by Hispanics spent over $2 billion ($2,408,471,000) on laundry and cleaning supplies in 2007.

When comparing the total spending figures in this report with total spending estimates from the Bureau of Economic Analysis, other government agencies, or trade associations, keep in mind that the Consumer Expenditure Survey includes only household spending, not spending by businesses or institutions. Sales data also differ from household spending totals because sales figures for consumer products include the value of goods sold to industries, government, and foreign markets, which can be a significant proportion of sales.

• **Market Shares (Biggest Customers)** New Strategist produces market share figures by converting total (aggregate) spending data into percentages. To calculate the percentage of total spending on an item that is controlled by each racial and ethnic group—i.e., its market share—each segment's total spending on an item is divided by aggregate household spending on the item.

Market shares reveal the biggest customers—the demographic segments that account for the largest share of spending on a particular product or service. This report examines the spending of minorities, but naturally minority market shares are relatively small. For many products and services, however, Asians, blacks, and Hispanics account for a disproportionate share of the market. The three groups together (with some overlap, because Hispanics may be of any race) account for a substantial share of household spending on many products and services. With competition for customers more heated than ever, and with minority populations growing rapidly, business prosperity increasingly depends on successfully targeting Asian, black, and Hispanic consumers.

For more information

To find out more about the Consumer Expenditure Survey, contact the specialists at the Bureau of Labor Statistics at (202) 691-6900, or visit the Consumer Expenditure Survey home page at http://www.bls.gov/cex/. The web site includes news releases, technical documentation, and current and historical summary-level data. The detailed average spending data shown in this report are available from the Bureau of Labor Statistics only by special request.

For a comprehensive look at detailed household spending data for other demographic characteristics such as age, income, and household type, see the 14th edition of *Household Spending: Who Spends How Much on What.* New Strategist's books are available in hardcopy or as downloads with links to the Excel version of each table. Find out more by visiting http://www.newstrategist.com or by calling 1-800-848-0842.

Household Spending Trends: 2000 to 2007

Between 2000 and 2007, spending by the average household rose by 8 percent, after adjusting for inflation—to $49,638. The 8 percent rise is substantial, but it masks the onset of the recession that officially began in December of that year. Households were grappling with the economic downturn even as the government was collecting the 2007 spending data. In fact, between 2006 and 2007 spending by the average household fell by several hundred dollars, after adjusting for inflation—a sign that recession was imminent.

An examination of the 2000 to 2007 spending trends reveals two opposing forces. On the one hand, the numbers show that some households were awash in the easy money that resulted from surging housing prices and the abuse of home equity loans. On the other hand, the cost of necessities soared between 2000 and 2007, and many households were forced to trim their spending well before the official start of the recession.

Average household spending on mortgage interest grew by an enormous 22 percent between 2000 and 2007, after adjusting for inflation, as the rate of homeownership reached a record high and some families bought larger homes than they could afford. Entertainment spending grew by 20 percent as some spent their home equity on big-screen TVs and other electronic toys. Average household spending on food away from home, other lodging (mostly hotel and motel expenses), alcoholic beverages, and public transportation (mostly airfares) also grew during those years.

Ominously, however, the cost of necessities was rising sharply. The average household spent 53 percent more on gasoline in 2007 than in 2000, after adjusting for inflation. Health insurance spending rose 31 percent, and education spending was up 24 percent. The middle class was being squeezed, and consumers were cutting back. Spending on used vehicles plummeted by 26 percent between 2000 and 2007. Spending on new vehicles fell by 19 percent. Spending on women's clothes fell 14 percent, and spending on shoes was down 21 percent. Despite the record high homeownership rate, spending on household furnishings and equipment fell by 4 percent.

Then the recession hit. Those who track the government's Consumer Expenditure Survey statistics would not have been surprised by the sharp decline in household spending that followed. For years, spending trends have suggested that American households are struggling. In 2007, they finally threw in the towel and spent less than in 2006, cutting back on a growing number of items, such as food away from home. American consumers are proving once again to be cautious spenders, with enormous consequences for our economy.

Households are being squeezed by the rising cost of necessities

(percent change in spending by the average household on selected products and services, 2000–07; in 2007 dollars)

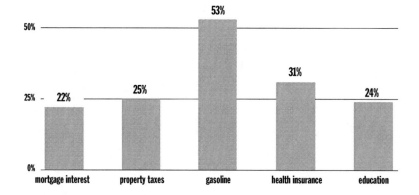

Table 1. Household spending trends, 2000 to 2007

(average annual spending of consumer units, 2000, 2006, and 2007; percent change, 2006–07 and 2000–07; in 2007 dollars)

	2007	2006	2000	percent change 2006–07	percent change 2000–07
Number of consumer units (in 000s)	120,171	118,843	109,367	1.1%	9.9%
Average before-tax income of consumer units	$63,091	$62,257	$53,761	1.3	17.4
Average annual spending of consumer units	49,638	49,776	45,809	−0.3	8.4
FOOD	6,133	6,285	6,211	−2.4	−1.2
Food at home	3,465	3,514	3,638	−1.4	−4.7
Cereals and bakery products	460	459	545	0.3	−15.7
Cereals and cereal products	143	147	188	−2.8	−23.9
Bakery products	317	313	358	1.4	−11.4
Meats, poultry, fish, and eggs	777	820	957	−5.2	−18.8
Beef	216	243	287	−11.0	−24.6
Pork	150	161	201	−7.1	−25.4
Other meats	104	108	122	−3.7	−14.5
Poultry	142	145	175	−2.1	−18.7
Fish and seafood	122	125	132	−2.8	−7.9
Eggs	43	38	41	13.0	5.0
Dairy products	387	378	391	2.3	−1.1
Fresh milk and cream	154	144	158	7.0	−2.4
Other dairy products	234	234	232	−0.2	0.7
Fruits and vegetables	600	609	627	−1.5	−4.4
Fresh fruits	202	201	196	0.7	2.9
Fresh vegetables	190	198	191	−4.3	−0.8
Processed fruits	112	112	138	−0.1	−19.1
Processed vegetables	96	98	101	−1.7	−5.1
Other food at home	1,241	1,247	1,116	−0.4	11.2
Sugar and other sweets	124	129	141	−3.5	−12.0
Fats and oils	91	88	100	2.9	−8.9
Miscellaneous foods	650	645	526	0.8	23.5
Nonalcoholic beverages	333	341	301	−2.5	10.6
Food prepared by consumer unit on trips	43	44	48	−2.8	−10.7
Food away from home	2,668	2,771	2,573	−3.7	3.7
ALCOHOLIC BEVERAGES	457	511	448	−10.6	2.0
HOUSING	16,920	16,832	14,833	0.5	14.1
Shelter	10,023	9,949	8,566	0.7	17.0
Owned dwellings	6,730	6,702	5,541	0.4	21.5
Mortgage interest and charges	3,890	3,860	3,178	0.8	22.4
Property taxes	1,709	1,696	1,371	0.8	24.6
Maintenance, repair, insurance, other expenses	1,131	1,147	993	−1.4	13.9
Rented dwellings	2,602	2,664	2,449	−2.3	6.2
Other lodging	691	583	576	18.5	20.1
Utilities, fuels, and public services	3,477	3,494	2,997	−0.5	16.0
Natural gas	480	523	370	−8.3	29.9
Electricity	1,303	1,302	1,097	0.1	18.8
Fuel oil and other fuels	151	142	117	6.4	29.3
Telephone services	1,110	1,118	1,056	−0.7	5.1
Water and other public services	434	408	356	6.3	21.8
Household services	984	975	824	0.9	19.5
Personal services	415	404	393	2.7	5.7
Other household services	569	571	431	−0.3	32.0
Housekeeping supplies	639	658	580	−2.9	10.1
Laundry and cleaning supplies	140	155	158	−9.9	−11.2
Other household products	347	339	272	2.2	27.5
Postage and stationery	152	164	152	−7.0	0.2

	2007	2006	2000	percent change 2006–07	percent change 2000–07
Household furnishings and equipment	**$1,797**	**$1,757**	**$1,865**	**2.3%**	**−3.7%**
Household textiles	133	158	128	−16.0	4.2
Furniture	446	476	471	−6.3	−5.3
Floor coverings	46	49	53	−6.8	−13.2
Major appliances	231	248	228	−6.8	1.5
Small appliances and miscellaneous housewares	101	112	105	−9.9	−3.6
Miscellaneous household equipment	840	713	880	17.9	−4.6
APPAREL AND RELATED SERVICES	**1,881**	**1,927**	**2,235**	**−2.4**	**−15.8**
Men and boys	**435**	**457**	**530**	**−4.7**	**−17.9**
Men, aged 16 or older	351	363	414	−3.3	−15.3
Boys, aged 2 to 15	84	94	116	−10.2	−27.3
Women and girls	**749**	**772**	**873**	**−3.0**	**−14.2**
Women, aged 16 or older	627	647	731	−3.1	−14.2
Girls, aged 2 to 15	122	125	142	−2.8	−14.1
Children under age 2	**93**	**99**	**99**	**−5.8**	**−5.8**
Footwear	**327**	**313**	**413**	**4.6**	**−20.8**
Other apparel products and services	**276**	**288**	**320**	**−4.2**	**−13.8**
TRANSPORTATION	**8,758**	**8,750**	**8,931**	**0.1**	**−1.9**
Vehicle purchases	**3,244**	**3,518**	**4,116**	**−7.8**	**−21.2**
Cars and trucks, new	1,572	1,849	1,933	−15.0	−18.7
Cars and trucks, used	1,567	1,613	2,131	−2.8	−26.5
Other vehicles	105	54	52	94.4	102.8
Gasoline and motor oil	**2,384**	**2,290**	**1,554**	**4.1**	**53.4**
Other vehicle expenses	**2,592**	**2,422**	**2,746**	**7.0**	**−5.6**
Vehicle finance charges	305	306	395	−0.5	−22.8
Maintenance and repairs	738	708	751	4.3	−1.8
Vehicle insurance	1,071	911	937	17.5	14.3
Vehicle rentals, leases, licenses, other charges	478	496	663	−3.6	−28.0
Public transportation	**538**	**519**	**514**	**3.6**	**4.6**
HEALTH CARE	**2,853**	**2,845**	**2,488**	**0.3**	**14.7**
Health insurance	1,545	1,507	1,184	2.5	30.5
Medical services	709	689	684	2.9	3.7
Drugs	481	529	501	−9.0	−4.0
Medical supplies	118	120	119	−1.9	−1.0
ENTERTAINMENT	**2,698**	**2,444**	**2,243**	**10.4**	**20.3**
Fees and admissions	658	623	620	5.6	6.1
Audio and visual equipment and services	987	932	749	5.9	31.8
Pets, toys, and playground equipment	560	424	402	32.2	39.2
Other entertainment products and services	493	464	473	6.3	4.2
PERSONAL CARE PRODUCTS AND SERVICES	**588**	**602**	**679**	**−2.3**	**−13.4**
READING	**118**	**120**	**176**	**−1.9**	**−32.9**
EDUCATION	**945**	**913**	**761**	**3.5**	**24.2**
TOBACCO PRODUCTS AND SMOKING SUPPLIES	**323**	**336**	**384**	**−4.0**	**−15.9**
MISCELLANEOUS	**808**	**870**	**934**	**−7.1**	**−13.5**
CASH CONTRIBUTIONS	**1,821**	**1,922**	**1,435**	**−5.3**	**26.9**
PERSONAL INSURANCE AND PENSIONS	**5,336**	**5,420**	**4,052**	**−1.6**	**31.7**
Life and other personal insurance	309	331	480	−6.7	−35.7
Pensions and Social Security*	5,027	5,089	3,571	−1.2	–
PERSONAL TAXES	**2,233**	**2,501**	**3,753**	**−10.7**	**−40.5**
Federal income taxes	1,569	1,760	2,901	−10.8	−45.9
State and local income taxes	468	534	677	−12.3	−30.8
Other taxes	196	208	176	−5.7	11.5
GIFTS FOR PEOPLE IN OTHER HOUSEHOLDS	**1,198**	**1,187**	**1,304**	**0.9**	**−8.1**

* Spending on pensions and Social Security in 2000 is not comparable with 2006 or 2007 numbers because of changes in methodology.
Note: Average spending is rounded to the nearest dollar, but the percent change calculation is based on unrounded figures. Spending by category does not add to total spending because gift spending is also included in the preceding product and service categories and personal taxes are not included in the total.
Source: Bureau of Labor Statistics, 2000, 2006, and 2007 Consumer Expenditure Surveys, Internet site http://www.bls.gov/cex/; calculations by New Strategist

Spending Overview, 2007

The economic clout of the nation's minority populations is growing. In 2007, households headed by Asians, blacks, and Hispanics spent nearly $1.4 trillion on food, clothing, housing, transportation, entertainment, and other products and services. This information comes from the Bureau of Labor Statistics' Consumer Expenditure Survey, a data collection effort that reveals the unique spending patterns of households headed by these consumers. This report presents the Consumer Expenditure Survey data by race and Hispanic origin, as well as analyses of the data that tell a compelling story about the growing importance of Asian, black, and Hispanic consumers.

In 2007, the $60,402 spent by the average Asian household surpassed the average spending of every other racial or ethnic group—including non-Hispanic whites—and exceeded the spending of the average household by 16 percent. The average black household spent $36,067 in 2007, or 27 percent less than average. Hispanic spending, at $41,501, was 16 percent below average. Non-Hispanic whites and others spent $53,003 on average in 2006, 7 percent more than the average household.

Cultural and lifestyle differences shape the unique spending patterns of each racial and ethnic group. Because Asians, blacks, and Hispanics have larger-than-average households, they are important consumers of children's products and services. Asians spend more on education than other racial and ethnic groups. Hispanics are the biggest spenders on laundry and cleaning supplies, and blacks spend the most on girls' clothes. This report details the spending of each racial and ethnic group, shows how much each group spends relative to the average household, and reveals how much of the spending on each individual product and service category each group controls.

Together, Asians, blacks, and Hispanics account for 23 percent of household spending—but there is some overlap among the groups because Hispanics may be of any race. For many products and services, the minority share of spending is even larger. Asians, blacks, and Hispanics account for 41 percent of the housing rental market, for example. They account for 34 percent of the market for fish and seafood and they control 35 percent of spending on infants' clothes.

As minority populations expand, their spending power is growing in every product and service category. Asians, blacks, and Hispanics are no longer niche markets, but important segments of customers in these economically troubled times.

Table 2. Average spending by race and Hispanic origin of householder, 2007

(average annual spending of consumer units by product and service category and by race and Hispanic origin of consumer unit reference person, 2007)

	total consumer units	Asian	black	Hispanic	non-Hispanic white and other
Number of consumer units (in 000s)	120,171	4,240	14,422	14,185	91,734
Average number of persons per consumer unit	2.5	2.8	2.6	3.2	2.3
Average before-tax income of consumer units	$63,091	$80,487	$44,381	$48,330	$68,285
Average annual spending of consumer units	49,638	60,402	36,067	41,501	53,003
FOOD	**6,133**	**7,139**	**4,601**	**5,933**	**6,399**
Food at home	**3,465**	**3,890**	**2,831**	**3,424**	**3,568**
Cereals and bakery products	460	469	365	410	481
Cereals and cereal products	143	195	127	154	143
Bakery products	317	275	237	255	338
Meats, poultry, fish, and eggs	777	1,026	834	890	752
Beef	216	221	185	255	215
Pork	150	160	185	162	142
Other meats	104	106	95	101	107
Poultry	142	158	189	193	127
Fish and seafood	122	321	138	119	120
Eggs	43	60	41	60	40
Dairy products	387	349	259	368	410
Fresh milk and cream	154	154	111	168	158
Other dairy products	234	196	147	200	252
Fruits and vegetables	600	887	455	652	615
Fresh fruits	202	309	131	227	209
Fresh vegetables	190	369	133	229	194
Processed fruits	112	116	107	106	114
Processed vegetables	96	93	83	91	98
Other food at home	1,241	1,159	919	1,104	1,310
Sugar and other sweets	124	133	88	97	134
Fats and oils	91	93	81	90	93
Miscellaneous foods	650	549	456	546	694
Nonalcoholic beverages	333	343	279	345	340
Food prepared by consumer unit on trips	43	40	15	27	50
Food away from home	**2,668**	**3,249**	**1,771**	**2,508**	**2,831**
ALCOHOLIC BEVERAGES	**457**	**290**	**198**	**262**	**525**
HOUSING	**16,920**	**22,554**	**13,494**	**15,573**	**17,662**
Shelter	**10,023**	**15,383**	**8,084**	**9,794**	**10,367**
Owned dwellings	6,730	10,387	4,110	5,419	7,346
Mortgage interest and charges	3,890	6,383	2,723	3,609	4,118
Property taxes	1,709	2,754	893	1,218	1,912
Maintenance, repair, insurance, other expenses	1,131	1,249	494	592	1,317
Rented dwellings	2,602	4,073	3,669	4,135	2,200
Other lodging	691	923	305	239	820
Utilities, fuels, and public services	**3,477**	**3,436**	**3,500**	**3,274**	**3,505**
Natural gas	480	577	475	378	497
Electricity	1,303	1,169	1,355	1,258	1,301
Fuel oil and other fuels	151	44	56	62	179
Telephone services	1,110	1,172	1,196	1,167	1,088
Water and other public services	434	475	418	409	440
Household services	**984**	**1,157**	**616**	**681**	**1,088**
Personal services	415	529	297	348	444
Other household services	569	627	319	333	644
Housekeeping supplies	**639**	**496**	**383**	**571**	**688**
Laundry and cleaning supplies	140	103	142	170	136
Other household products	347	238	184	245	386
Postage and stationery	152	155	58	157	166

	total consumer units	Asian	black	Hispanic	non-Hispanic white and other
Household furnishings and equipment	$1,797	$2,081	$910	$1,253	$2,014
Household textiles	133	125	51	112	149
Furniture	446	858	313	364	478
Floor coverings	46	35	32	15	54
Major appliances	231	196	119	136	263
Small appliances and miscellaneous housewares	101	103	58	98	108
Miscellaneous household equipment	840	765	336	528	962
APPAREL AND RELATED SERVICES	1,881	2,709	1,743	1,994	1,886
Men and boys	435	602	344	539	435
Men, aged 16 or older	351	512	236	425	358
Boys, aged 2 to 15	84	91	108	113	77
Women and girls	749	1,234	671	636	777
Women, aged 16 or older	627	1,080	513	505	663
Girls, aged 2 to 15	122	155	158	131	115
Children under age 2	93	107	103	140	85
Footwear	327	514	387	408	306
Other apparel products and services	276	252	238	272	283
TRANSPORTATION	8,758	10,921	6,458	8,035	9,234
Vehicle purchases	3,244	4,007	2,223	2,876	3,463
Cars and trucks, new	1,572	2,797	729	1,271	1,752
Cars and trucks, used	1,567	1,210	1,460	1,541	1,588
Other vehicles	105	–	34	63	123
Gasoline and motor oil	2,384	2,391	1,935	2,304	2,466
Other vehicle expenses	2,592	2,978	2,001	2,525	2,697
Vehicle finance charges	305	236	252	314	312
Maintenance and repairs	738	729	505	557	802
Vehicle insurance	1,071	1,550	872	1,280	1,073
Vehicle rentals, leases, licenses, other charges	478	463	371	375	510
Public transportation	538	1,545	299	330	608
HEALTH CARE	2,853	2,170	1,689	1,486	3,244
Health insurance	1,545	1,378	1,001	744	1,752
Medical services	709	487	370	468	799
Drugs	481	220	262	213	556
Medical supplies	118	86	57	62	136
ENTERTAINMENT	2,698	2,454	1,288	1,674	3,072
Fees and admissions	658	895	212	316	779
Audio and visual equipment and services	987	973	753	815	1,050
Pets, toys, and playground equipment	560	316	173	315	657
Other entertainment products and services	493	270	149	229	586
PERSONAL CARE PRODUCTS AND SERVICES	588	564	485	526	614
READING	118	98	46	38	141
EDUCATION	945	1,627	700	415	1,065
TOBACCO PRODUCTS AND SMOKING SUPPLIES	323	135	219	165	363
MISCELLANEOUS	808	719	453	478	913
CASH CONTRIBUTIONS	1,821	2,153	1,178	1,083	2,035
PERSONAL INSURANCE AND PENSIONS	5,336	6,868	3,515	3,837	5,851
Life and other personal insurance	309	353	245	109	350
Pensions and Social Security	5,027	6,515	3,271	3,729	5,501
PERSONAL TAXES	2,233	2,295	771	703	2,697
Federal income taxes	1,569	1,489	511	463	1,905
State and local income taxes	468	628	175	172	559
Other taxes	196	179	85	68	233
GIFTS FOR PEOPLE IN OTHER HOUSEHOLDS	1,198	1,455	698	679	1,355

Note: "Asian" and "black" include Hispanics and non-Hispanics who identify themselves as being of the respective race alone. "Hispanic" includes people of any race who identify themselves as Hispanic. "Other" includes people who identify themselves as non-Hispanic and as Alaska Native, American Indian, Asian (who are also included in the "Asian" column), Native Hawaiian or other Pacific Islander, as well as non-Hispanics reporting more than one race. Spending by category does not add to total spending because gift spending is also included in the preceding product and service categories and personal taxes are not included in the total. "–" means sample is too small to make a reliable estimate.
Source: Bureau of Labor Statistics, 2007 Consumer Expenditure Survey, Internet site http://www.bls.gov/cex/

Table 3. Indexed spending by race and Hispanic origin of householder, 2007

(indexed average annual spending of consumer units by product and service category and by race and Hispanic origin of consumer unit reference person, 2007; index definition: an index of 100 is the average for all consumer units; an index of 132 means that spending by consumer units in that group is 32 percent above the average for all consumer units; an index of 68 indicates spending that is 32 percent below the average for all consumer units)

	total consumer units	Asian	black	Hispanic	non-Hispanic white and other
Average spending of consumer units, total	$49,638	$60,402	$36,067	$41,501	$53,003
Average spending of consumer units, index	100	122	73	84	107
FOOD	100	116	75	97	104
Food at home	100	112	82	99	103
Cereals and bakery products	100	102	79	89	105
Cereals and cereal products	100	136	89	108	100
Bakery products	100	87	75	80	107
Meats, poultry, fish, and eggs	100	132	107	115	97
Beef	100	102	86	118	100
Pork	100	107	123	108	95
Other meats	100	102	91	97	103
Poultry	100	111	133	136	89
Fish and seafood	100	263	113	98	98
Eggs	100	140	95	140	93
Dairy products	100	90	67	95	106
Fresh milk and cream	100	100	72	95	103
Other dairy products	100	84	63	109	108
Fruits and vegetables	100	148	76	109	103
Fresh fruits	100	153	65	112	103
Fresh vegetables	100	194	70	121	102
Processed fruits	100	104	96	95	102
Processed vegetables	100	97	86	95	102
Other food at home	100	93	74	89	106
Sugar and other sweets	100	107	71	78	108
Fats and oils	100	102	89	99	102
Miscellaneous foods	100	84	70	84	107
Nonalcoholic beverages	100	103	84	104	102
Food prepared by consumer unit on trips	100	93	35	63	116
Food away from home	100	122	66	94	106
ALCOHOLIC BEVERAGES	100	63	43	57	115
HOUSING	100	133	80	92	104
Shelter	100	153	81	98	103
Owned dwellings	100	154	61	81	109
Mortgage interest and charges	100	164	70	93	106
Property taxes	100	161	52	71	112
Maintenance, repair, insurance, other expenses	100	110	44	52	116
Rented dwellings	100	157	141	159	85
Other lodging	100	134	44	35	119
Utilities, fuels, and public services	100	99	101	94	101
Natural gas	100	120	99	79	104
Electricity	100	90	104	97	100
Fuel oil and other fuels	100	29	37	41	119
Telephone services	100	106	108	105	98
Water and other public services	100	109	96	94	101
Household services	100	118	63	69	111
Personal services	100	127	72	84	107
Other household services	100	110	56	59	113
Housekeeping supplies	100	78	60	89	108
Laundry and cleaning supplies	100	74	101	121	97
Other household products	100	69	53	71	111
Postage and stationery	100	102	38	103	109

	total consumer units	Asian	black	Hispanic	non-Hispanic white and other
Household furnishings and equipment	100	116	51	70	112
Household textiles	100	94	38	84	112
Furniture	100	192	70	82	107
Floor coverings	100	76	70	33	117
Major appliances	100	85	52	59	114
Small appliances and miscellaneous housewares	100	102	57	97	107
Miscellaneous household equipment	100	91	40	63	115
APPAREL AND RELATED SERVICES	100	144	93	106	100
Men and boys	100	138	79	124	100
Men, aged 16 or older	100	146	67	121	102
Boys, aged 2 to 15	100	108	129	135	92
Women and girls	100	165	90	85	104
Women, aged 16 or older	100	172	82	81	106
Girls, aged 2 to 15	100	127	130	107	94
Children under age 2	100	115	111	151	91
Footwear	100	157	118	125	94
Other apparel products and services	100	91	86	99	103
TRANSPORTATION	100	125	74	92	105
Vehicle purchases	100	124	69	89	107
Cars and trucks, new	100	178	46	81	111
Cars and trucks, used	100	77	93	98	101
Other vehicles	100	–	32	60	117
Gasoline and motor oil	100	100	81	97	103
Other vehicle expenses	100	115	77	97	104
Vehicle finance charges	100	77	83	103	102
Maintenance and repairs	100	99	68	75	109
Vehicle insurance	100	145	81	120	100
Vehicle rentals, leases, licenses, other charges	100	97	78	78	107
Public transportation	100	287	56	61	113
HEALTH CARE	100	76	59	52	114
Health insurance	100	89	65	48	113
Medical services	100	69	52	66	113
Drugs	100	46	54	44	116
Medical supplies	100	73	48	53	115
ENTERTAINMENT	100	91	48	62	114
Fees and admissions	100	136	32	48	118
Audio and visual equipment and services	100	99	76	83	106
Pets, toys, and playground equipment	100	56	31	56	117
Other entertainment products and services	100	55	30	46	119
PERSONAL CARE PRODUCTS AND SERVICES	100	96	82	89	104
READING	100	83	39	32	119
EDUCATION	100	172	74	44	113
TOBACCO PRODUCTS AND SMOKING SUPPLIES	100	42	68	51	112
MISCELLANEOUS	100	89	56	59	113
CASH CONTRIBUTIONS	100	118	65	59	112
PERSONAL INSURANCE AND PENSIONS	100	129	66	72	110
Life and other personal insurance	100	114	79	35	113
Pensions and Social Security	100	130	65	74	109
PERSONAL TAXES	100	103	35	31	121
Federal income taxes	100	95	33	30	121
State and local income taxes	100	134	37	37	119
Other taxes	100	91	43	35	119
GIFTS FOR PEOPLE IN OTHER HOUSEHOLDS	100	121	58	57	113

Note: "Asian" and "black" include Hispanics and non-Hispanics who identify themselves as being of the respective race alone. "Hispanic" includes people of any race who identify themselves as Hispanic. "Other" includes people who identify themselves as non-Hispanic and as Alaska Native, American Indian, Asian (who are also included in the "Asian" column), Native Hawaiian or other Pacific Islander, as well as non-Hispanics reporting more than one race. "–" means sample is too small to make a reliable estimate.
Source: Calculations by New Strategist based on the Bureau of Labor Statistics' 2007 Consumer Expenditure Survey

Table 4. Total spending by race and Hispanic origin of householder, 2007

(total annual spending by race and Hispanic origin groups, 2007; consumer units and dollars in thousands)

	total consumer units	Asian	black	Hispanic	non-Hispanic white and other
Number of consumer units	120,171	4,240	14,422	14,185	91,734
Total spending of all consumer units	$5,965,048,098	$256,104,480	$520,158,274	$588,691,685	$4,862,177,202
FOOD	737,008,743	30,269,360	66,355,622	84,159,605	587,005,866
Food at home	416,392,515	16,493,600	40,828,682	48,569,440	327,306,912
Cereals and bakery products	55,278,660	1,988,560	5,264,030	5,815,850	44,124,054
Cereals and cereal products	17,184,453	826,800	1,831,594	2,184,490	13,117,962
Bakery products	38,094,207	1,166,000	3,418,014	3,617,175	31,006,092
Meats, poultry, fish, and eggs	93,372,867	4,350,240	12,027,948	12,624,650	68,983,968
Beef	25,956,936	937,040	2,668,070	3,617,175	19,722,810
Pork	18,025,650	678,400	2,668,070	2,297,970	13,026,228
Other meats	12,497,784	449,440	1,370,090	1,432,685	9,815,538
Poultry	17,064,282	669,920	2,725,758	2,737,705	11,650,218
Fish and seafood	14,660,862	1,361,040	1,990,236	1,688,015	11,008,080
Eggs	5,167,353	254,400	591,302	851,100	3,669,360
Dairy products	46,506,177	1,479,760	3,735,298	5,220,080	37,610,940
Fresh milk and cream	18,506,334	652,960	1,600,842	2,383,080	14,493,972
Other dairy products	28,120,014	831,040	2,120,034	2,837,000	23,116,968
Fruits and vegetables	72,102,600	3,760,880	6,562,010	9,248,620	56,416,410
Fresh fruits	24,274,542	1,310,160	1,889,282	3,219,995	19,172,406
Fresh vegetables	22,832,490	1,564,560	1,918,126	3,248,365	17,796,396
Processed fruits	13,459,152	491,840	1,543,154	1,503,610	10,457,676
Processed vegetables	11,536,416	394,320	1,197,026	1,290,835	8,989,932
Other food at home	149,132,211	4,914,160	13,253,818	15,660,240	120,171,540
Sugar and other sweets	14,901,204	563,920	1,269,136	1,375,945	12,292,356
Fats and oils	10,935,561	394,320	1,168,182	1,276,650	8,531,262
Miscellaneous foods	78,111,150	2,327,760	6,576,432	7,745,010	63,663,396
Nonalcoholic beverages	40,016,943	1,454,320	4,023,738	4,893,825	31,189,560
Food prepared by consumer unit on trips	5,167,353	169,600	216,330	382,995	4,586,700
Food away from home	320,616,228	13,775,760	25,541,362	35,575,980	259,698,954
ALCOHOLIC BEVERAGES	54,918,147	1,229,600	2,855,556	3,716,470	48,160,350
HOUSING	2,033,293,320	95,628,960	194,610,468	220,903,005	1,620,205,908
Shelter	1,204,473,933	65,223,920	116,587,448	138,927,890	951,006,378
Owned dwellings	808,750,830	44,040,880	59,274,420	76,868,515	673,877,964
Mortgage interest and charges	467,465,190	27,063,920	39,271,106	51,193,665	377,760,612
Property taxes	205,372,239	11,676,960	12,878,846	17,277,330	175,395,408
Maintenance, repair, insurance, other expenses	135,913,401	5,295,760	7,124,468	8,397,520	120,813,678
Rented dwellings	312,684,942	17,269,520	52,914,318	58,654,975	201,814,800
Other lodging	83,038,161	3,913,520	4,398,710	3,390,215	75,221,880
Utilities, fuels, and public services	417,834,567	14,568,640	50,477,000	46,441,690	321,527,670
Natural gas	57,682,080	2,446,480	6,850,450	5,361,930	45,591,798
Electricity	156,582,813	4,956,560	19,541,810	17,844,730	119,345,934
Fuel oil and other fuels	18,145,821	186,560	807,632	879,470	16,420,386
Telephone	133,389,810	4,969,280	17,248,712	16,553,895	99,806,592
Water and other public services	52,154,214	2,014,000	6,028,396	5,801,665	40,362,960
Household services	118,248,264	4,905,680	8,883,952	9,659,985	99,806,592
Personal services	49,870,965	2,242,960	4,283,334	4,936,380	40,729,896
Other household services	68,377,299	2,658,480	4,600,618	4,723,605	59,076,696
Housekeeping supplies	76,789,269	2,103,040	5,523,626	8,099,635	63,112,992
Laundry and cleaning supplies	16,823,940	436,720	2,047,924	2,411,450	12,475,824
Other household products	41,699,337	1,009,120	2,653,648	3,475,325	35,409,324
Postage and stationery	18,265,992	657,200	836,476	2,227,045	15,227,844

	total consumer units	Asian	black	Hispanic	non-Hispanic white and other
Household furnishings and equipment	**$215,947,287**	**$8,823,440**	**$13,124,020**	**$17,773,805**	**$184,752,276**
Household textiles	15,982,743	530,000	735,522	1,588,720	13,668,366
Furniture	53,596,266	3,637,920	4,514,086	5,163,340	43,848,852
Floor coverings	5,527,866	148,400	461,504	212,775	4,953,636
Major appliances	27,759,501	831,040	1,716,218	1,929,160	24,126,042
Small appliances and miscellaneous housewares	12,137,271	436,720	836,476	1,390,130	9,907,272
Miscellaneous household equipment	100,943,640	3,243,600	4,845,792	7,489,680	88,248,108
APPAREL AND RELATED SERVICES	**226,041,651**	**11,486,160**	**25,137,546**	**28,284,890**	**173,010,324**
Men and boys	**52,274,385**	**2,552,480**	**4,961,168**	**7,645,715**	**39,904,290**
Men, aged 16 or older	42,180,021	2,170,880	3,403,592	6,028,625	32,840,772
Boys, aged 2 to 15	10,094,364	385,840	1,557,576	1,602,905	7,063,518
Women and girls	**90,008,079**	**5,232,160**	**9,677,162**	**9,021,660**	**71,277,318**
Women, aged 16 or older	75,347,217	4,579,200	7,398,486	7,163,425	60,819,642
Girls, aged 2 to 15	14,660,862	657,200	2,278,676	1,858,235	10,549,410
Children under age 2	**11,175,903**	**453,680**	**1,485,466**	**1,985,900**	**7,797,390**
Footwear	**39,295,917**	**2,179,360**	**5,581,314**	**5,787,480**	**28,070,604**
Other apparel products and services	**33,167,196**	**1,068,480**	**3,432,436**	**3,858,320**	**25,960,722**
TRANSPORTATION	**1,052,457,618**	**46,305,040**	**93,137,276**	**113,976,475**	**847,071,756**
Vehicle purchases	**389,834,724**	**16,989,680**	**32,060,106**	**40,796,060**	**317,674,842**
Cars and trucks, new	188,908,812	11,859,280	10,513,638	18,029,135	160,717,968
Cars and trucks, used	188,307,957	5,130,400	21,056,120	21,859,085	145,673,592
Other vehicles	12,617,955	–	490,348	893,655	11,283,282
Gasoline and motor oil	**286,487,664**	**10,137,840**	**27,906,570**	**32,682,240**	**226,216,044**
Other vehicle expenses	**311,483,232**	**12,626,720**	**28,858,422**	**35,817,125**	**247,406,598**
Vehicle finance charges	36,652,155	1,000,640	3,634,344	4,454,090	28,621,008
Maintenance and repairs	88,686,198	3,090,960	7,283,110	7,901,045	73,570,668
Vehicle insurance	128,703,141	6,572,000	12,575,984	18,156,800	98,430,582
Vehicle rentals, leases, licenses, other charges	57,441,738	1,963,120	5,350,562	5,319,375	46,784,340
Public transportation	**64,651,998**	**6,550,800**	**4,312,178**	**4,681,050**	**55,774,272**
HEALTH CARE	**342,847,863**	**9,200,800**	**24,358,758**	**21,078,910**	**297,585,096**
Health insurance	185,664,195	5,842,720	14,436,422	10,553,640	160,717,968
Medical services	85,201,239	2,064,880	5,336,140	6,638,580	73,295,466
Drugs	57,802,251	932,800	3,778,564	3,021,405	51,004,104
Medical supplies	14,180,178	364,640	822,054	879,470	12,475,824
ENTERTAINMENT	**324,221,358**	**10,404,960**	**18,575,536**	**23,745,690**	**281,806,848**
Fees and admissions	79,072,518	3,794,800	3,057,464	4,482,460	71,460,786
Television, radio, and sound equipment	118,608,777	4,125,520	10,859,766	11,560,775	96,320,700
Pets, toys, and playground equipment	67,295,760	1,339,840	2,495,006	4,468,275	60,269,238
Other entertainment products and services	59,244,303	1,144,800	2,148,878	3,248,365	53,756,124
PERSONAL CARE PRODUCTS AND SERVICES	**70,660,548**	**2,391,360**	**6,994,670**	**7,461,310**	**56,324,676**
READING	**14,180,178**	**415,520**	**663,412**	**539,030**	**12,934,494**
EDUCATION	**113,561,595**	**6,898,480**	**10,095,400**	**5,886,775**	**97,696,710**
TOBACCO PRODUCTS AND SMOKING SUPPLIES	**38,815,233**	**572,400**	**3,158,418**	**2,340,525**	**33,299,442**
MISCELLANEOUS	**97,098,168**	**3,048,560**	**6,533,166**	**6,780,430**	**83,753,142**
CASH CONTRIBUTIONS	**218,831,391**	**9,128,720**	**16,989,116**	**15,362,355**	**186,678,690**
PERSONAL INSURANCE AND PENSIONS	**641,232,456**	**29,120,320**	**50,693,330**	**54,427,845**	**536,735,634**
Life and other personal insurance	37,132,839	1,496,720	3,533,390	1,546,165	32,106,900
Pensions and Social Security	604,099,617	27,623,600	47,174,362	52,895,865	504,628,734
PERSONAL TAXES	**268,341,843**	**9,730,800**	**11,119,362**	**9,972,055**	**247,406,598**
Federal income taxes	188,548,299	6,313,360	7,369,642	6,567,655	174,753,270
State and local income taxes	56,240,028	2,662,720	2,523,850	2,439,820	51,279,306
Other taxes	23,553,516	758,960	1,225,870	964,580	21,374,022
GIFTS FOR PEOPLE IN OTHER HOUSEHOLDS	**143,964,858**	**6,169,200**	**10,066,556**	**9,631,615**	**124,299,570**

Note: "Asian" and "black" include Hispanics and non-Hispanics who identify themselves as being of the respective race alone. "Hispanic" includes people of any race who identify themselves as Hispanic. "Other" includes people who identify themselves as non-Hispanic and as Alaska Native, American Indian, Asian (who are also included in the "Asian" column), Native Hawaiian or other Pacific Islander, as well as non-Hispanics reporting more than one race. "–" means sample is too small to make a reliable estimate.
Source: Calculations by New Strategist based on the Bureau of Labor Statistics' 2007 Consumer Expenditure Survey

Table 5. Market shares by race and Hispanic origin, 2007

(percentage of total annual spending accounted for by race and Hispanic origin groups, 2007)

	total consumer units	Asian	black	Hispanic	non-Hispanic white and other
Share of total consumer units	100.0%	3.5%	12.0%	11.8%	76.3%
Share of total before-tax income	100.0	4.5	8.4	9.0	82.6
Share of total spending	100.0	4.3	8.7	9.9	81.5
FOOD	100.0	4.1	9.0	11.4	79.6
Food at home	100.0	4.0	9.8	11.7	78.6
Cereals and bakery products	100.0	3.6	9.5	10.5	79.8
Cereals and cereal products	100.0	4.8	10.7	12.7	76.3
Bakery products	100.0	3.1	9.0	9.5	81.4
Meats, poultry, fish, and eggs	100.0	4.7	12.9	13.5	73.9
Beef	100.0	3.6	10.3	13.9	76.0
Pork	100.0	3.8	14.8	12.7	72.3
Other meats	100.0	3.6	11.0	11.5	78.5
Poultry	100.0	3.9	16.0	16.0	68.3
Fish and seafood	100.0	9.3	13.6	11.5	75.1
Eggs	100.0	4.9	11.4	16.5	71.0
Dairy products	100.0	3.2	8.0	11.2	80.9
Fresh milk and cream	100.0	3.5	8.7	12.9	78.3
Other dairy products	100.0	3.0	7.5	10.1	82.2
Fruits and vegetables	100.0	5.2	9.1	12.8	78.2
Fresh fruits	100.0	5.4	7.8	13.3	79.0
Fresh vegetables	100.0	6.9	8.4	14.2	77.9
Processed fruits	100.0	3.7	11.5	11.2	77.7
Processed vegetables	100.0	3.4	10.4	11.2	77.9
Other food at home	100.0	3.3	8.9	10.5	80.6
Sugar and other sweets	100.0	3.8	8.5	9.2	82.5
Fats and oils	100.0	3.6	10.7	11.7	78.0
Miscellaneous foods	100.0	3.0	8.4	9.9	81.5
Nonalcoholic beverages	100.0	3.6	10.1	12.2	77.9
Food prepared by consumer unit on trips	100.0	3.3	4.2	7.4	88.8
Food away from home	100.0	4.3	8.0	11.1	81.0
ALCOHOLIC BEVERAGES	100.0	2.2	5.2	6.8	87.7
HOUSING	100.0	4.7	9.6	10.9	79.7
Shelter	100.0	5.4	9.7	11.5	79.0
Owned dwellings	100.0	5.4	7.3	9.5	83.3
Mortgage interest and charges	100.0	5.8	8.4	11.0	80.8
Property taxes	100.0	5.7	6.3	8.4	85.4
Maintenance, repair, insurance, other expenses	100.0	3.9	5.2	6.2	88.9
Rented dwellings	100.0	5.5	16.9	18.8	64.5
Other lodging	100.0	4.7	5.3	4.1	90.6
Utilities, fuels, and public services	100.0	3.5	12.1	11.1	77.0
Natural gas	100.0	4.2	11.9	9.3	79.0
Electricity	100.0	3.2	12.5	11.4	76.2
Fuel oil and other fuels	100.0	1.0	4.5	4.8	90.5
Telephone	100.0	3.7	12.9	12.4	74.8
Water and other public services	100.0	3.9	11.6	11.1	77.4
Household services	100.0	4.1	7.5	8.2	84.4
Personal services	100.0	4.5	8.6	9.9	81.7
Other household services	100.0	3.9	6.7	6.9	86.4
Housekeeping supplies	100.0	2.7	7.2	10.5	82.2
Laundry and cleaning supplies	100.0	2.6	12.2	14.3	74.2
Other household products	100.0	2.4	6.4	8.3	84.9
Postage and stationery	100.0	3.6	4.6	12.2	83.4

	total consumer units	Asian	black	Hispanic	non-Hispanic white and other
Household furnishings and equipment	**100.0%**	**4.1%**	**6.1%**	**8.2%**	**85.6%**
Household textiles	100.0	3.3	4.6	9.9	85.5
Furniture	100.0	6.8	8.4	9.6	81.8
Floor coverings	100.0	2.7	8.3	3.8	89.6
Major appliances	100.0	3.0	6.2	6.9	86.9
Small appliances and miscellaneous housewares	100.0	3.6	6.9	11.5	81.6
Miscellaneous household equipment	100.0	3.2	4.8	7.4	87.4
APPAREL AND RELATED SERVICES	**100.0**	**5.1**	**11.1**	**12.5**	**76.5**
Men and boys	**100.0**	**4.9**	**9.5**	**14.6**	**76.3**
Men, aged 16 or older	100.0	5.1	8.1	14.3	77.9
Boys, aged 2 to 15	100.0	3.8	15.4	15.9	70.0
Women and girls	**100.0**	**5.8**	**10.8**	**10.0**	**79.2**
Women, aged 16 or older	100.0	6.1	9.8	9.5	80.7
Girls, aged 2 to 15	100.0	4.5	15.5	12.7	72.0
Children under age 2	**100.0**	**4.1**	**13.3**	**17.8**	**69.8**
Footwear	**100.0**	**5.5**	**14.2**	**14.7**	**71.4**
Other apparel products and services	**100.0**	**3.2**	**10.3**	**11.6**	**78.3**
TRANSPORTATION	**100.0**	**4.4**	**8.8**	**10.8**	**80.5**
Vehicle purchases	**100.0**	**4.4**	**8.2**	**10.5**	**81.5**
Cars and trucks, new	100.0	6.3	5.6	9.5	85.1
Cars and trucks, used	100.0	2.7	11.2	11.6	77.4
Other vehicles	100.0	–	3.9	7.1	89.4
Gasoline and motor oil	**100.0**	**3.5**	**9.7**	**11.4**	**79.0**
Other vehicle expenses	**100.0**	**4.1**	**9.3**	**11.5**	**79.4**
Vehicle finance charges	100.0	2.7	9.9	12.2	78.1
Maintenance and repairs	100.0	3.5	8.2	8.9	83.0
Vehicle insurance	100.0	5.1	9.8	14.1	76.5
Vehicle rentals, leases, licenses, other charges	100.0	3.4	9.3	9.3	81.4
Public transportation	**100.0**	**10.1**	**6.7**	**7.2**	**86.3**
HEALTH CARE	**100.0**	**2.7**	**7.1**	**6.1**	**86.8**
Health insurance	100.0	3.1	7.8	5.7	86.6
Medical services	100.0	2.4	6.3	7.8	86.0
Drugs	100.0	1.6	6.5	5.2	88.2
Medical supplies	100.0	2.6	5.8	6.2	88.0
ENTERTAINMENT	**100.0**	**3.2**	**5.7**	**7.3**	**86.9**
Fees and admissions	100.0	4.8	3.9	5.7	90.4
Television, radio, and sound equipment	100.0	3.5	9.2	9.7	81.2
Pets, toys, and playground equipment	100.0	2.0	3.7	6.6	89.6
Other entertainment products and services	100.0	1.9	3.6	5.5	90.7
PERSONAL CARE PRODUCTS AND SERVICES	**100.0**	**3.4**	**9.9**	**10.6**	**79.7**
READING	**100.0**	**2.9**	**4.7**	**3.8**	**91.2**
EDUCATION	**100.0**	**6.1**	**8.9**	**5.2**	**86.0**
TOBACCO PRODUCTS AND SMOKING SUPPLIES	**100.0**	**1.5**	**8.1**	**6.0**	**85.8**
MISCELLANEOUS	**100.0**	**3.1**	**6.7**	**7.0**	**86.3**
CASH CONTRIBUTIONS	**100.0**	**4.2**	**7.8**	**7.0**	**85.3**
PERSONAL INSURANCE AND PENSIONS	**100.0**	**4.5**	**7.9**	**8.5**	**83.7**
Life and other personal insurance	100.0	4.0	9.5	4.2	86.5
Pensions and Social Security	100.0	4.6	7.8	8.8	83.5
PERSONAL TAXES	**100.0**	**3.6**	**4.1**	**3.7**	**92.2**
Federal income taxes	100.0	3.3	3.9	3.5	92.7
State and local income taxes	100.0	4.7	4.5	4.3	91.2
Other taxes	100.0	3.2	5.2	4.1	90.7
GIFTS FOR PEOPLE IN OTHER HOUSEHOLDS	**100.0**	**4.3**	**7.0**	**6.7**	**86.3**

Note: "Asian" and "black" include Hispanics and non-Hispanics who identify themselves as being of the respective race alone. "Hispanic" includes people of any race who identify themselves as Hispanic. "Other" includes people who identify themselves as non-Hispanic and as Alaska Native, American Indian, Asian (who are also included in the "Asian" column), Native Hawaiian or other Pacific Islander, as well as non-Hispanics reporting more than one race. "–" means sample is too small to make a reliable estimate.
Source: Calculations by New Strategist based on the Bureau of Labor Statistics' 2007 Consumer Expenditure Survey

Spending on Apparel, 2007

Americans are spending ever less on apparel. In 2007, the average household spent $1,881 on clothes, shoes, and related items. This figure is 16 percent below the inflation-adjusted $2,235 spent by the average household on apparel in 2000. The average household cut spending on all apparel categories during the time period. Spending on women's clothing fell 14 percent, and spending on footwear declined 21 percent.Overall, Americans devoted 3.8 percent of their spending to clothes, shoes, and related products and services in 2007, down from 4.9 percent in 2000.

Asian households are the biggest spenders on apparel. In 2007, they spent 44 percent more than the average household on this category and devoted $2,709 to apparel. Hispanics also spend more than average on clothes, their apparel spending at 6 percent above average. Non-Hispanic whites spent an average amount on apparel, and blacks 7 percent less.

Asians, blacks, and Hispanics outspend the average household on a number of apparel categories. All three groups spend more than average on men's footwear and girls' clothes, for example. Blacks spend 71 percent more than average on girls' shoes, while Hispanics spend over twice the average amount on boys' shoes. Together, blacks and Hispanics control 29 percent of the footwear market. Hispanics spend 50 percent more than the average household on clothes for infants, and 21 percent more than average on men's clothes. Asians spend 72 percent more than average on women's clothes. Asians, blacks, and Hispanics dominate the market for coin-operated laundries and account for 57 percent of household spending on this service.

Table 6. Apparel: Average spending by race and Hispanic origin, 2007

(average annual spending of consumer units on apparel, accessories, and related services, by race and Hispanic origin of consumer unit reference person, 2007)

	total consumer units	Asian	black	Hispanic	non-Hispanic white and other
Number of consumer units (in 000s)	120,171	4,240	14,422	14,185	91,734
Average number of persons per consumer unit	2.5	2.8	2.6	3.2	2.3
Average before-tax income of consumer units	$63,091.00	$80,487.00	$44,381.00	$48,330.00	$68,285.00
Average spending of consumer units, total	49,637.95	60,402.09	36,067.28	41,501.12	53,002.87
Apparel, average spending	**1,880.72**	**2,708.59**	**1,742.58**	**1,994.44**	**1,885.81**
MEN'S APPAREL	**351.05**	**511.55**	**236.18**	**425.39**	**358.42**
Suits	23.47	47.56	27.16	12.27	24.57
Sport coats and tailored jackets	10.94	22.47	12.10	7.86	11.23
Coats and jackets	30.11	33.21	16.10	34.81	31.57
Underwear	14.21	18.26	14.41	16.88	13.78
Hosiery	14.69	24.32	9.39	10.86	16.03
Nightwear	1.42	1.20	1.26	0.87	1.52
Accessories	28.84	31.91	15.06	29.24	30.87
Sweaters and vests	16.69	29.62	6.87	27.24	16.69
Active sportswear	19.54	22.84	7.60	23.70	20.78
Shirts	93.00	113.18	61.31	115.75	94.75
Pants and shorts	94.21	157.60	61.88	139.71	92.90
Uniforms	3.20	4.17	2.98	5.68	2.85
Costumes	0.75	–	0.06	0.52	0.89
BOYS' (AGED 2 TO 15) APPAREL	**84.32**	**90.56**	**108.01**	**113.27**	**76.51**
Coats and jackets	5.40	6.30	9.81	7.11	4.56
Sweaters	2.13	2.14	2.04	2.95	2.01
Shirts	24.44	35.41	27.50	39.48	21.79
Underwear	5.46	5.74	8.35	5.99	4.93
Nightwear	1.12	0.58	0.61	0.78	1.25
Hosiery	4.10	1.40	5.48	4.85	3.78
Accessories	5.65	7.68	6.36	3.50	5.83
Suits, sport coats, and vests	1.31	0.68	1.81	1.18	1.25
Pants and shorts	28.46	22.52	36.44	36.29	26.05
Uniforms	3.73	4.89	7.93	8.07	2.48
Active sportswear	1.68	2.29	1.01	2.38	1.67
Costumes	0.87	0.92	0.67	0.69	0.92
WOMEN'S APPAREL	**627.31**	**1,079.71**	**512.88**	**504.98**	**662.53**
Coats and jackets	52.75	133.49	32.20	29.83	59.11
Dresses	60.41	99.54	75.41	60.05	58.06
Sport coats and tailored jackets	6.68	7.19	3.54	3.72	7.63
Sweaters and vests	48.94	51.13	18.24	39.67	55.26
Shirts, blouses, and tops	141.23	226.33	124.30	114.37	147.47
Skirts	17.10	13.00	9.98	5.48	19.83
Pants and shorts	112.31	212.54	88.01	102.65	117.39
Active sportswear	28.97	38.71	14.98	14.74	33.15
Nightwear	25.65	22.18	18.89	17.22	27.86
Undergarments	33.96	29.91	35.92	25.43	35.17
Hosiery	17.11	26.47	15.99	11.86	18.02
Suits	16.60	21.32	24.95	6.43	16.83
Accessories	58.19	–	41.00	67.38	59.47
Uniforms	4.83	4.14	7.47	4.62	4.44
Costumes	2.58	–	1.98	1.51	2.84

	total consumer units	Asian	black	Hispanic	non-Hispanic white and other
GIRLS' (AGED 2 TO 15) APPAREL	**$121.62**	**$154.53**	**$157.63**	**$130.85**	**$114.96**
Coats and jackets	6.27	14.36	21.48	2.02	4.50
Dresses and suits	11.09	14.87	24.15	9.22	9.32
Shirts, blouses, and sweaters	39.01	62.71	42.71	53.08	36.56
Skirts, pants, and shorts	30.26	27.42	33.85	31.41	29.58
Active sportswear	11.05	1.74	8.79	13.18	11.09
Underwear and nightwear	8.14	9.71	8.82	4.67	8.64
Hosiery	4.41	2.74	6.30	4.32	4.13
Accessories	6.43	–	3.99	7.09	6.72
Uniforms	3.05	0.83	6.98	4.45	2.21
Costumes	1.92	0.56	0.54	1.41	2.21
CHILDREN'S (UNDER AGE 2) APPAREL	**93.36**	**106.77**	**103.40**	**140.34**	**84.96**
Coats, jackets, and snowsuits	2.44	3.77	3.43	2.20	2.31
Outerwear including dresses	25.16	18.15	25.00	29.06	24.57
Underwear	46.89	49.05	48.65	85.11	41.11
Nightwear and loungewear	4.45	5.17	5.61	5.54	4.09
Accessories	14.43	30.64	20.70	18.42	12.87
FOOTWEAR	**327.06**	**513.93**	**386.95**	**407.61**	**305.90**
Men's	102.60	150.19	118.66	149.48	93.31
Boys'	29.95	24.92	50.20	61.38	22.31
Women's	160.33	315.58	159.72	150.35	161.64
Girls'	34.18	23.24	58.37	46.40	28.65
OTHER APPAREL PRODUCTS AND SERVICES	**275.99**	**251.54**	**237.53**	**272.00**	**282.54**
Material for making clothes	6.65	8.96	3.53	3.35	7.59
Sewing patterns and notions	6.77	1.13	3.26	6.24	7.40
Watches	20.55	38.23	23.77	25.68	19.29
Jewelry	125.79	84.05	63.71	77.02	142.87
Shoe repair and other shoe services	1.43	0.22	0.67	0.68	1.67
Coin-operated apparel laundry and dry cleaning	40.75	51.81	67.40	113.75	25.39
Apparel alteration, repair, and tailoring services	6.24	5.29	4.82	3.94	6.83
Clothing rental	2.15	0.57	0.95	2.08	2.34
Watch and jewelry repair	3.65	1.73	1.30	2.06	4.25
Professional laundry, dry cleaning	61.30	58.83	67.11	36.64	64.23
Clothing storage	0.70	0.73	1.01	0.56	0.67

Note: "Asian" and "black" include Hispanics and non-Hispanics who identify themselves as being of the respective race alone. "Hispanic" includes people of any race who identify themselves as Hispanic. "Other" includes people who identify themselves as non-Hispanic and as Alaska Native, American Indian, Asian (who are also included in the "Asian" column), Native Hawaiian or other Pacific Islander, as well as non-Hispanics reporting more than one race. Subcategories may not add to total because some are not shown. "–" means sample is too small to make a reliable estimate.
Source: Bureau of Labor Statistics, unpublished data from the 2007 Consumer Expenditure Survey

Table 7. Apparel: Indexed spending by race and Hispanic origin, 2007

(indexed average annual spending of consumer units on apparel, accessories, and related services, by race and Hispanic origin of consumer unit reference person, 2007; index definition: an index of 100 is the average for all consumer units; an index of 132 means that spending by consumer units in that group is 32 percent above the average for all consumer units; an index of 68 indicates spending that is 32 percent below the average for all consumer units)

	total consumer units	Asian	black	Hispanic	non-Hispanic white and other
Average spending of consumer units, total	$49,638	$60,402	$36,067	$41,501	$53,003
Average spending of consumer units, index	100	122	73	84	107
Apparel, spending index	**100**	**144**	**93**	**106**	**100**
MEN'S APPAREL	**100**	**146**	**67**	**121**	**102**
Suits	100	203	116	52	105
Sport coats and tailored jackets	100	205	111	72	103
Coats and jackets	100	110	53	116	105
Underwear	100	129	101	119	97
Hosiery	100	166	64	74	109
Nightwear	100	85	89	61	107
Accessories	100	111	52	101	107
Sweaters and vests	100	177	41	163	100
Active sportswear	100	117	39	121	106
Shirts	100	122	66	124	102
Pants and shorts	100	167	66	148	99
Uniforms	100	130	93	178	89
Costumes	100	–	8	69	119
BOYS' (AGED 2 TO 15) APPAREL	**100**	**107**	**128**	**134**	**91**
Coats and jackets	100	117	182	132	84
Sweaters	100	100	96	138	94
Shirts	100	145	113	162	89
Underwear	100	105	153	110	90
Nightwear	100	52	54	70	112
Hosiery	100	34	134	118	92
Accessories	100	136	113	62	103
Suits, sport coats, and vests	100	52	138	90	95
Pants and shorts	100	79	128	128	92
Uniforms	100	131	213	216	66
Active sportswear	100	136	60	142	99
Costumes	100	106	77	79	106
WOMEN'S APPAREL	**100**	**172**	**82**	**80**	**106**
Coats and jackets	100	253	61	57	112
Dresses	100	165	125	99	96
Sport coats and tailored jackets	100	108	53	56	114
Sweaters and vests	100	104	37	81	113
Shirts, blouses, and tops	100	160	88	81	104
Skirts	100	76	58	32	116
Pants and shorts	100	189	78	91	105
Active sportswear	100	134	52	51	114
Nightwear	100	86	74	67	109
Undergarments	100	88	106	75	104
Hosiery	100	155	93	69	105
Suits	100	128	150	39	101
Accessories	100	–	70	116	102
Uniforms	100	86	155	96	92
Costumes	100	–	77	59	110

	total consumer units	Asian	black	Hispanic	non-Hispanic white and other
GIRLS' (AGED 2 TO 15) APPAREL	**100**	**127**	**130**	**108**	**95**
Coats and jackets	100	229	343	32	72
Dresses and suits	100	134	218	83	84
Shirts, blouses, and sweaters	100	161	109	136	94
Skirts, pants, and shorts	100	91	112	104	98
Active sportswear	100	16	80	119	100
Underwear and nightwear	100	119	108	57	106
Hosiery	100	62	143	98	94
Accessories	100	–	62	110	105
Uniforms	100	27	229	146	72
Costumes	100	29	28	73	115
CHILDREN'S (UNDER AGE 2) APPAREL	**100**	**114**	**111**	**150**	**91**
Coats, jackets, and snowsuits	100	155	141	90	95
Outerwear including dresses	100	72	99	116	98
Underwear	100	105	104	182	88
Nightwear and loungewear	100	116	126	124	92
Accessories	100	212	143	128	89
FOOTWEAR	**100**	**157**	**118**	**125**	**94**
Men's	100	146	116	146	91
Boys'	100	83	168	205	74
Women's	100	197	100	94	101
Girls'	100	68	171	136	84
OTHER APPAREL PRODUCTS AND SERVICES	**100**	**91**	**86**	**99**	**102**
Material for making clothes	100	135	53	50	114
Sewing patterns and notions	100	17	48	92	109
Watches	100	186	116	125	94
Jewelry	100	67	51	61	114
Shoe repair and other shoe services	100	15	47	48	117
Coin-operated apparel laundry and dry cleaning	100	127	165	279	62
Apparel alteration, repair, and tailoring services	100	85	77	63	109
Clothing rental	100	27	44	97	109
Watch and jewelry repair	100	47	36	56	116
Professional laundry, dry cleaning	100	96	109	60	105
Clothing storage	100	104	144	80	96

Note: "Asian" and "black" include Hispanics and non-Hispanics who identify themselves as being of the respective race alone. "Hispanic" includes people of any race who identify themselves as Hispanic. "Other" includes people who identify themselves as non-Hispanic and as Alaska Native, American Indian, Asian (who are also included in the "Asian" column), Native Hawaiian or other Pacific Islander, as well as non-Hispanics reporting more than one race. "–" means sample is too small to make a reliable estimate.
Source: Calculations by New Strategist based on the Bureau of Labor Statistics' 2007 Consumer Expenditure Survey

Table 8. Apparel: Total spending by race and Hispanic origin, 2007

(total annual spending on apparel, accessories, and related services, by race and Hispanic origin groups, 2007; consumer units and dollars in thousands)

	total consumer units	Asian	black	Hispanic	non-Hispanic white and other
Number of consumer units	120,171	4,240	14,422	14,185	91,734
Total spending of all consumer units	$5,965,042,089	$256,104,862	$520,162,312	$588,693,387	$4,862,165,277
Apparel, total spending	226,008,003	11,484,422	25,131,489	28,291,131	172,992,895
MEN'S APPAREL	**42,186,030**	**2,168,972**	**3,406,188**	**6,034,157**	**32,879,300**
Suits	2,820,413	201,654	391,702	174,050	2,253,904
Sport coats and tailored jackets	1,314,671	95,273	174,506	111,494	1,030,173
Coats and jackets	3,618,349	140,810	232,194	493,780	2,896,042
Underwear	1,707,630	77,422	207,821	239,443	1,264,095
Hosiery	1,765,312	103,117	135,423	154,049	1,470,496
Nightwear	170,643	5,088	18,172	12,341	139,436
Accessories	3,465,732	135,298	217,195	414,769	2,831,829
Sweaters and vests	2,005,654	125,589	99,079	386,399	1,531,040
Active sportswear	2,348,141	96,842	109,607	336,185	1,906,233
Shirts	11,175,903	479,883	884,213	1,641,914	8,691,797
Pants and shorts	11,321,310	668,224	892,433	1,981,786	8,522,089
Uniforms	384,547	17,681	42,978	80,571	261,442
Costumes	90,128	–	865	7,376	81,643
BOYS' (AGED 2 TO 15) APPAREL	**10,132,819**	**383,974**	**1,557,720**	**1,606,735**	**7,018,568**
Coats and jackets	648,923	26,712	141,480	100,855	418,307
Sweaters	255,964	9,074	29,421	41,846	184,385
Shirts	2,936,979	150,138	396,605	560,024	1,998,884
Underwear	656,134	24,338	120,424	84,968	452,249
Nightwear	134,592	2,459	8,797	11,064	114,668
Hosiery	492,701	5,936	79,033	68,797	346,755
Accessories	678,966	32,563	91,724	49,648	534,809
Suits, sport coats, and vests	157,424	2,883	26,104	16,738	114,668
Pants and shorts	3,420,067	95,485	525,538	514,774	2,389,671
Uniforms	448,238	20,734	114,366	114,473	227,500
Active sportswear	201,887	9,710	14,566	33,760	153,196
Costumes	104,549	3,901	9,663	9,788	84,395
WOMEN'S APPAREL	**75,384,470**	**4,577,970**	**7,396,755**	**7,163,141**	**60,776,527**
Coats and jackets	6,339,020	565,998	464,388	423,139	5,422,397
Dresses	7,259,530	422,050	1,087,563	851,809	5,326,076
Sport coats and tailored jackets	802,742	30,486	51,054	52,768	699,930
Sweaters and vests	5,881,169	216,791	263,057	562,719	5,069,221
Shirts, blouses, and tops	16,971,750	959,639	1,792,655	1,622,338	13,528,013
Skirts	2,054,924	55,120	143,932	77,734	1,819,085
Pants and shorts	13,496,405	901,170	1,269,280	1,456,090	10,768,654
Active sportswear	3,481,354	164,130	216,042	209,087	3,040,982
Nightwear	3,082,386	94,043	272,432	244,266	2,555,709
Undergarments	4,081,007	126,818	518,038	360,725	3,226,285
Hosiery	2,056,126	112,233	230,608	168,234	1,653,047
Suits	1,994,839	90,397	359,829	91,210	1,543,883
Accessories	6,992,750	–	591,302	955,785	5,455,421
Uniforms	580,426	17,554	107,732	65,535	407,299
Costumes	310,041	–	28,556	21,419	260,525

	total consumer units	Asian	black	Hispanic	non-Hispanic white and other
GIRLS' (AGED 2 TO 15) APPAREL	**$14,615,197**	**$655,207**	**$2,273,340**	**$1,856,107**	**$10,545,741**
Coats and jackets	753,472	60,886	309,785	28,654	412,803
Dresses and suits	1,332,696	63,049	348,291	130,786	854,961
Shirts, blouses, and sweaters	4,687,871	265,890	615,964	752,940	3,353,795
Skirts, pants, and shorts	3,636,374	116,261	488,185	445,551	2,713,492
Active sportswear	1,327,890	7,378	126,769	186,958	1,017,330
Underwear and nightwear	978,192	41,170	127,202	66,244	792,582
Hosiery	529,954	11,618	90,859	61,279	378,861
Accessories	772,700	–	57,544	100,572	616,452
Uniforms	366,522	3,519	100,666	63,123	202,732
Costumes	230,728	2,374	7,788	20,001	202,732
CHILDREN'S (UNDER AGE 2) APPAREL	**11,219,165**	**452,705**	**1,491,235**	**1,990,723**	**7,793,721**
Coats, jackets, and snowsuits	293,217	15,985	49,467	31,207	211,906
Outerwear including dresses	3,023,502	76,956	360,550	412,216	2,253,904
Underwear	5,634,818	207,972	701,630	1,207,285	3,771,185
Nightwear and loungewear	534,761	21,921	80,907	78,585	375,192
Accessories	1,734,068	129,914	298,535	261,288	1,180,617
FOOTWEAR	**39,303,127**	**2,179,063**	**5,580,593**	**5,781,948**	**28,061,431**
Men's	12,329,545	636,806	1,711,315	2,120,374	8,559,700
Boys'	3,599,121	105,661	723,984	870,675	2,046,586
Women's	19,267,016	1,338,059	2,303,482	2,132,715	14,827,884
Girls'	4,107,445	98,538	841,812	658,184	2,628,179
OTHER APPAREL PRODUCTS AND SERVICES	**33,165,994**	**1,066,530**	**3,425,658**	**3,858,320**	**25,918,524**
Material for making clothes	799,137	37,990	50,910	47,520	696,261
Sewing patterns and notions	813,558	4,791	47,016	88,514	678,832
Watches	2,469,514	162,095	342,811	364,271	1,769,549
Jewelry	15,116,310	356,372	918,826	1,092,529	13,106,037
Shoe repair and other shoe services	171,845	933	9,663	9,646	153,196
Coin-operated apparel laundry and dry cleaning	4,896,968	219,674	972,043	1,613,544	2,329,126
Apparel alteration, repair, and tailoring services	749,867	22,430	69,514	55,889	626,543
Clothing rental	258,368	2,417	13,701	29,505	214,658
Watch and jewelry repair	438,624	7,335	18,749	29,221	389,870
Professional laundry, dry cleaning	7,366,482	249,439	967,860	519,738	5,892,075
Clothing storage	84,120	3,095	14,566	7,944	61,462

Note: "Asian" and "black" include Hispanics and non-Hispanics who identify themselves as being of the respective race alone. "Hispanic" includes people of any race who identify themselves as Hispanic. "Other" includes people who identify themselves as non-Hispanic and as Alaska Native, American Indian, Asian (who are also included in the "Asian" column), Native Hawaiian or other Pacific Islander, as well as non-Hispanics reporting more than one race. Numbers may not add to total because of rounding and missing subcategories. "–" means sample is too small to make a reliable estimate.
Source: Calculations by New Strategist based on the Bureau of Labor Statistics' 2007 Consumer Expenditure Survey

Table 9. Apparel: Market shares by race and Hispanic origin, 2007

(percentage of total annual spending on apparel, accessories, and related services accounted for by race and Hispanic origin groups, 2007)

	total consumer units	Asian	black	Hispanic	non-Hispanic white and other
Share of total consumer units	100.0%	3.5%	12.0%	11.8%	76.3%
Share of total before-tax income	100.0	4.5	8.4	9.0	82.6
Share of total spending	100.0	4.3	8.7	9.9	81.5
Share of apparel spending	100.0	5.1	11.1	12.5	76.5
MEN'S APPAREL	100.0	5.1	8.1	14.3	77.9
Suits	100.0	7.1	13.9	6.2	79.9
Sport coats and tailored jackets	100.0	7.2	13.3	8.5	78.4
Coats and jackets	100.0	3.9	6.4	13.6	80.0
Underwear	100.0	4.5	12.2	14.0	74.0
Hosiery	100.0	5.8	7.7	8.7	83.3
Nightwear	100.0	3.0	10.6	7.2	81.7
Accessories	100.0	3.9	6.3	12.0	81.7
Sweaters and vests	100.0	6.3	4.9	19.3	76.3
Active sportswear	100.0	4.1	4.7	14.3	81.2
Shirts	100.0	4.3	7.9	14.7	77.8
Pants and shorts	100.0	5.9	7.9	17.5	75.3
Uniforms	100.0	4.6	11.2	21.0	68.0
Costumes	100.0	–	1.0	8.2	90.6
BOYS' (AGED 2 TO 15) APPAREL	100.0	3.8	15.4	15.9	69.3
Coats and jackets	100.0	4.1	21.8	15.5	64.5
Sweaters	100.0	3.5	11.5	16.3	72.0
Shirts	100.0	5.1	13.5	19.1	68.1
Underwear	100.0	3.7	18.4	12.9	68.9
Nightwear	100.0	1.8	6.5	8.2	85.2
Hosiery	100.0	1.2	16.0	14.0	70.4
Accessories	100.0	4.8	13.5	7.3	78.8
Suits, sport coats, and vests	100.0	1.8	16.6	10.6	72.8
Pants and shorts	100.0	2.8	15.4	15.1	69.9
Uniforms	100.0	4.6	25.5	25.5	50.8
Active sportswear	100.0	4.8	7.2	16.7	75.9
Costumes	100.0	3.7	9.2	9.4	80.7
WOMEN'S APPAREL	100.0	6.1	9.8	9.5	80.6
Coats and jackets	100.0	8.9	7.3	6.7	85.5
Dresses	100.0	5.8	15.0	11.7	73.4
Sport coats and tailored jackets	100.0	3.8	6.4	6.6	87.2
Sweaters and vests	100.0	3.7	4.5	9.6	86.2
Shirts, blouses, and tops	100.0	5.7	10.6	9.6	79.7
Skirts	100.0	2.7	7.0	3.8	88.5
Pants and shorts	100.0	6.7	9.4	10.8	79.8
Active sportswear	100.0	4.7	6.2	6.0	87.4
Nightwear	100.0	3.1	8.8	7.9	82.9
Undergarments	100.0	3.1	12.7	8.8	79.1
Hosiery	100.0	5.5	11.2	8.2	80.4
Suits	100.0	4.5	18.0	4.6	77.4
Accessories	100.0	–	8.5	13.7	78.0
Uniforms	100.0	3.0	18.6	11.3	70.2
Costumes	100.0	–	9.2	6.9	84.0

	total consumer units	Asian	black	Hispanic	non-Hispanic white and other
GIRLS' (AGED 2 TO 15) APPAREL	**100.0%**	**4.5%**	**15.6%**	**12.7%**	**72.2%**
Coats and jackets	100.0	8.1	41.1	3.8	54.8
Dresses and suits	100.0	4.7	26.1	9.8	64.2
Shirts, blouses, and sweaters	100.0	5.7	13.1	16.1	71.5
Skirts, pants, and shorts	100.0	3.2	13.4	12.3	74.6
Active sportswear	100.0	0.6	9.5	14.1	76.6
Underwear and nightwear	100.0	4.2	13.0	6.8	81.0
Hosiery	100.0	2.2	17.1	11.6	71.5
Accessories	100.0	–	7.4	13.0	79.8
Uniforms	100.0	1.0	27.5	17.2	55.3
Costumes	100.0	1.0	3.4	8.7	87.9
CHILDREN'S (UNDER AGE 2) APPAREL	**100.0**	**4.0**	**13.3**	**17.7**	**69.5**
Coats, jackets, and snowsuits	100.0	5.5	16.9	10.6	72.3
Outerwear including dresses	100.0	2.5	11.9	13.6	74.5
Underwear	100.0	3.7	12.5	21.4	66.9
Nightwear and loungewear	100.0	4.1	15.1	14.7	70.2
Accessories	100.0	7.5	17.2	15.1	68.1
FOOTWEAR	**100.0**	**5.5**	**14.2**	**14.7**	**71.4**
Men's	100.0	5.2	13.9	17.2	69.4
Boys'	100.0	2.9	20.1	24.2	56.9
Women's	100.0	6.9	12.0	11.1	77.0
Girls'	100.0	2.4	20.5	16.0	64.0
OTHER APPAREL PRODUCTS AND SERVICES	**100.0**	**3.2**	**10.3**	**11.6**	**78.1**
Material for making clothes	100.0	4.8	6.4	5.9	87.1
Sewing patterns and notions	100.0	0.6	5.8	10.9	83.4
Watches	100.0	6.6	13.9	14.8	71.7
Jewelry	100.0	2.4	6.1	7.2	86.7
Shoe repair and other shoe services	100.0	0.5	5.6	5.6	89.1
Coin-operated apparel laundry and dry cleaning	100.0	4.5	19.8	32.9	47.6
Apparel alteration, repair, and tailoring services	100.0	3.0	9.3	7.5	83.6
Clothing rental	100.0	0.9	5.3	11.4	83.1
Watch and jewelry repair	100.0	1.7	4.3	6.7	88.9
Professional laundry, dry cleaning	100.0	3.4	13.1	7.1	80.0
Clothing storage	100.0	3.7	17.3	9.4	73.1

Note: "Asian" and "black" include Hispanics and non-Hispanics who identify themselves as being of the respective race alone. "Hispanic" includes people of any race who identify themselves as Hispanic. "Other" includes people who identify themselves as non-Hispanic and as Alaska Native, American Indian, Asian (who are also included in the "Asian" column), Native Hawaiian or other Pacific Islander, as well as non-Hispanics reporting more than one race. "–" means sample is too small to make a reliable estimate.
Source: Calculations by New Strategist based on the Bureau of Labor Statistics' 2007 Consumer Expenditure Survey

Spending on Entertainment, 2007

Entertainment spending has grown since 2000, despite the volatility of the economy. The average household spent $2,698 on entertainment in 2007, up from an inflation-adjusted $2,243 in 2000—a 20 percent rise. Overall, Americans devoted 5.4 percent of their spending to entertainment in 2007; the percentage was 4.9 in 2000. The average American household now spends substantially more on entertainment than it does on clothes.

Asians, blacks, and Hispanics spend less than the average household on entertainment. Asians devoted $2,454 to entertainment in 2007, or 9 percent less than the average household. Hispanics spent $1,674 on entertainment, fully 38 percent less than average. Blacks spend the least on entertainment—only $1,288 in 2006, just less than half the average. Behind the below average spending of blacks and Hispanics are their lower incomes. Also, the younger age of the Asian, black, and Hispanic populations means they have less leisure time than non-Hispanic whites, many of whom are retired.

In some entertainment categories, Asians, blacks, and Hispanics spend considerably more than the average household. Asians spend more than twice the average on recreation expenses on trips, for example. Blacks spend 53 percent more than average on the installation of television sets, and Hispanics spend 61 percent more than the average household on sound components and component systems. All three groups spend far less than the average household on pets.

Table 10. Entertainment: Average spending by race and Hispanic origin, 2007

(average annual spending of consumer units on entertainment, by race and Hispanic origin of consumer unit reference person, 2007)

	total consumer units	Asian	black	Hispanic	non-Hispanic white and other
Number of consumer units (in 000s)	120,171	4,240	14,422	14,185	91,734
Average number of persons per consumer unit	2.5	2.8	2.6	3.2	2.3
Average before-tax income of consumer units	$63,091.00	$80,487.00	$44,381.00	$48,330.00	$68,285.00
Average spending of consumer units, total	49,637.95	60,402.09	36,067.28	41,501.12	53,002.87
Entertainment, average spending	**2,697.99**	**2,453.63**	**1,287.51**	**1,674.37**	**3,071.72**
FEES AND ADMISSIONS	**658.07**	**894.95**	**212.20**	**315.63**	**779.24**
Recreation expenses on trips	27.89	57.55	10.92	18.14	32.03
Social, recreation, civic club membership	123.48	113.92	40.51	57.73	146.61
Fees for participant sports	116.94	140.81	22.59	28.14	144.01
Participant sports on trips	31.96	26.70	1.93	6.94	40.50
Movie, theater, amusement park, and other admissions	116.53	115.92	61.92	87.17	129.60
Movie, other admissions on trips	42.82	55.49	19.14	24.78	49.26
Admission to sports events	50.75	29.73	13.50	21.09	61.14
Admission to sports events on trips	14.27	18.50	6.38	8.26	16.42
Fees for recreational lessons	105.56	278.77	24.39	45.24	127.63
Other entertainment services on trips	27.89	57.55	10.92	18.14	32.03
AUDIO AND VISUAL EQUIPMENT AND SERVICES	**986.81**	**972.99**	**753.29**	**814.98**	**1,049.92**
Radios	2.74	0.65	0.80	1.62	3.21
Television sets	162.24	216.66	92.65	140.11	176.70
Tape recorders and players	3.38	3.87	2.41	3.97	3.51
Cable and satellite television services	555.13	439.14	534.00	447.25	575.12
Miscellaneous sound equipment	2.54	6.06	0.36	1.52	3.02
Satellite radio service	12.01	7.55	7.38	10.27	12.98
Sound equipment accessories	13.79	4.11	3.42	9.41	16.00
Online gaming services	1.55	1.50	0.68	0.87	1.79
VCRs and video disc players	14.83	14.19	7.67	15.66	15.81
Video game hardware and software	63.10	137.02	7.29	53.70	72.99
Video cassettes, tapes, and discs	38.32	26.16	27.24	31.40	41.14
Streamed and downloaded video	1.03	0.68	0.22	0.65	1.22
Repair of TV, radio, and sound equipment	4.26	4.65	4.77	2.44	4.45
Rental of television sets	0.72	–	0.37	1.19	0.70
Personal digital audio players	17.39	20.47	11.44	14.07	19.04
Sound components and component systems	13.21	4.75	6.57	21.25	13.03
Satellite dishes	0.98	–	–	0.48	1.21
Compact discs, records, and audio tapes	27.39	19.40	23.32	24.49	28.50
Streamed and downloaded audio	3.68	2.91	1.90	1.40	4.30
Rental of VCR, radio, and sound equipment	0.31	–	0.10	–	0.39
Musical instruments and accessories	14.99	27.22	1.44	7.06	18.32
Rental and repair of musical instruments	1.29	3.13	0.39	0.53	1.55
Rental of video cassettes, tapes, discs, films	30.87	26.19	17.38	25.36	33.80
Installation of television sets	0.98	2.52	1.50	0.30	1.00
PETS, TOYS, HOBBIES, PLAYGROUND EQUIPMENT	**560.14**	**316.11**	**172.82**	**315.20**	**656.68**
Pets	**430.80**	**174.07**	**116.82**	**225.74**	**510.39**
Pet food	146.88	60.71	46.87	89.06	171.68
Pet purchase, supplies, and medicines	139.06	70.93	46.19	95.30	160.29
Pet services	31.68	5.25	6.72	12.78	38.48
Veterinarian services	113.18	37.18	17.04	28.60	139.94
Toys, games, hobbies, and tricycles	**119.93**	**124.28**	**55.00**	**86.40**	**134.60**
Stamp and coin collecting	**4.02**	**–**	**0.65**	**0.22**	**5.14**
Playground equipment	**5.38**	**1.36**	**0.36**	**2.85**	**6.56**

	total consumer units	Asian	black	Hispanic	non-Hispanic white and other
OTHER ENTERTAINMENT SUPPLIES, EQUIPMENT, SERVICES	**$492.95**	**$269.58**	**$149.20**	**$228.55**	**$585.88**
Unmotored recreational vehicles	**72.01**	**–**	**35.14**	**4.81**	**88.06**
Boat without motor and boat trailers	21.51	–	–	4.81	27.43
Trailer and other attachable campers	50.50	–	35.14	–	60.63
Motorized recreational vehicles	**147.76**	**8.19**	**33.10**	**82.05**	**175.68**
Motorized camper	58.58	–	–	77.79	64.71
Other vehicle	31.10	–	–	1.81	40.46
Motorboats	58.09	8.19	33.10	2.45	70.51
Rental of recreational vehicles	**8.00**	**7.27**	**2.01**	**4.48**	**9.47**
Docking and landing fees	**4.42**	**–**	**0.62**	**2.00**	**5.39**
Sports, recreation, exercise equipment	**154.40**	**169.97**	**25.82**	**61.69**	**187.60**
Athletic gear, game tables, exercise equipment	65.55	90.89	11.27	38.83	77.67
Bicycles	16.72	7.10	5.74	5.99	20.08
Camping equipment	11.39	10.76	3.97	3.33	13.66
Hunting and fishing equipment	29.66	14.84	2.12	2.57	37.74
Winter sports equipment	4.06	2.42	0.76	1.42	4.98
Water sports equipment	4.49	0.51	0.54	0.94	5.64
Other sports equipment	7.03	14.29	1.25	4.67	8.34
Global positioning system devices	13.07	29.12	–	–	16.94
Rental and repair of miscellaneous sports equipment	2.43	0.05	0.17	3.94	2.54
Photographic equipment and supplies	**79.45**	**68.26**	**31.22**	**60.63**	**89.84**
Film	4.69	3.45	2.76	3.63	5.15
Other photographic supplies	0.78	–	0.12	0.39	0.93
Photo processing	15.98	13.12	6.47	5.96	19.00
Repair and rental of photographic equipment	0.63	0.17	0.56	0.11	0.72
Photographic equipment	32.24	34.57	12.05	21.01	37.09
Photographer fees	25.13	16.96	9.26	29.52	26.94
Fireworks	**2.44**	**1.33**	**2.30**	**0.53**	**2.73**
Pinball, electronic video games	**1.04**	**0.16**	**0.54**	**–**	**1.27**
Live entertainment for catered affairs	**9.18**	**0.97**	**8.18**	**2.66**	**10.32**
Rental of party supplies for catered affairs	**9.36**	**1.67**	**9.31**	**7.78**	**9.59**

Note: "Asian" and "black" include Hispanics and non-Hispanics who identify themselves as being of the respective race alone. "Hispanic" includes people of any race who identify themselves as Hispanic. "Other" includes people who identify themselves as non-Hispanic and as Alaska Native, American Indian, Asian (who are also included in the "Asian" column), Native Hawaiian or other Pacific Islander, as well as non-Hispanics reporting more than one race. Subcategories may not add to total because some are not shown. "–" means sample is too small to make a reliable estimate.
Source: Bureau of Labor Statistics, unpublished data from the 2007 Consumer Expenditure Survey

Table 11. Entertainment: Indexed spending by race and Hispanic origin, 2007

(indexed average annual spending of consumer units on entertainment by race and Hispanic origin of consumer unit reference person, 2007; index definition: an index of 100 is the average for all consumer units; an index of 132 means that spending by consumer units in that group is 32 percent above the average for all consumer units; an index of 68 indicates spending that is 32 percent below the average for all consumer units)

	total consumer units	Asian	black	Hispanic	non-Hispanic white and other
Average spending of consumer units, total	$49,638	$60,402	$36,067	$41,501	$53,003
Average spending of consumer units, index	100	122	73	84	107
Entertainment, spending index	100	91	48	62	114
FEES AND ADMISSIONS	100	136	32	48	118
Recreation expenses on trips	100	206	39	65	115
Social, recreation, civic club membership	100	92	33	47	119
Fees for participant sports	100	120	19	24	123
Participant sports on trips	100	84	6	22	127
Movie, theater, amusement park, and other admissions	100	99	53	75	111
Movie, other admissions on trips	100	130	45	58	115
Admission to sports events	100	59	27	42	120
Admission to sports events on trips	100	130	45	58	115
Fees for recreational lessons	100	264	23	43	121
Other entertainment services on trips	100	206	39	65	115
AUDIO AND VISUAL EQUIPMENT AND SERVICES	100	99	76	83	106
Radios	100	24	29	59	117
Television sets	100	134	57	86	109
Tape recorders and players	100	114	71	117	104
Cable and satellite television services	100	79	96	81	104
Miscellaneous sound equipment	100	239	14	60	119
Satellite radio service	100	63	61	86	108
Sound equipment accessories	100	30	25	68	116
Online gaming services	100	97	44	56	115
VCRs and video disc players	100	96	52	106	107
Video game hardware and software	100	217	12	85	116
Video cassettes, tapes, and discs	100	68	71	82	107
Streamed and downloaded video	100	66	21	63	118
Repair of TV, radio, and sound equipment	100	109	112	57	104
Rental of television sets	100	–	51	165	97
Personal digital audio players	100	118	66	81	109
Sound components and component systems	100	36	50	161	99
Satellite dishes	100	–	–	49	123
Compact discs, records, and audio tapes	100	71	85	89	104
Streamed and downloaded audio	100	79	52	38	117
Rental of VCR, radio, and sound equipment	100	–	32	–	126
Musical instruments and accessories	100	182	10	47	122
Rental and repair of musical instruments	100	243	30	41	120
Rental of video cassettes, tapes, discs, films	100	85	56	82	109
Installation of television sets	100	257	153	31	102
PETS, TOYS, HOBBIES, PLAYGROUND EQUIPMENT	100	56	31	56	117
Pets	100	40	27	52	118
Pet food	100	41	32	61	117
Pet purchase, supplies, and medicines	100	51	33	69	115
Pet services	100	17	21	40	121
Veterinarian services	100	33	15	25	124
Toys, games, hobbies, and tricycles	100	104	46	72	112
Stamp and coin collecting	100	–	16	5	128
Playground equipment	100	25	7	53	122

	total consumer units	Asian	black	Hispanic	non-Hispanic white and other
OTHER ENTERTAINMENT SUPPLIES, EQUIPMENT, SERVICES	**100**	**55**	**30**	**46**	**119**
Unmotored recreational vehicles	**100**	**–**	**49**	**7**	**122**
Boat without motor and boat trailers	100	–	–	22	128
Trailer and other attachable campers	100	–	70	–	120
Motorized recreational vehicles	**100**	**6**	**22**	**56**	**119**
Motorized camper	100	–	–	133	110
Other vehicle	100	–	–	6	130
Motorboats	100	14	57	4	121
Rental of recreational vehicles	**100**	**91**	**25**	**56**	**118**
Docking and landing fees	**100**	**–**	**14**	**45**	**122**
Sports, recreation, exercise equipment	**100**	**110**	**17**	**40**	**122**
Athletic gear, game tables, exercise equipment	100	139	17	59	118
Bicycles	100	42	34	36	120
Camping equipment	100	94	35	29	120
Hunting and fishing equipment	100	50	7	9	127
Winter sports equipment	100	60	19	35	123
Water sports equipment	100	11	12	21	126
Other sports equipment	100	203	18	66	119
Global positioning system devices	100	223	–	–	130
Rental and repair of miscellaneous sports equipment	100	2	7	162	105
Photographic equipment and supplies	**100**	**86**	**39**	**76**	**113**
Film	100	74	59	77	110
Other photographic supplies	100	–	15	50	119
Photo processing	100	82	40	37	119
Repair and rental of photographic equipment	100	27	89	17	114
Photographic equipment	100	107	37	65	115
Photographer fees	100	67	37	117	107
Fireworks	**100**	**55**	**94**	**22**	**112**
Pinball, electronic video games	**100**	**15**	**52**	**–**	**122**
Live entertainment for catered affairs	**100**	**11**	**89**	**29**	**112**
Rental of party supplies for catered affairs	**100**	**18**	**99**	**83**	**102**

Note: "Asian" and "black" include Hispanics and non-Hispanics who identify themselves as being of the respective race alone. "Hispanic" includes people of any race who identify themselves as Hispanic. "Other" includes people who identify themselves as non-Hispanic and as Alaska Native, American Indian, Asian (who are also included in the "Asian" column), Native Hawaiian or other Pacific Islander, as well as non-Hispanics reporting more than one race. "–" means sample is too small to make a reliable estimate.
Source: Calculations by New Strategist based on the Bureau of Labor Statistics' 2007 Consumer Expenditure Survey

Table 12. Entertainment: Total spending by race and Hispanic origin, 2007

(total annual spending on entertainment, by consumer unit race and Hispanic origin groups, 2007; consumer units and dollars in thousands)

	total consumer units	Asian	black	Hispanic	non-Hispanic white and other
Number of consumer units	120,171	4,240	14,422	14,185	91,734
Total spending of all consumer units	$5,965,042,089	$256,104,862	$520,162,312	$588,693,387	$4,862,165,277
Entertainment, total spending	324,220,156	10,403,391	18,568,469	23,750,938	281,781,162
FEES AND ADMISSIONS	79,080,930	3,794,588	3,060,348	4,477,212	71,482,802
Recreation expenses on trips	3,351,569	244,012	157,488	257,316	2,938,240
Social, recreation, civic club membership	14,838,715	483,021	584,235	818,900	13,449,122
Fees for participant sports	14,052,797	597,034	325,793	399,166	13,210,613
Participant sports on trips	3,840,665	113,208	27,834	98,444	3,715,227
Movie, theater, amusement park, and other admissions	14,003,527	491,501	893,010	1,236,506	11,888,726
Movie, other admissions on trips	5,145,722	235,278	276,037	351,504	4,518,817
Admission to sports events	6,098,678	126,055	194,697	299,162	5,608,617
Admission to sports events on trips	1,714,840	78,440	92,012	117,168	1,506,272
Fees for recreational lessons	12,685,251	1,181,985	351,753	641,729	11,708,010
Other entertainment services on trips	3,351,569	244,012	157,488	257,316	2,938,240
AUDIO AND VISUAL EQUIPMENT AND SERVICES	118,585,945	4,125,478	10,863,948	11,560,491	96,313,361
Radios	329,269	2,756	11,538	22,980	294,466
Television sets	19,496,543	918,638	1,336,198	1,987,460	16,209,398
Tape recorders and players	406,178	16,409	34,757	56,314	321,986
Cable and satellite television services	66,710,527	1,861,954	7,701,348	6,344,241	52,758,058
Miscellaneous sound equipment	305,234	25,694	5,192	21,561	277,037
Satellite radio service	1,443,254	32,012	106,434	145,680	1,190,707
Sound equipment accessories	1,657,158	17,426	49,323	133,481	1,467,744
Online gaming services	186,265	6,360	9,807	12,341	164,204
VCRs and video disc players	1,782,136	60,166	110,617	222,137	1,450,315
Video game hardware and software	7,582,790	580,965	105,136	761,735	6,695,665
Video cassettes, tapes, and discs	4,604,953	110,918	392,855	445,409	3,773,937
Streamed and downloaded video	123,776	2,883	3,173	9,220	111,915
Repair of TV, radio, and sound equipment	511,928	19,716	68,793	34,611	408,216
Rental of television sets	86,523	–	5,336	16,880	64,214
Personal digital audio players	2,089,774	86,793	164,988	199,583	1,746,615
Sound components and component systems	1,587,459	20,140	94,753	301,431	1,195,294
Satellite dishes	117,768	–	–	6,809	110,998
Compact discs, records, and audio tapes	3,291,484	82,256	336,321	347,391	2,614,419
Streamed and downloaded audio	442,229	12,338	27,402	19,859	394,456
Rental of VCR, radio, and sound equipment	37,253	–	1,442	–	35,776
Musical instruments and accessories	1,801,363	115,413	20,768	100,146	1,680,567
Rental and repair of musical instruments	155,021	13,271	5,625	7,518	142,188
Rental of video cassettes, tapes, discs, films	3,709,679	111,046	250,654	359,732	3,100,609
Installation of television sets	117,768	10,685	21,633	4,256	91,734
PETS, TOYS, HOBBIES, AND PLAYGROUND EQUIPMENT	67,312,584	1,340,306	2,492,410	4,471,112	60,239,883
Pets	51,769,667	738,057	1,684,778	3,202,122	46,820,116
Pet food	17,650,716	257,410	675,959	1,263,316	15,748,893
Pet purchase, supplies, and medicines	16,710,979	300,743	666,152	1,351,831	14,704,043
Pet services	3,807,017	22,260	96,916	181,284	3,529,924
Veterinarian services	13,600,954	157,643	245,751	405,691	12,837,256
Toys, games, hobbies, and tricycles	14,412,108	526,947	793,210	1,225,584	12,347,396
Stamp and coin collecting	483,087	–	9,374	3,121	471,513
Playground equipment	646,520	5,766	5,192	40,427	601,775

	total consumer units	Asian	black	Hispanic	non-Hispanic white and other
OTHER ENTERTAINMENT SUPPLIES, EQUIPMENT, SERVICES	**$59,238,294**	**$1,143,019**	**$2,151,762**	**$3,241,982**	**$53,745,116**
Unmotored recreational vehicles	**8,653,514**	**–**	**506,789**	**68,230**	**8,078,096**
Boat without motor and boat trailers	2,584,878	–	–	68,230	2,516,264
Trailer and other attachable campers	6,068,636	–	506,789	–	5,561,832
Motorized recreational vehicles	**17,756,467**	**34,726**	**477,368**	**1,163,879**	**16,115,829**
Motorized camper	7,039,617	–	–	1,103,451	5,936,107
Other vehicle	3,737,318	–	–	25,675	3,711,558
Motorboats	6,980,733	34,726	477,368	34,753	6,468,164
Rental of recreational vehicles	**961,368**	**30,825**	**28,988**	**63,549**	**868,721**
Docking and landing fees	**531,156**	**–**	**8,942**	**28,370**	**494,446**
Sports, recreation, exercise equipment	**18,554,402**	**720,673**	**372,376**	**875,073**	**17,209,298**
Athletic gear, game tables, exercise equipment	7,877,209	385,374	162,536	550,804	7,124,980
Bicycles	2,009,259	30,104	82,782	84,968	1,842,019
Camping equipment	1,368,748	45,622	57,255	47,236	1,253,086
Hunting and fishing equipment	3,564,272	62,922	30,575	36,455	3,462,041
Winter sports equipment	487,894	10,261	10,961	20,143	456,835
Water sports equipment	539,568	2,162	7,788	13,334	517,380
Other sports equipment	844,802	60,590	18,028	66,244	765,062
Global positioning system devices	1,570,635	123,469	–	–	1,553,974
Rental and repair of miscellaneous sports equipment	292,016	212	2,452	55,889	233,004
Photographic equipment and supplies	**9,547,586**	**289,422**	**450,255**	**860,037**	**8,241,383**
Film	563,602	14,628	39,805	51,492	472,430
Other photographic supplies	93,733	–	1,731	5,532	85,313
Photo processing	1,920,333	55,629	93,310	84,543	1,742,946
Repair and rental of photographic equipment	75,708	721	8,076	1,560	66,048
Photographic equipment	3,874,313	146,577	173,785	298,027	3,402,414
Photographer fees	3,019,897	71,910	133,548	418,741	2,471,314
Fireworks	**293,217**	**5,639**	**33,171**	**7,518**	**250,434**
Pinball, electronic video games	**124,978**	**678**	**7,788**	**–**	**116,502**
Live entertainment for catered affairs	**1,103,170**	**4,113**	**117,972**	**37,732**	**946,695**
Rental of party supplies for catered affairs	**1,124,801**	**7,081**	**134,269**	**110,359**	**879,729**

Note: "Asian" and "black" include Hispanics and non-Hispanics who identify themselves as being of the respective race alone. "Hispanic" includes people of any race who identify themselves as Hispanic. "Other" includes people who identify themselves as non-Hispanic and as Alaska Native, American Indian, Asian (who are also included in the "Asian" column), Native Hawaiian or other Pacific Islander, as well as non-Hispanics reporting more than one race. Numbers may not add to total because of rounding and missing subcategories. "–" means sample is too small to make a reliable estimate.
Source: Calculations by New Strategist based on the Bureau of Labor Statistics' 2007 Consumer Expenditure Survey

Table 13. Entertainment: Market shares by race and Hispanic origin, 2007

(percentage of total annual spending on entertainment accounted for by consumer unit race and Hispanic origin groups, 2007)

	total consumer units	Asian	black	Hispanic	non-Hispanic white and other
Share of total consumer units	100.0%	3.5%	12.0%	11.8%	76.3%
Share of total before-tax income	100.0	4.5	8.4	9.0	82.6
Share of total spending	100.0	4.3	8.7	9.9	81.5
Share of entertainment spending	100.0	3.2	5.7	7.3	86.9
FEES AND ADMISSIONS	100.0	4.8	3.9	5.7	90.4
Recreation expenses on trips	100.0	7.3	4.7	7.7	87.7
Social, recreation, civic club membership	100.0	3.3	3.9	5.5	90.6
Fees for participant sports	100.0	4.2	2.3	2.8	94.0
Participant sports on trips	100.0	2.9	0.7	2.6	96.7
Movie, theater, amusement park, and other admissions	100.0	3.5	6.4	8.8	84.9
Movie, other admissions on trips	100.0	4.6	5.4	6.8	87.8
Admission to sports events	100.0	2.1	3.2	4.9	92.0
Admission to sports events on trips	100.0	4.6	5.4	6.8	87.8
Fees for recreational lessons	100.0	9.3	2.8	5.1	92.3
Other entertainment services on trips	100.0	7.3	4.7	7.7	87.7
AUDIO AND VISUAL EQUIPMENT AND SERVICES	100.0	3.5	9.2	9.7	81.2
Radios	100.0	0.8	3.5	7.0	89.4
Television sets	100.0	4.7	6.9	10.2	83.1
Tape recorders and players	100.0	4.0	8.6	13.9	79.3
Cable and satellite television services	100.0	2.8	11.5	9.5	79.1
Miscellaneous sound equipment	100.0	8.4	1.7	7.1	90.8
Satellite radio service	100.0	2.2	7.4	10.1	82.5
Sound equipment accessories	100.0	1.1	3.0	8.1	88.6
Online gaming services	100.0	3.4	5.3	6.6	88.2
VCRs and video disc players	100.0	3.4	6.2	12.5	81.4
Video game hardware and software	100.0	7.7	1.4	10.0	88.3
Video cassettes, tapes, and discs	100.0	2.4	8.5	9.7	82.0
Streamed and downloaded video	100.0	2.3	2.6	7.4	90.4
Repair of TV, radio, and sound equipment	100.0	3.9	13.4	6.8	79.7
Rental of television sets	100.0	–	6.2	19.5	74.2
Personal digital audio players	100.0	4.2	7.9	9.6	83.6
Sound components and component systems	100.0	1.3	6.0	19.0	75.3
Satellite dishes	100.0	–	–	5.8	94.3
Compact discs, records, and audio tapes	100.0	2.5	10.2	10.6	79.4
Streamed and downloaded audio	100.0	2.8	6.2	4.5	89.2
Rental of VCR, radio, and sound equipment	100.0	–	3.9	–	96.0
Musical instruments and accessories	100.0	6.4	1.2	5.6	93.3
Rental and repair of musical instruments	100.0	8.6	3.6	4.8	91.7
Rental of video cassettes, tapes, discs, films	100.0	3.0	6.8	9.7	83.6
Installation of television sets	100.0	9.1	18.4	3.6	77.9
PETS, TOYS, HOBBIES, PLAYGROUND EQUIPMENT	100.0	2.0	3.7	6.6	89.5
Pets	100.0	1.4	3.3	6.2	90.4
Pet food	100.0	1.5	3.8	7.2	89.2
Pet purchase, supplies, and medicines	100.0	1.8	4.0	8.1	88.0
Pet services	100.0	0.6	2.5	4.8	92.7
Veterinarian services	100.0	1.2	1.8	3.0	94.4
Toys, games, hobbies, and tricycles	100.0	3.7	5.5	8.5	85.7
Stamp and coin collecting	100.0	–	1.9	0.6	97.6
Playground equipment	100.0	0.9	0.8	6.3	93.1

	total consumer units	Asian	black	Hispanic	non-Hispanic white and other
OTHER ENTERTAINMENT SUPPLIES, EQUIPMENT, SERVICES	100.0%	1.9%	3.6%	5.5%	90.7%
Unmotored recreational vehicles	100.0	–	5.9	0.8	93.4
Boat without motor and boat trailers	100.0	–	–	2.6	97.3
Trailer and other attachable campers	100.0	–	8.4	–	91.6
Motorized recreational vehicles	100.0	0.2	2.7	6.6	90.8
Motorized camper	100.0	–	–	15.7	84.3
Other vehicle	100.0	–	–	0.7	99.3
Motorboats	100.0	0.5	6.8	0.5	92.7
Rental of recreational vehicles	100.0	3.2	3.0	6.6	90.4
Docking and landing fees	100.0	–	1.7	5.3	93.1
Sports, recreation, exercise equipment	100.0	3.9	2.0	4.7	92.8
Athletic gear, game tables, exercise equipment	100.0	4.9	2.1	7.0	90.5
Bicycles	100.0	1.5	4.1	4.2	91.7
Camping equipment	100.0	3.3	4.2	3.5	91.5
Hunting and fishing equipment	100.0	1.8	0.9	1.0	97.1
Winter sports equipment	100.0	2.1	2.2	4.1	93.6
Water sports equipment	100.0	0.4	1.4	2.5	95.9
Other sports equipment	100.0	7.2	2.1	7.8	90.6
Global positioning system devices	100.0	7.9	–	–	98.9
Rental and repair of miscellaneous sports equipment	100.0	0.1	0.8	19.1	79.8
Photographic equipment and supplies	100.0	3.0	4.7	9.0	86.3
Film	100.0	2.6	7.1	9.1	83.8
Other photographic supplies	100.0	–	1.8	5.9	91.0
Photo processing	100.0	2.9	4.9	4.4	90.8
Repair and rental of photographic equipment	100.0	1.0	10.7	2.1	87.2
Photographic equipment	100.0	3.8	4.5	7.7	87.8
Photographer fees	100.0	2.4	4.4	13.9	81.8
Fireworks	100.0	1.9	11.3	2.6	85.4
Pinball, electronic video games	100.0	0.5	6.2	–	93.2
Live entertainment for catered affairs	100.0	0.4	10.7	3.4	85.8
Rental of party supplies for catered affairs	100.0	0.6	11.9	9.8	78.2

Note: "Asian" and "black" include Hispanics and non-Hispanics who identify themselves as being of the respective race alone. "Hispanic" includes people of any race who identify themselves as Hispanic. "Other" includes people who identify themselves as non-Hispanic and as Alaska Native, American Indian, Asian (who are also included in the "Asian" column), Native Hawaiian or other Pacific Islander, as well as non-Hispanics reporting more than one race. "–" means sample is too small to make a reliable estimate.
Source: Calculations by New Strategist based on the Bureau of Labor Statistics' 2007 Consumer Expenditure Survey

Spending on Financial Products and Services, 2007

Trends in spending on financial products and services have been mixed since 2000. Spending on cash contributions (a category that includes child support as well as gifts to charities) rose 27 percent between 2000 and 2007, after adjusting for inflation. Spending on life and other personal insurance fell 36 percent. Households spent considerably less on federal and state taxes, but other taxes rose 11 percent.

Minority households spend 11 to 44 percent less than average on financial products and services overall, but exceed average spending in some categories. Asians spend nearly twice the average on cash contributions to educational institutions and 31 percent more than average on support for college students. Hispanics spend 44 percent more than average on child support and 23 percent more than average on cash gifts to members of other households. Child support is the only financial item on which black householders spend more than average and non-Hispanic whites spend less.

Black and Hispanic households spend, respectively, 35 and 41 percent less than average on cash contributions, but Asians spend 18 percent more than average on this item. Asians also spend well above average on personal insurance and pensions, while other minorities spend considerably less than average on these categories because many work in low-paying, entry-level jobs.

Table 14. Financial: Average spending by race and Hispanic origin, 2007

(average annual spending of consumer units on financial products and services, cash contributions, and miscellaneous items, by race and Hispanic origin of consumer unit reference person, 2007)

	total consumer units	Asian	black	Hispanic	non-Hispanic white and other
Number of consumer units (in 000s)	120,171	4,240	14,422	14,185	91,734
Average number of persons per consumer unit	2.5	2.8	2.6	3.2	2.3
Average before-tax income of consumer units	$63,091.00	$80,487.00	$44,381.00	$48,330.00	$68,285.00
Average spending of consumer units, total	49,637.95	60,402.09	36,067.28	41,501.12	53,002.87
FINANCIAL PRODUCTS AND SERVICES	**807.56**	**719.11**	**453.19**	**477.69**	**912.95**
Lottery and gambling losses	72.53	60.64	37.24	43.12	82.07
Legal fees	156.59	169.54	72.60	68.61	183.11
Funeral expenses	58.28	36.01	53.91	35.16	62.44
Safe deposit box rental	3.42	7.06	0.78	0.72	4.25
Checking accounts, other bank service charges	20.77	13.63	20.56	16.28	21.47
Cemetery lots, vaults, and maintenance fees	15.39	10.05	12.26	8.70	16.89
Accounting fees	77.08	69.22	25.08	38.96	91.09
Miscellaneous personal services	41.61	46.31	19.68	20.41	47.96
Dating services	0.40	0.83	–	0.09	0.50
Finance charges, except mortgage and vehicles	167.63	119.20	126.45	138.83	178.90
Occupational expenses	48.95	36.52	31.75	34.69	53.91
Expenses for other properties	126.00	132.32	42.57	61.22	148.90
Credit card memberships	1.66	2.74	0.68	0.80	1.95
Shopping club membership fees	7.09	10.80	3.56	7.62	7.55
Vacation clubs	8.16	4.23	6.06	2.48	9.35
CASH CONTRIBUTIONS	**1,821.49**	**2,152.67**	**1,177.86**	**1,082.91**	**2,034.60**
Support for college students	99.06	130.13	70.63	26.01	114.68
Alimony expenditures	30.19	2.17	7.98	17.01	35.67
Child support expenditures	198.01	88.89	227.75	285.24	179.78
Gifts of stocks, bonds, and mutual funds to members of other households	62.25	–	0.50	0.86	81.33
Cash contributions to charities	275.94	229.45	41.28	39.45	348.90
Cash contributions to church, religious organizations	684.76	742.48	674.85	205.71	759.76
Cash contributions to educational institutions	51.10	100.73	4.51	2.48	65.88
Cash contributions to political organizations	10.47	3.16	5.18	1.50	12.68
Cash gifts to members of other households	409.71	307.54	145.16	504.65	435.93
PERSONAL INSURANCE AND PENSIONS	**5,336.15**	**6,868.29**	**3,515.42**	**3,837.48**	**5,851.03**
Life and other personal insurance	**309.47**	**352.82**	**244.68**	**108.66**	**350.47**
Life, endowment, annuity, other personal insurance	298.19	341.73	240.14	104.71	337.01
Other nonhealth insurance	11.28	11.10	4.54	3.95	13.45
Pensions and Social Security	**5,026.69**	**6,515.46**	**3,270.74**	**3,728.81**	**5,500.56**
Deductions for government retirement	74.57	104.44	45.11	38.82	84.59
Deductions for railroad retirement	2.93	–	0.50	–	3.76
Deductions for private pensions	558.59	661.08	226.56	162.01	671.08
Nonpayroll deposit to retirement plans	482.66	485.80	126.98	80.27	599.91
Deductions for Social Security	3,907.94	5,264.13	2,871.59	3,447.72	4,141.22
PERSONAL TAXES	**2,233.48**	**2,295.26**	**771.13**	**702.80**	**2,696.62**
Federal income taxes	1,569.13	1,488.53	511.44	462.85	1,904.73
Federal income tax deducted	1,839.50	1,712.71	1,155.33	1,215.13	2,042.42
Additional federal income tax paid	557.66	484.10	108.15	126.58	693.98
Federal income tax refunds	-828.02	−708.28	−752.04	−878.85	−831.67
State and local income taxes	468.06	627.56	174.66	172.23	558.59
State and local income tax deducted	478.96	555.28	280.42	230.44	547.73
Additional state and local income tax paid	106.59	209.89	6.79	24.43	134.79
State and local income tax refunds	−117.49	−137.60	−112.55	−82.64	−123.93
Other taxes	196.28	179.17	85.03	67.71	233.30

Note: "Asian" and "black" include Hispanics and non-Hispanics who identify themselves as being of the respective race alone. "Hispanic" includes people of any race who identify themselves as Hispanic. "Other" includes people who identify themselves as non-Hispanic and as Alaska Native, American Indian, Asian (who are also included in the "Asian" column), Native Hawaiian or other Pacific Islander, as well as non-Hispanics reporting more than one race. Subcategories may not add to total because some are not shown. "–" means sample is too small to make a reliable estimate.
Source: Bureau of Labor Statistics, unpublished tables from the 2007 Consumer Expenditure Survey

Table 15. Financial: Indexed spending by race and Hispanic origin, 2007

(indexed average annual spending of consumer units on financial products and services, cash contributions, and miscellaneous items, by race and Hispanic origin of consumer unit reference person, 2007; index definition: an index of 100 is the average for all consumer units; an index of 132 means that spending by consumer units in that group is 32 percent above the average for all consumer units; an index of 68 indicates spending that is 32 percent below the average for all consumer units)

	total consumer units	Asian	black	Hispanic	non-Hispanic white and other
Average spending of consumer units, total	$49,638	$60,402	$36,067	$41,501	$53,003
Average spending of consumer units, index	100	122	73	84	107
FINANCIAL PRODUCTS AND SERVICES	**100**	**89**	**56**	**59**	**113**
Lottery and gambling losses	100	84	51	59	113
Legal fees	100	108	46	44	117
Funeral expenses	100	62	93	60	107
Safe deposit box rental	100	206	23	21	124
Checking accounts, other bank service charges	100	66	99	78	103
Cemetery lots, vaults, and maintenance fees	100	65	80	57	110
Accounting fees	100	90	33	51	118
Miscellaneous personal services	100	111	47	49	115
Dating services	100	208	–	23	125
Finance charges, except mortgage and vehicles	100	71	75	83	107
Occupational expenses	100	75	65	71	110
Expenses for other properties	100	105	34	49	118
Credit card memberships	100	165	41	48	117
Shopping club membership fees	100	152	50	107	106
Vacation clubs	100	52	74	30	115
CASH CONTRIBUTIONS	**100**	**118**	**65**	**59**	**112**
Support for college students	100	131	71	26	116
Alimony expenditures	100	7	26	56	118
Child support expenditures	100	45	115	144	91
Gifts of stocks, bonds, and mutual funds to members of other households	100	–	1	1	131
Cash contributions to charities	100	83	15	14	126
Cash contributions to church, religious organizations	100	108	99	30	111
Cash contributions to educational institutions	100	197	9	5	129
Cash contributions to political organizations	100	30	49	14	121
Cash gifts to members of other households	100	75	35	123	106
PERSONAL INSURANCE AND PENSIONS	**100**	**129**	**66**	**72**	**110**
Life and other personal insurance	**100**	**114**	**79**	**35**	**113**
Life, endowment, annuity, other personal insurance	100	115	81	35	113
Other nonhealth insurance	100	98	40	35	119
Pensions and Social Security	**100**	**130**	**65**	**74**	**109**
Deductions for government retirement	100	140	60	52	113
Deductions for railroad retirement	100	–	17	–	128
Deductions for private pensions	100	118	41	29	120
Nonpayroll deposit to retirement plans	100	101	26	17	124
Deductions for Social Security	100	135	73	88	106
PERSONAL TAXES	**100**	**103**	**35**	**31**	**121**
Federal income taxes	100	95	33	29	121
Federal income tax deducted	100	93	63	66	111
Additional federal income tax paid	100	87	19	23	124
Federal income tax refunds	100	86	91	106	100
State and local income taxes	100	134	37	37	119
State and local income tax deducted	100	116	59	48	114
Additional state and local income tax paid	100	197	6	23	126
State and local income tax refunds	100	117	96	70	105
Other taxes	100	91	43	34	119

Note: "Asian" and "black" include Hispanics and non-Hispanics who identify themselves as being of the respective race alone. "Hispanic" includes people of any race who identify themselves as Hispanic. "Other" includes people who identify themselves as non-Hispanic and as Alaska Native, American Indian, Asian (who are also included in the "Asian" column), Native Hawaiian or other Pacific Islander, as well as non-Hispanics reporting more than one race. "–" means sample is too small to make a reliable estimate.
Source: Calculations by New Strategist based on the Bureau of Labor Statistics' 2007 Consumer Expenditure Survey

Table 16. Financial: Total spending by race and Hispanic origin, 2007

(total annual spending on financial products and services, cash contributions, and miscellaneous items, by consumer unit race and Hispanic origin groups, 2007; consumer units and dollars in thousands)

	total consumer units	Asian	black	Hispanic	non-Hispanic white and other
Number of consumer units	120,171	4,240	14,422	14,185	91,734
Total spending of all consumer units	$5,965,042,089	$256,104,862	$520,162,312	$588,693,387	$4,862,165,277
FINANCIAL PRODUCTS AND SERVICES	97,045,293	3,049,026	6,535,906	6,776,033	83,748,555
Lottery and gambling losses	8,716,003	257,114	537,075	611,657	7,528,609
Legal fees	18,817,577	718,850	1,047,037	973,233	16,797,413
Funeral expenses	7,003,566	152,682	777,490	498,745	5,727,871
Safe deposit box rental	410,985	29,934	11,249	10,213	389,870
Checking accounts, other bank service charges	2,495,952	57,791	296,516	230,932	1,969,529
Cemetery lots, vaults, and maintenance fees	1,849,432	42,612	176,814	123,410	1,549,387
Accounting fees	9,262,781	293,493	361,704	552,648	8,356,050
Miscellaneous personal services	5,000,315	196,354	283,825	289,516	4,399,563
Dating services	48,068	3,519	–	1,277	45,867
Finance charges, except mortgage and vehicles	20,144,265	505,408	1,823,662	1,969,304	16,411,213
Occupational expenses	5,882,370	154,845	457,899	492,078	4,945,380
Expenses for other properties	15,141,546	561,037	613,945	868,406	13,659,193
Credit card memberships	199,484	11,618	9,807	11,348	178,881
Shopping club membership fees	852,012	45,792	51,342	108,090	692,592
Vacation clubs	980,595	17,935	87,397	35,179	857,713
CASH CONTRIBUTIONS	218,890,275	9,127,321	16,987,097	15,361,078	186,641,996
Support for college students	11,904,139	551,751	1,018,626	368,952	10,520,055
Alimony expenditures	3,627,962	9,201	115,088	241,287	3,272,152
Child support expenditures	23,795,060	376,894	3,284,611	4,046,129	16,491,939
Gifts of stocks, bonds, and mutual funds to members of other households	7,480,645	–	7,211	12,199	7,460,726
Cash contributions to charities	33,159,986	972,868	595,340	559,598	32,005,993
Cash contributions to church, religious organizations	82,288,294	3,148,115	9,732,687	2,917,996	69,695,824
Cash contributions to educational institutions	6,140,738	427,095	65,043	35,179	6,043,436
Cash contributions to political organizations	1,258,190	13,398	74,706	21,278	1,163,187
Cash gifts to members of other households	49,235,260	1,303,970	2,093,498	7,158,460	39,989,603
PERSONAL INSURANCE AND PENSIONS	641,250,482	29,121,550	50,699,387	54,434,654	536,738,386
Life and other personal insurance	37,189,319	1,495,957	3,528,775	1,541,342	32,150,015
Life, endowment, annuity, other personal insurance	35,833,790	1,448,935	3,463,299	1,485,311	30,915,275
Other nonhealth insurance	1,355,529	47,064	65,476	56,031	1,233,822
Pensions and Social Security	604,062,364	27,625,550	47,170,612	52,893,170	504,588,371
Deductions for government retirement	8,961,151	442,826	650,576	550,662	7,759,779
Deductions for railroad retirement	352,101	–	7,211	–	344,920
Deductions for private pensions	67,126,319	2,802,979	3,267,448	2,298,112	61,560,853
Nonpayroll deposit to retirement plans	58,001,735	2,059,792	1,831,306	1,138,630	55,032,144
Deductions for Social Security	469,621,058	22,319,911	41,414,071	48,905,908	379,890,675
PERSONAL TAXES	268,399,525	9,731,902	11,121,237	9,969,218	247,371,739
Federal income taxes	188,563,921	6,311,367	7,375,988	6,565,527	174,728,502
Federal income tax deducted	221,054,555	7,261,890	16,662,169	17,236,619	187,359,356
Additional federal income tax paid	67,014,560	2,052,584	1,559,739	1,795,537	63,661,561
Federal income tax refunds	–99,503,991	–3,003,107	–10,845,921	–12,466,487	–76,292,416
State and local income taxes	56,247,238	2,660,854	2,518,947	2,443,083	51,241,695
State and local income tax deducted	57,557,102	2,354,387	4,044,217	3,268,791	50,245,464
Additional state and local income tax paid	12,809,027	889,934	97,925	346,540	12,364,826
State and local income tax refunds	–14,118,891	–583,424	–1,623,196	–1,172,248	–11,368,595
Other taxes	23,587,164	759,681	1,226,303	960,466	21,401,542

Note: "Asian" and "black" include Hispanics and non-Hispanics who identify themselves as being of the respective race alone. "Hispanic" includes people of any race who identify themselves as Hispanic. "Other" includes people who identify themselves as non-Hispanic and as Alaska Native, American Indian, Asian (who are also included in the "Asian" column), Native Hawaiian or other Pacific Islander, as well as non-Hispanics reporting more than one race. Numbers may not add to total because of rounding and missing subcategories. "–" means sample is too small to make a reliable estimate.
Source: Calculations by New Strategist based on the Bureau of Labor Statistics' 2007 Consumer Expenditure Survey

Table 17. Financial: Market shares by race and Hispanic origin, 2007

(percentage of total annual spending on financial products and services, cash contributions, and miscellaneous items accounted for by consumer unit race and Hispanic origin groups, 2007)

	total consumer units	Asian	black	Hispanic	non-Hispanic white and other
Share of total consumer units	100.0%	3.5%	12.0%	11.8%	76.3%
Share of total before-tax income	100.0	4.5	8.4	9.0	82.6
Share of total spending	100.0	4.3	8.7	9.9	81.5
FINANCIAL PRODUCTS AND SERVICES	100.0	3.1	6.7	7.0	86.3
Lottery and gambling losses	100.0	2.9	6.2	7.0	86.4
Legal fees	100.0	3.8	5.6	5.2	89.3
Funeral expenses	100.0	2.2	11.1	7.1	81.8
Safe deposit box rental	100.0	7.3	2.7	2.5	94.9
Checking accounts, other bank service charges	100.0	2.3	11.9	9.3	78.9
Cemetery lots, vaults, and maintenance fees	100.0	2.3	9.6	6.7	83.8
Accounting fees	100.0	3.2	3.9	6.0	90.2
Miscellaneous personal services	100.0	3.9	5.7	5.8	88.0
Dating services	100.0	7.3	–	2.7	95.4
Finance charges, except mortgage and vehicles	100.0	2.5	9.1	9.8	81.5
Occupational expenses	100.0	2.6	7.8	8.4	84.1
Expenses for other properties	100.0	3.7	4.1	5.7	90.2
Credit card memberships	100.0	5.8	4.9	5.7	89.7
Shopping club membership fees	100.0	5.4	6.0	12.7	81.3
Vacation clubs	100.0	1.8	8.9	3.6	87.5
CASH CONTRIBUTIONS	100.0	4.2	7.8	7.0	85.3
Support for college students	100.0	4.6	8.6	3.1	88.4
Alimony expenditures	100.0	0.3	3.2	6.7	90.2
Child support expenditures	100.0	1.6	13.8	17.0	69.3
Gifts of stocks, bonds, and mutual funds to members of other households	100.0	–	0.1	0.2	99.7
Cash contributions to charities	100.0	2.9	1.8	1.7	96.5
Cash contributions to church, religious organizations	100.0	3.8	11.8	3.5	84.7
Cash contributions to educational institutions	100.0	7.0	1.1	0.6	98.4
Cash contributions to political organizations	100.0	1.1	5.9	1.7	92.4
Cash gifts to members of other households	100.0	2.6	4.3	14.5	81.2
PERSONAL INSURANCE AND PENSIONS	100.0	4.5	7.9	8.5	83.7
Life and other personal insurance	100.0	4.0	9.5	4.1	86.4
Life, endowment, annuity, other personal insurance	100.0	4.0	9.7	4.1	86.3
Other nonhealth insurance	100.0	3.5	4.8	4.1	91.0
Pensions and Social Security	100.0	4.6	7.8	8.8	83.5
Deductions for government retirement	100.0	4.9	7.3	6.1	86.6
Deductions for railroad retirement	100.0	–	2.0	–	98.0
Deductions for private pensions	100.0	4.2	4.9	3.4	91.7
Nonpayroll deposit to retirement plans	100.0	3.6	3.2	2.0	94.9
Deductions for Social Security	100.0	4.8	8.8	10.4	80.9
PERSONAL TAXES	100.0	3.6	4.1	3.7	92.2
Federal income taxes	100.0	3.3	3.9	3.5	92.7
Federal income tax deducted	100.0	3.3	7.5	7.8	84.8
Additional federal income tax paid	100.0	3.1	2.3	2.7	95.0
Federal income tax refunds	100.0	3.0	10.9	12.5	76.7
State and local income taxes	100.0	4.7	4.5	4.3	91.1
State and local income tax deducted	100.0	4.1	7.0	5.7	87.3
Additional state and local income tax paid	100.0	6.9	0.8	2.7	96.5
State and local income tax refunds	100.0	4.1	11.5	8.3	80.5
Other taxes	100.0	3.2	5.2	4.1	90.7

Note: "Asian" and "black" include Hispanics and non-Hispanics who identify themselves as being of the respective race alone. "Hispanic" includes people of any race who identify themselves as Hispanic. "Other" includes people who identify themselves as non-Hispanic and as Alaska Native, American Indian, Asian (who are also included in the "Asian" column), Native Hawaiian or other Pacific Islander, as well as non-Hispanics reporting more than one race. "–" means sample is too small to make a reliable estimate.
Source: Calculations by New Strategist based on the Bureau of Labor Statistics' 2007 Consumer Expenditure Survey

Spending on Food and Alcoholic Beverages, 2007

The average household spent 4 percent more on food away from home (primarily sit-down meals and take-outs from restaurants) in 2007 than in 2000, after adjusting for inflation. Spending on food at home (groceries) fell 5 percent during those years. Overall, Americans devoted 12.3 percent of their expenditures to food in 2007, down from 13.6 percent in 2000. Spending on alcoholic beverages increased by 2 percent between 2000 and 2007, after adjusting for inflation.

Asians spend the most on food overall because they are the most-affluent households. In 2007, Asian households devoted $7,139 to food, 16 percent more than the average household. Asian households spend 12 percent more than average on food at home (groceries) and 22 percent more on food away from home—primarily restaurant meals. Asians spend 94 percent more than average on fresh vegetables and more than four times the average on rice.

Hispanic households are average spenders on food even though they have the largest households—an average of 3.2 persons per Hispanic household versus 2.5 people in the average household. Hispanics spend 6 percent less than average on food away from home—yet they spend well more than the average household on breakfast and brunch away from home. Blacks spend 25 percent less than the average household on food overall, but they spend more than the average household on a number of grocery categories including pork, poultry, fresh fish and shellfish, sugar, fats and oils, noncarbonated fruit-flavored drinks, and breakfast and brunch at employer and school cafeterias.

Asians, blacks, and Hispanics spend significantly less than the average household on alcoholic beverages.

Table 18. Food and Alcohol: Average spending by race and Hispanic origin, 2007

(average annual spending of consumer units on food and alcoholic beverages, by race and Hispanic origin of consumer unit reference person, 2007)

	total consumer units	Asian	black	Hispanic	non-Hispanic white and other
Number of consumer units (in 000s)	120,171	4,240	14,422	14,185	91,734
Average number of persons per consumer unit	2.5	2.8	2.6	3.2	2.3
Average before-tax income of consumer units	$63,091.00	$80,487.00	$44,381.00	$48,330.00	$68,285.00
Average spending of consumer units, total	49,637.95	60,402.09	36,067.28	41,501.12	53,002.87
Food, average spending	**6,133.40**	**7,138.72**	**4,601.32**	**5,932.72**	**6,399.38**
Alcoholic beverages, average spending	**456.59**	**290.40**	**198.11**	**262.42**	**525.09**
FOOD AT HOME	**3,465.01**	**3,890.15**	**2,830.69**	**3,424.36**	**3,568.41**
Cereals and bakery products	**459.55**	**469.49**	**364.52**	**409.52**	**481.09**
Cereals and cereal products	142.68	194.88	127.31	154.46	143.39
Flour	5.14	13.97	3.99	7.14	5.03
Prepared flour mixes	11.60	5.21	8.82	9.32	12.35
Ready-to-eat and cooked cereals	84.57	71.32	78.79	83.42	85.61
Rice	16.60	69.79	16.89	29.79	14.68
Pasta, cornmeal, and other cereal products	24.77	34.57	18.83	24.79	25.71
Bakery products	316.87	274.61	237.21	255.06	337.70
Bread	89.18	84.99	72.16	86.78	92.11
White bread	33.86	32.48	31.68	38.75	33.48
Bread, other than white	55.32	52.51	40.48	48.03	58.62
Cookies and crackers	76.59	51.40	57.22	52.50	82.93
Cookies	44.89	33.92	36.29	33.66	47.77
Crackers	31.70	17.48	20.93	18.83	35.16
Frozen and refrigerated bakery products	26.27	21.64	22.46	19.29	27.82
Other bakery products	124.83	116.59	85.37	96.49	134.85
Biscuits and rolls	44.32	50.45	26.78	32.60	48.66
Cakes and cupcakes	40.26	34.15	32.86	28.53	43.05
Bread and cracker products	4.10	1.35	1.60	1.98	4.79
Sweetrolls, coffee cakes, doughnuts	21.18	22.23	12.82	23.93	22.07
Pies, tarts, turnovers	14.96	8.41	11.31	9.44	16.28
Meats, poultry, fish, and eggs	**776.87**	**1,025.54**	**833.51**	**890.32**	**752.24**
Beef	216.25	220.99	185.05	255.44	215.37
Ground beef	89.11	59.81	91.49	99.85	87.15
Roast	34.38	56.09	27.89	32.55	35.60
Chuck roast	9.72	18.45	8.86	10.75	9.70
Round roast	6.92	–	5.23	6.10	7.29
Other roast	17.73	16.72	13.79	15.70	18.61
Steak	76.31	69.99	51.15	94.10	77.64
Round steak	11.77	12.77	6.38	22.36	11.08
Sirloin steak	20.03	12.60	10.82	21.44	21.24
Other steak	44.51	44.62	33.95	50.30	45.32
Other beef	16.45	35.09	14.53	28.94	14.97
Pork	149.64	159.71	185.45	161.73	142.45
Bacon	27.84	24.60	30.00	22.54	28.27
Pork chops	28.87	15.92	50.11	29.90	25.41
Ham	31.85	26.45	31.56	41.18	30.64
Ham, not canned	31.14	25.55	31.28	40.05	29.91
Canned ham	0.72	0.90	0.27	1.12	0.73
Sausage	25.58	29.08	35.14	22.45	24.53
Other pork	35.50	63.66	38.64	45.66	33.60

	total consumer units	Asian	black	Hispanic	non-Hispanic white and other
Other meats	$104.49	$105.93	$95.18	$100.68	$106.77
Frankfurters	18.73	18.61	22.09	21.09	17.87
Lunch meats (cold cuts)	76.14	54.20	62.76	63.47	79.99
Bologna, liverwurst, salami	19.22	15.25	18.57	17.48	19.56
Other lunch meats	56.92	38.95	44.19	45.99	60.44
Lamb, organ meats, and others	9.62	–	10.34	16.12	8.90
Poultry	141.85	157.71	188.51	193.37	127.36
Fresh and frozen chicken	113.50	130.36	149.80	175.63	99.14
Fresh and frozen whole chicken	29.80	49.45	35.80	56.02	25.15
Fresh and frozen chicken parts	83.70	80.91	114.00	119.61	73.98
Other poultry	28.35	27.35	38.71	17.74	28.23
Fish and seafood	121.93	321.22	138.15	118.97	119.82
Canned fish and seafood	16.35	13.99	14.63	13.47	17.01
Fresh fish and shellfish	63.81	220.50	77.87	66.59	61.28
Frozen fish and shellfish	41.77	86.72	45.65	38.91	41.54
Eggs	42.71	59.98	41.18	60.14	40.47
Dairy products	**387.39**	**349.43**	**258.92**	**368.28**	**409.98**
Fresh milk and cream	153.68	153.62	111.42	168.26	158.07
Fresh milk, all types	138.15	145.16	104.51	155.29	140.85
Cream	15.53	8.46	6.91	12.96	17.21
Other dairy products	233.71	195.81	147.49	200.02	251.92
Butter	20.11	17.07	12.66	11.36	22.51
Cheese	117.15	70.57	68.19	106.02	126.38
Ice cream and related products	57.37	68.84	38.47	43.17	62.29
Miscellaneous dairy products	39.07	39.33	28.18	39.46	40.74
Fruits and vegetables	**599.87**	**886.90**	**454.66**	**652.11**	**614.69**
Fresh fruits	201.74	308.69	131.49	226.72	208.95
Apples	34.95	52.77	24.39	34.06	36.70
Bananas	28.32	40.32	22.99	36.36	28.01
Oranges	22.19	44.21	16.67	31.92	21.65
Citrus fruits, excluding oranges	17.77	32.04	9.74	28.67	17.45
Other fresh fruits	98.51	139.36	57.70	95.71	105.13
Fresh vegetables	190.29	368.71	132.73	228.79	193.58
Potatoes	31.19	45.03	25.01	31.58	32.07
Lettuce	23.79	39.38	17.36	25.56	24.52
Tomatoes	35.05	49.74	27.16	54.69	33.45
Other fresh vegetables	100.26	234.55	63.21	116.97	103.54
Processed fruits	112.32	116.16	107.21	106.01	114.06
Frozen fruits and fruit juices	11.09	5.16	7.67	7.39	12.15
Frozen orange juice	3.93	2.09	2.74	3.34	4.21
Frozen fruits	4.97	2.00	2.77	1.97	5.73
Frozen fruit juices, excluding orange	2.20	1.07	2.16	2.09	2.22
Canned fruits	19.47	9.62	16.48	13.44	20.79
Dried fruits	8.08	12.19	4.17	5.57	9.03
Fresh fruit juice	17.21	22.69	16.94	17.94	17.13
Canned and bottled fruit juice	56.46	66.50	61.94	61.67	54.96
Processed vegetables	95.52	93.34	83.23	90.59	98.10
Frozen vegetables	31.34	31.50	27.61	17.91	33.80
Canned and dried vegetables and juices	64.18	61.85	55.62	72.67	64.29
Canned beans	12.82	9.40	12.99	15.46	12.41
Canned corn	5.37	3.15	6.22	6.37	5.09
Canned miscellaneous vegetables	18.53	11.97	14.46	14.13	19.77
Dried peas	0.16	0.11	0.22	0.12	0.16
Dried beans	2.73	4.19	2.58	8.14	1.98
Dried miscellaneous vegetables	8.05	8.01	7.96	9.29	7.88
Fresh and canned vegetable juices	15.56	12.15	11.05	18.67	15.84

	total consumer units	Asian	black	Hispanic	non-Hispanic white and other
Sugar and other sweets	$124.49	$133.11	$87.82	$96.77	$134.02
Candy and chewing gum	80.35	91.37	48.88	53.71	88.96
Sugar	16.49	19.57	20.65	23.80	14.79
Artificial sweeteners	5.83	2.93	3.97	2.66	6.57
Jams, preserves, other sweets	21.81	19.23	14.32	16.61	23.71
Fats and oils	91.26	93.45	81.10	89.77	93.08
Margarine	7.04	3.41	5.06	4.57	7.72
Fats and oils	30.63	52.90	36.87	47.26	27.28
Salad dressings	27.15	17.84	23.15	19.52	28.86
Nondairy cream and imitation milk	13.56	9.87	6.41	11.85	14.91
Peanut butter	12.87	9.43	9.62	6.57	14.30
Miscellaneous foods	649.50	549.48	456.38	546.04	693.75
Frozen prepared foods	136.74	114.78	96.53	84.96	150.24
Frozen meals	71.36	66.22	54.57	39.84	78.37
Other frozen prepared foods	65.38	48.56	41.96	45.12	71.87
Canned and packaged soups	40.05	40.52	28.81	27.91	43.48
Potato chips, nuts, and other snacks	127.93	98.18	84.49	95.67	139.13
Potato chips and other snacks	95.81	72.27	66.36	76.16	103.07
Nuts	32.12	25.90	18.13	19.51	36.07
Condiments and seasonings	108.01	107.16	78.57	82.25	116.20
Salt, spices, and other seasonings	24.07	32.50	20.49	24.02	24.60
Olives, pickles, relishes	12.80	7.05	7.80	8.08	14.25
Sauces and gravies	46.54	45.55	36.54	39.43	49.13
Baking needs and miscellaneous products	24.60	22.05	13.74	10.72	28.22
Other canned or packaged prepared foods	236.77	188.84	167.99	255.25	244.70
Prepared salads	32.63	19.99	19.98	17.01	36.78
Prepared desserts	12.30	7.25	7.59	10.22	13.31
Baby food	42.34	33.69	41.47	60.10	39.91
Miscellaneous prepared foods	148.07	127.91	98.57	167.10	153.02
Nonalcoholic beverages	333.09	342.91	278.59	345.02	339.72
Cola	84.96	60.60	62.77	99.04	86.42
Other carbonated drinks	46.79	27.15	34.86	55.33	47.46
Tea	28.63	50.03	24.98	22.47	30.03
Coffee	51.07	67.43	26.12	41.02	56.31
Roasted coffee	32.00	32.46	16.04	26.30	35.25
Instant and freeze-dried coffee	19.07	34.97	10.08	14.72	21.07
Noncarbonated fruit-flavored drinks	23.96	15.07	31.74	33.61	21.39
Other noncarbonated beverages and ice	36.47	45.41	38.69	31.96	36.76
Bottled water	60.72	77.21	59.43	61.60	60.73
Food prepared by consumer unit on trips	43.00	39.85	15.19	26.53	49.84
FOOD AWAY FROM HOME	2,668.39	3,248.57	1,770.63	2,508.36	2,830.97
Meals at restaurants, carry-outs, other	2,221.83	2,656.75	1,557.14	2,200.79	2,326.25
Lunch	761.38	991.80	548.77	838.77	782.92
At fast-food restaurants*	358.00	473.29	299.94	439.81	355.43
At full-service restaurants	307.84	388.33	158.82	293.43	332.63
At vending machines, mobile vendors	9.85	5.16	5.10	19.68	9.19
At employer and school cafeterias	85.68	125.02	84.92	85.85	85.67
Dinner	1,073.51	1,158.51	724.95	929.21	1,146.84
At fast-food restaurants*	334.88	340.53	337.36	383.79	327.35
At full-service restaurants	730.76	808.76	381.30	538.88	811.20
At vending machines, mobile vendors	2.23	1.70	1.13	3.05	2.28
At employer and school cafeterias	5.63	7.52	5.16	3.48	6.00
Snacks and nonalcoholic beverages	171.82	244.68	106.32	176.89	181.31
At fast-food restaurants*	109.46	144.32	60.12	109.05	117.24
At full-service restaurants	28.39	66.80	14.01	26.69	30.85
At vending machines, mobile vendors	27.72	24.81	26.80	36.12	26.65
At employer and school cafeterias	6.25	8.75	5.40	5.03	6.58

	total consumer units	Asian	black	Hispanic	non-Hispanic white and other
Breakfast and brunch	$215.13	$261.76	$177.08	$255.91	$215.18
At fast-food restaurants*	112.13	133.65	110.78	147.30	107.40
At full-service restaurants	88.22	98.46	48.48	88.56	94.26
At vending machines, mobile vendors	4.14	8.49	2.39	9.17	3.69
At employer and school cafeterias	10.63	21.15	15.43	10.88	9.83
Board (including at school)	**23.69**	**10.44**	**15.83**	**7.17**	**27.44**
Catered affairs	**74.07**	**157.08**	**14.15**	**51.98**	**86.84**
Food on trips	**245.53**	**323.70**	**89.22**	**142.25**	**286.08**
School lunches	**71.09**	**61.47**	**68.26**	**65.48**	**72.34**
Meals as pay	**32.18**	**39.14**	**26.04**	**40.70**	**32.01**
ALCOHOLIC BEVERAGES	**456.59**	**290.40**	**198.11**	**262.42**	**525.09**
At home	**239.71**	**165.21**	**138.77**	**166.18**	**266.54**
Beer and ale	114.93	71.92	80.20	119.38	120.61
Whiskey	8.64	8.97	5.89	0.52	10.21
Wine	97.21	58.39	34.20	41.19	114.80
Other alcoholic beverages	18.92	25.93	18.48	5.09	20.93
Away from home	**216.89**	**125.19**	**59.34**	**96.24**	**258.55**
Beer and ale	75.29	32.35	15.02	35.75	90.14
At fast-food restaurants*	10.96	3.35	3.07	6.18	12.85
At full-service restaurants	63.02	29.01	11.32	29.57	75.70
At vending machines, mobile vendors	1.29	–	0.63	–	1.57
Wine	36.91	16.41	12.17	19.94	43.10
At fast-food restaurants*	1.53	–	0.18	1.21	1.78
At full-service restaurants	35.29	16.41	11.99	18.72	41.21
Other alcoholic beverages	61.07	45.26	23.45	21.32	72.46
At fast-food restaurants*	4.29	2.65	2.31	0.62	5.12
At full-service restaurants	56.62	42.61	20.95	20.28	67.23
Alcoholic beverages purchased on trips	43.62	31.16	8.70	19.24	52.85

The category fast-food restaurants also includes take-out, delivery, concession stands, buffets, and cafeterias other than employer and school.

Note: "Asian" and "black" include Hispanics and non-Hispanics who identify themselves as being of the respective race alone. "Hispanic" includes people of any race who identify themselves as Hispanic. "Other" includes people who identify themselves as non-Hispanic and as Alaska Native, American Indian, Asian (who are also included in the "Asian" column), Native Hawaiian or other Pacific Islander, as well as non-Hispanics reporting more than one race. Subcategories may not add to total because some are not shown. "–" means sample is too small to make a reliable estimate.

Source: Bureau of Labor Statistics, unpublished tables from the 2007 Consumer Expenditure Survey

Table 19. Food and Alcohol: Indexed spending by race and Hispanic origin, 2007

(indexed average annual spending of consumer units on food and alcoholic beverages, by race and Hispanic origin of consumer unit reference person, 2007; index definition: an index of 100 is the average for all consumer units; an index of 132 means that spending by consumer units in that group is 32 percent above the average for all consumer units; an index of 68 indicates spending that is 32 percent below the average for all consumer units)

	total consumer units	Asian	black	Hispanic	non-Hispanic white and other
Average spending of consumer units, total	$49,638	$60,402	$36,067	$41,501	$53,003
Average spending of consumer units, index	100	122	73	84	107
Food, spending index	**100**	**116**	**75**	**97**	**104**
Alcoholic beverages, spending index	**100**	**64**	**43**	**57**	**115**
FOOD AT HOME	**100**	**112**	**82**	**99**	**103**
Cereals and bakery products	**100**	**102**	**79**	**89**	**105**
Cereals and cereal products	100	137	89	108	100
Flour	100	272	78	139	98
Prepared flour mixes	100	45	76	80	106
Ready-to-eat and cooked cereals	100	84	93	99	101
Rice	100	420	102	179	88
Pasta, cornmeal, and other cereal products	100	140	76	100	104
Bakery products	100	87	75	80	107
Bread	100	95	81	97	103
White bread	100	96	94	114	99
Bread, other than white	100	95	73	87	106
Cookies and crackers	100	67	75	69	108
Cookies	100	76	81	75	106
Crackers	100	55	66	59	111
Frozen and refrigerated bakery products	100	82	85	73	106
Other bakery products	100	93	68	77	108
Biscuits and rolls	100	114	60	74	110
Cakes and cupcakes	100	85	82	71	107
Bread and cracker products	100	33	39	48	117
Sweetrolls, coffee cakes, doughnuts	100	105	61	113	104
Pies, tarts, turnovers	100	56	76	63	109
Meats, poultry, fish, and eggs	**100**	**132**	**107**	**115**	**97**
Beef	100	102	86	118	100
Ground beef	100	67	103	112	98
Roast	100	163	81	95	104
Chuck roast	100	190	91	111	100
Round roast	100	–	76	88	105
Other roast	100	94	78	89	105
Steak	100	92	67	123	102
Round steak	100	108	54	190	94
Sirloin steak	100	63	54	107	106
Other steak	100	100	76	113	102
Other beef	100	213	88	176	91
Pork	100	107	124	108	95
Bacon	100	88	108	81	102
Pork chops	100	55	174	104	88
Ham	100	83	99	129	96
Ham, not canned	100	82	100	129	96
Canned ham	100	125	38	156	101
Sausage	100	114	137	88	96
Other pork	100	179	109	129	95

	total consumer units	Asian	black	Hispanic	non-Hispanic white and other
Other meats	100	101	91	96	102
Frankfurters	100	99	118	113	95
Lunch meats (cold cuts)	100	71	82	83	105
Bologna, liverwurst, salami	100	79	97	91	102
Other lunch meats	100	68	78	81	106
Lamb, organ meats, and others	100	–	107	168	93
Poultry	100	111	133	136	90
Fresh and frozen chicken	100	115	132	155	87
Fresh and frozen whole chicken	100	166	120	188	84
Fresh and frozen chicken parts	100	97	136	143	88
Other poultry	100	96	137	63	100
Fish and seafood	100	263	113	98	98
Canned fish and seafood	100	86	89	82	104
Fresh fish and shellfish	100	346	122	104	96
Frozen fish and shellfish	100	208	109	93	99
Eggs	100	140	96	141	95
Dairy products	**100**	**90**	**67**	**95**	**106**
Fresh milk and cream	100	100	73	109	103
Fresh milk, all types	100	105	76	112	102
Cream	100	54	44	83	111
Other dairy products	100	84	63	86	108
Butter	100	85	63	56	112
Cheese	100	60	58	90	108
Ice cream and related products	100	120	67	75	109
Miscellaneous dairy products	100	101	72	101	104
Fruits and vegetables	**100**	**148**	**76**	**109**	**102**
Fresh fruits	100	153	65	112	104
Apples	100	151	70	97	105
Bananas	100	142	81	128	99
Oranges	100	199	75	144	98
Citrus fruits, excluding oranges	100	180	55	161	98
Other fresh fruits	100	141	59	97	107
Fresh vegetables	100	194	70	120	102
Potatoes	100	144	80	101	103
Lettuce	100	166	73	107	103
Tomatoes	100	142	77	156	95
Other fresh vegetables	100	234	63	117	103
Processed fruits	100	103	95	94	102
Frozen fruits and fruit juices	100	47	69	67	110
Frozen orange juice	100	53	70	85	107
Frozen fruits	100	40	56	40	115
Frozen fruit juices, excluding orange	100	49	98	95	101
Canned fruits	100	49	85	69	107
Dried fruits	100	151	52	69	112
Fresh fruit juice	100	132	98	104	100
Canned and bottled fruit juice	100	118	110	109	97
Processed vegetables	100	98	87	95	103
Frozen vegetables	100	101	88	57	108
Canned and dried vegetables and juices	100	96	87	113	100
Canned beans	100	73	101	121	97
Canned corn	100	59	116	119	95
Canned miscellaneous vegetables	100	65	78	76	107
Dried peas	100	69	138	75	100
Dried beans	100	153	95	298	73
Dried miscellaneous vegetables	100	100	99	115	98
Fresh and canned vegetable juices	100	78	71	120	102

	total consumer units	Asian	black	Hispanic	non-Hispanic white and other
Sugar and other sweets	**100**	**107**	**71**	**78**	**108**
Candy and chewing gum	100	114	61	67	111
Sugar	100	119	125	144	90
Artificial sweeteners	100	50	68	46	113
Jams, preserves, other sweets	100	88	66	76	109
Fats and oils	**100**	**102**	**89**	**98**	**102**
Margarine	100	48	72	65	110
Fats and oils	100	173	120	154	89
Salad dressings	100	66	85	72	106
Nondairy cream and imitation milk	100	73	47	87	110
Peanut butter	100	73	75	51	111
Miscellaneous foods	**100**	**85**	**70**	**84**	**107**
Frozen prepared foods	100	84	71	62	110
Frozen meals	100	93	76	56	110
Other frozen prepared foods	100	74	64	69	110
Canned and packaged soups	100	101	72	70	109
Potato chips, nuts, and other snacks	100	77	66	75	109
Potato chips and other snacks	100	75	69	79	108
Nuts	100	81	56	61	112
Condiments and seasonings	100	99	73	76	108
Salt, spices, and other seasonings	100	135	85	100	102
Olives, pickles, relishes	100	55	61	63	111
Sauces and gravies	100	98	79	85	106
Baking needs and miscellaneous products	100	90	56	44	115
Other canned or packaged prepared foods	100	80	71	108	103
Prepared salads	100	61	61	52	113
Prepared desserts	100	59	62	83	108
Baby food	100	80	98	142	94
Miscellaneous prepared foods	100	86	67	113	103
Nonalcoholic beverages	**100**	**103**	**84**	**104**	**102**
Cola	100	71	74	117	102
Other carbonated drinks	100	58	75	118	101
Tea	100	175	87	78	105
Coffee	100	132	51	80	110
Roasted coffee	100	101	50	82	110
Instant and freeze-dried coffee	100	183	53	77	110
Noncarbonated fruit-flavored drinks	100	63	132	140	89
Other noncarbonated beverages and ice	100	125	106	88	101
Bottled water	100	127	98	101	100
Food prepared by consumer unit on trips	**100**	**93**	**35**	**62**	**116**
FOOD AWAY FROM HOME	**100**	**122**	**66**	**94**	**106**
Meals at restaurants, carry-outs, other	**100**	**120**	**70**	**99**	**105**
Lunch	100	130	72	110	103
At fast-food restaurants*	100	132	84	123	99
At full-service restaurants	100	126	52	95	108
At vending machines, mobile vendors	100	52	52	200	93
At employer and school cafeterias	100	146	99	100	100
Dinner	100	108	68	87	107
At fast-food restaurants*	100	102	101	115	98
At full-service restaurants	100	111	52	74	111
At vending machines, mobile vendors	100	76	51	137	102
At employer and school cafeterias	100	134	92	62	107
Snacks and nonalcoholic beverages	100	142	62	103	106
At fast-food restaurants*	100	132	55	100	107
At full-service restaurants	100	235	49	94	109
At vending machines, mobile vendors	100	90	97	130	96
At employer and school cafeterias	100	140	86	80	105

	total consumer units	Asian	black	Hispanic	non-Hispanic white and other
Breakfast and brunch	100	122	82	119	100
At fast-food restaurants*	100	119	99	131	96
At full-service restaurants	100	112	55	100	107
At vending machines, mobile vendors	100	205	58	221	89
At employer and school cafeterias	100	199	145	102	92
Board (including at school)	**100**	**44**	**67**	**30**	**116**
Catered affairs	**100**	**212**	**19**	**70**	**117**
Food on trips	**100**	**132**	**36**	**58**	**117**
School lunches	**100**	**86**	**96**	**92**	**102**
Meals as pay	**100**	**122**	**81**	**126**	**99**
ALCOHOLIC BEVERAGES	**100**	**64**	**43**	**57**	**115**
At home	**100**	**69**	**58**	**69**	**111**
Beer and ale	100	63	70	104	105
Whiskey	100	104	68	6	118
Wine	100	60	35	42	118
Other alcoholic beverages	100	137	98	27	111
Away from home	**100**	**58**	**27**	**44**	**119**
Beer and ale	100	43	20	47	120
At fast-food restaurants*	100	31	28	56	117
At full-service restaurants	100	46	18	47	120
At vending machines, mobile vendors	100	–	49	–	122
Wine	100	44	33	54	117
At fast-food restaurants*	100	–	12	79	116
At full-service restaurants	100	47	34	53	117
Other alcoholic beverages	100	74	38	35	119
At fast-food restaurants*	100	62	54	14	119
At full-service restaurants	100	75	37	36	119
Alcoholic beverages purchased on trips	100	71	20	44	121

* The category fast-food restaurants also includes take-out, delivery, concession stands, buffets, and cafeterias other than employer and school.
Note: "Asian" and "black" include Hispanics and non-Hispanics who identify themselves as being of the respective race alone. "Hispanic" includes people of any race who identify themselves as Hispanic. "Other" includes people who identify themselves as non-Hispanic and as Alaska Native, American Indian, Asian (who are also included in the "Asian" column), Native Hawaiian or other Pacific Islander, as well as non-Hispanics reporting more than one race. "–" means sample is too small to make a reliable estimate.
Source: Calculations by New Strategist based on the Bureau of Labor Statistics' 2007 Consumer Expenditure Survey

Table 20. Food and Alcohol: Total spending by race and Hispanic origin, 2007

(total annual spending on food and alcoholic beverages, by consumer unit race and Hispanic origin groups, 2007; consumer units and dollars in thousands)

	total consumer units	Asian	black	Hispanic	non-Hispanic white and other
Number of consumer units	120,171	4,240	14,422	14,185	91,734
Total spending of all consumer units	$5,965,042,089	$256,104,862	$520,162,312	$588,693,387	$4,862,165,277
Food, total spending	737,056,811	30,268,173	66,360,237	84,155,633	587,040,725
Alcoholic beverages, total spending	54,868,877	1,231,296	2,857,142	3,722,428	48,168,606
FOOD AT HOME	**416,393,717**	**16,494,236**	**40,824,211**	**48,574,547**	**327,344,523**
Cereals and bakery products	**55,224,583**	**1,990,638**	**5,257,107**	**5,809,041**	**44,132,310**
Cereals and cereal products	17,145,998	826,291	1,836,065	2,191,015	13,153,738
Flour	617,679	59,233	57,544	101,281	461,422
Prepared flour mixes	1,393,984	22,090	127,202	132,204	1,132,915
Ready-to-eat and cooked cereals	10,162,861	302,397	1,136,309	1,183,313	7,853,348
Rice	1,994,839	295,910	243,588	422,571	1,346,655
Pasta, cornmeal, and other cereal products	2,976,636	146,577	271,566	351,646	2,358,481
Bakery products	38,078,585	1,164,346	3,421,043	3,618,026	30,978,572
Bread	10,716,850	360,358	1,040,692	1,230,974	8,449,619
White bread	4,068,990	137,715	456,889	549,669	3,071,254
Bread, other than white	6,647,860	222,642	583,803	681,306	5,377,447
Cookies and crackers	9,203,897	217,936	825,227	744,713	7,607,501
Cookies	5,394,476	143,821	523,374	477,467	4,382,133
Crackers	3,809,421	74,115	301,852	267,104	3,225,367
Frozen and refrigerated bakery products	3,156,892	91,754	323,918	273,629	2,552,040
Other bakery products	15,000,946	494,342	1,231,206	1,368,711	12,370,330
Biscuits and rolls	5,325,979	213,908	386,221	462,431	4,463,776
Cakes and cupcakes	4,838,084	144,796	473,907	404,698	3,949,149
Bread and cracker products	492,701	5,724	23,075	28,086	439,406
Sweetrolls, coffee cakes, doughnuts	2,545,222	94,255	184,890	339,447	2,024,569
Pies, tarts, turnovers	1,797,758	35,658	163,113	133,906	1,493,430
Meats, poultry, fish, and eggs	**93,357,245**	**4,348,290**	**12,020,881**	**12,629,189**	**69,005,984**
Beef	25,986,979	936,998	2,668,791	3,623,416	19,756,752
Ground beef	10,708,438	253,594	1,319,469	1,416,372	7,994,618
Roast	4,131,479	237,822	402,230	461,722	3,265,730
Chuck roast	1,168,062	78,228	127,779	152,489	889,820
Round roast	831,583	–	75,427	86,529	668,741
Other roast	2,130,632	70,893	198,879	222,705	1,707,170
Steak	9,170,249	296,758	737,685	1,334,809	7,122,228
Round steak	1,414,413	54,145	92,012	317,177	1,016,413
Sirloin steak	2,407,025	53,424	156,046	304,126	1,948,430
Other steak	5,348,811	189,189	489,627	713,506	4,157,385
Other beef	1,976,813	148,782	209,552	410,514	1,373,258
Pork	17,982,388	677,170	2,674,560	2,294,140	13,067,508
Bacon	3,345,561	104,304	432,660	319,730	2,593,320
Pork chops	3,469,337	67,501	722,686	424,132	2,330,961
Ham	3,827,446	112,148	455,158	584,138	2,810,730
Ham, not canned	3,742,125	108,332	451,120	568,109	2,743,764
Canned ham	86,523	3,816	3,894	15,887	66,966
Sausage	3,073,974	123,299	506,789	318,453	2,250,235
Other pork	4,266,071	269,918	557,266	647,687	3,082,262

	total consumer units	Asian	black	Hispanic	non-Hispanic white and other
Other meats	$12,556,668	$449,143	$1,372,686	$1,428,146	$9,794,439
Frankfurters	2,250,803	78,906	318,582	299,162	1,639,287
Lunch meats (cold cuts)	9,149,820	229,808	905,125	900,322	7,337,803
Bologna, liverwurst, salami	2,309,687	64,660	267,817	247,954	1,794,317
Other lunch meats	6,840,133	165,148	637,308	652,368	5,544,403
Lamb, organ meats, and others	1,156,045	–	149,123	228,662	816,433
Poultry	17,046,256	668,690	2,718,691	2,742,953	11,683,242
Fresh and frozen chicken	13,639,409	552,726	2,160,416	2,491,312	9,094,509
Fresh and frozen whole chicken	3,581,096	209,668	516,308	794,644	2,307,110
Fresh and frozen chicken parts	10,058,313	343,058	1,644,108	1,696,668	6,786,481
Other poultry	3,406,848	115,964	558,276	251,642	2,589,651
Fish and seafood	14,652,450	1,361,973	1,992,399	1,687,589	10,991,568
Canned fish and seafood	1,964,796	59,318	210,994	191,072	1,560,395
Fresh fish and shellfish	7,668,112	934,920	1,123,041	944,579	5,621,460
Frozen fish and shellfish	5,019,543	367,693	658,364	551,938	3,810,630
Eggs	5,132,503	254,315	593,898	853,086	3,712,475
Dairy products	**46,553,044**	**1,481,583**	**3,734,144**	**5,224,052**	**37,609,105**
Fresh milk and cream	18,467,879	651,349	1,606,899	2,386,768	14,500,393
Fresh milk, all types	16,601,624	615,478	1,507,243	2,202,789	12,920,734
Cream	1,866,256	35,870	99,656	183,838	1,578,742
Other dairy products	28,085,164	830,234	2,127,101	2,837,284	23,109,629
Butter	2,416,639	72,377	182,583	161,142	2,064,932
Cheese	14,078,033	299,217	983,436	1,503,894	11,593,343
Ice cream and related products	6,894,210	291,882	554,814	612,366	5,714,111
Miscellaneous dairy products	4,695,081	166,759	406,412	559,740	3,737,243
Fruits and vegetables	**72,086,978**	**3,760,456**	**6,557,107**	**9,250,180**	**56,387,972**
Fresh fruits	24,243,298	1,308,846	1,896,349	3,216,023	19,167,819
Apples	4,199,976	223,745	351,753	483,141	3,366,638
Bananas	3,403,243	170,957	331,562	515,767	2,569,469
Oranges	2,666,594	187,450	240,415	452,785	1,986,041
Citrus fruits, excluding oranges	2,135,439	135,850	140,470	406,684	1,600,758
Other fresh fruits	11,838,045	590,886	832,149	1,357,646	9,643,995
Fresh vegetables	22,867,340	1,563,330	1,914,232	3,245,386	17,757,868
Potatoes	3,748,133	190,927	360,694	447,962	2,941,909
Lettuce	2,858,868	166,971	250,366	362,569	2,249,318
Tomatoes	4,211,994	210,898	391,702	775,778	3,068,502
Other fresh vegetables	12,048,344	994,492	911,615	1,659,219	9,498,138
Processed fruits	13,497,607	492,518	1,546,183	1,503,752	10,463,180
Frozen fruits and fruit juices	1,332,696	21,878	110,617	104,827	1,114,568
Frozen orange juice	472,272	8,862	39,516	47,378	386,200
Frozen fruits	597,250	8,480	39,949	27,944	525,636
Frozen fruit juices, excluding orange	264,376	4,537	31,152	29,647	203,649
Canned fruits	2,339,729	40,789	237,675	190,646	1,907,150
Dried fruits	970,982	51,686	60,140	79,010	828,358
Fresh fruit juice	2,068,143	96,206	244,309	254,479	1,571,403
Canned and bottled fruit juice	6,784,855	281,960	893,299	874,789	5,041,701
Processed vegetables	11,478,734	395,762	1,200,343	1,285,019	8,999,105
Frozen vegetables	3,766,159	133,560	398,191	254,053	3,100,609
Canned and dried vegetables and juices	7,712,575	262,244	802,152	1,030,824	5,897,579
Canned beans	1,540,592	39,856	187,342	219,300	1,138,419
Canned corn	645,318	13,356	89,705	90,358	466,926
Canned miscellaneous vegetables	2,226,769	50,753	208,542	200,434	1,813,581
Dried peas	19,227	466	3,173	1,702	14,677
Dried beans	328,067	17,766	37,209	115,466	181,633
Dried miscellaneous vegetables	967,377	33,962	114,799	131,779	722,864
Fresh and canned vegetable juices	1,869,861	51,516	159,363	264,834	1,453,067

	total consumer units	Asian	black	Hispanic	non-Hispanic white and other
Sugar and other sweets	**$14,960,088**	**$564,386**	**$1,266,540**	**$1,372,682**	**$12,294,191**
Candy and chewing gum	9,655,740	387,409	704,947	761,876	8,160,657
Sugar	1,981,620	82,977	297,814	337,603	1,356,746
Artificial sweeteners	700,597	12,423	57,255	37,732	602,692
Jams, preserves, other sweets	2,620,930	81,535	206,523	235,613	2,175,013
Fats and oils	**10,966,805**	**396,228**	**1,169,624**	**1,273,387**	**8,538,601**
Margarine	846,004	14,458	72,975	64,825	708,186
Fats and oils	3,680,838	224,296	531,739	670,383	2,502,504
Salad dressings	3,262,643	75,642	333,869	276,891	2,647,443
Nondairy cream and imitation milk	1,629,519	41,849	92,445	168,092	1,367,754
Peanut butter	1,546,601	39,983	138,740	93,195	1,311,796
Miscellaneous foods	**78,051,065**	**2,329,795**	**6,581,912**	**7,745,577**	**63,640,463**
Frozen prepared foods	16,432,183	486,667	1,392,156	1,205,158	13,782,116
Frozen meals	8,575,403	280,773	787,009	565,130	7,189,194
Other frozen prepared foods	7,856,780	205,894	605,147	640,027	6,592,923
Canned and packaged soups	4,812,849	171,805	415,498	395,903	3,988,594
Potato chips, nuts, and other snacks	15,373,476	416,283	1,218,515	1,357,079	12,762,951
Potato chips and other snacks	11,513,584	306,425	957,044	1,080,330	9,455,023
Nuts	3,859,893	109,816	261,471	276,749	3,308,845
Condiments and seasonings	12,979,670	454,358	1,133,137	1,166,716	10,659,491
Salt, spices, and other seasonings	2,892,516	137,800	295,507	340,724	2,256,656
Olives, pickles, relishes	1,538,189	29,892	112,492	114,615	1,307,210
Sauces and gravies	5,592,758	193,132	526,980	559,315	4,506,891
Baking needs and miscellaneous products	2,956,207	93,492	198,158	152,063	2,588,733
Other canned or packaged prepared foods	28,452,888	800,682	2,422,752	3,620,721	22,447,310
Prepared salads	3,921,180	84,758	288,152	241,287	3,373,977
Prepared desserts	1,478,103	30,740	109,463	144,971	1,220,980
Baby food	5,088,040	142,846	598,080	852,519	3,661,104
Miscellaneous prepared foods	17,793,720	542,338	1,421,577	2,370,314	14,037,137
Nonalcoholic beverages	**40,027,758**	**1,453,938**	**4,017,825**	**4,894,109**	**31,163,874**
Cola	10,209,728	256,944	905,269	1,404,882	7,927,652
Other carbonated drinks	5,622,801	115,116	502,751	784,856	4,353,696
Tea	3,440,496	212,127	360,262	318,737	2,754,772
Coffee	6,137,133	285,903	376,703	581,869	5,165,542
Roasted coffee	3,845,472	137,630	231,329	373,066	3,233,624
Instant and freeze-dried coffee	2,291,661	148,273	145,374	208,803	1,932,835
Noncarbonated fruit-flavored drinks	2,879,297	63,897	457,754	476,758	1,962,190
Other noncarbonated beverages and ice	4,382,636	192,538	557,987	453,353	3,372,142
Bottled water	7,296,783	327,370	857,099	873,796	5,571,006
Food prepared by consumer unit on trips	**5,167,353**	**168,964**	**219,070**	**376,328**	**4,572,023**
FOOD AWAY FROM HOME	**320,663,095**	**13,773,937**	**25,536,026**	**35,581,087**	**259,696,202**
Meals at restaurants, carry-outs, other	**266,999,533**	**11,264,620**	**22,457,073**	**31,218,206**	**213,396,218**
Lunch	91,495,796	4,205,232	7,914,361	11,897,952	71,820,383
At fast-food restaurants*	43,021,218	2,006,750	4,325,735	6,238,705	32,605,016
At full-service restaurants	36,993,441	1,646,519	2,290,502	4,162,305	30,513,480
At vending machines, mobile vendors	1,183,684	21,878	73,552	279,161	843,035
At employer and school cafeterias	10,296,251	530,085	1,224,716	1,217,782	7,858,852
Dinner	129,004,770	4,912,082	10,455,229	13,180,844	105,204,221
At fast-food restaurants*	40,242,864	1,443,847	4,865,406	5,444,061	30,029,125
At full-service restaurants	87,816,160	3,429,142	5,499,109	7,644,013	74,414,621
At vending machines, mobile vendors	267,981	7,208	16,297	43,264	209,154
At employer and school cafeterias	676,563	31,885	74,418	49,364	550,404
Snacks and nonalcoholic beverages	20,647,781	1,037,443	1,533,347	2,509,185	16,632,292
At fast-food restaurants*	13,153,918	611,917	867,051	1,546,874	10,754,894
At full-service restaurants	3,411,655	283,232	202,052	378,598	2,829,994
At vending machines, mobile vendors	3,331,140	105,194	386,510	512,362	2,444,711
At employer and school cafeterias	751,069	37,100	77,879	71,351	603,610

	total consumer units	Asian	black	Hispanic	non-Hispanic white and other
Breakfast and brunch	$25,852,387	$1,109,862	$2,553,848	$3,630,083	$19,739,322
At fast-food restaurants*	13,474,774	566,676	1,597,669	2,089,451	9,852,232
At full-service restaurants	10,601,486	417,470	699,179	1,256,224	8,646,847
At vending machines, mobile vendors	497,508	35,998	34,469	130,076	338,498
At employer and school cafeterias	1,277,418	89,676	222,531	154,333	901,745
Board (including at school)	**2,846,851**	**44,266**	**228,300**	**101,706**	**2,517,181**
Catered affairs	**8,901,066**	**666,019**	**204,071**	**737,336**	**7,966,181**
Food on trips	**29,505,586**	**1,372,488**	**1,286,731**	**2,017,816**	**26,243,263**
School lunches	**8,542,956**	**260,633**	**984,446**	**928,834**	**6,636,038**
Meals as pay	**3,867,103**	**165,954**	**375,549**	**577,330**	**2,936,405**
ALCOHOLIC BEVERAGES	**54,868,877**	**1,231,296**	**2,857,142**	**3,722,428**	**48,168,606**
At home	**28,806,190**	**700,490**	**2,001,341**	**2,357,263**	**24,450,780**
Beer and ale	13,811,253	304,941	1,156,644	1,693,405	11,064,038
Whiskey	1,038,277	38,033	84,946	7,376	936,604
Wine	11,681,823	247,574	493,232	584,280	10,531,063
Other alcoholic beverages	2,273,635	109,943	266,519	72,202	1,919,993
Away from home	**26,063,888**	**530,806**	**855,801**	**1,365,164**	**23,717,826**
Beer and ale	9,047,675	137,164	216,618	507,114	8,268,903
At fast-food restaurants*	1,317,074	14,204	44,276	87,663	1,178,782
At full-service restaurants	7,573,176	123,002	163,257	419,450	6,944,264
At vending machines, mobile vendors	155,021	–	9,086	–	144,022
Wine	4,435,512	69,578	175,516	282,849	3,953,735
At fast-food restaurants*	183,862	–	2,596	17,164	163,287
At full-service restaurants	4,240,835	69,578	172,920	265,543	3,780,358
Other alcoholic beverages	7,338,843	191,902	338,196	302,424	6,647,046
At fast-food restaurants*	515,534	11,236	33,315	8,795	469,678
At full-service restaurants	6,804,082	180,666	302,141	287,672	6,167,277
Alcoholic beverages purchased on trips	5,241,859	132,118	125,471	272,919	4,848,142

* The category fast-food restaurants also includes take-out, delivery, concession stands, buffets, and cafeterias other than employer and school.
Note: "Asian" and "black" include Hispanics and non-Hispanics who identify themselves as being of the respective race alone. "Hispanic" includes people of any race who identify themselves as Hispanic. "Other" includes people who identify themselves as non-Hispanic and as Alaska Native, American Indian, Asian (who are also included in the "Asian" column), Native Hawaiian or other Pacific Islander, as well as non-Hispanics reporting more than one race. Numbers may not add to total because of rounding and missing subcategories. "–" means sample is too small to make a reliable estimate.
Source: Calculations by New Strategist based on the Bureau of Labor Statistics' 2007 Consumer Expenditure Survey

Table 21. Food and Alcohol: Market shares by race and Hispanic origin, 2007

(percentage of total annual spending on food and alcoholic beverages accounted for by consumer unit race and Hispanic origin groups, 2007)

	total consumer units	Asian	black	Hispanic	non-Hispanic white and other
Share of total consumer units	100.0%	3.5%	12.0%	11.8%	76.3%
Share of total before-tax income	100.0	4.5	8.4	9.0	82.6
Share of total spending	100.0	4.3	8.7	9.9	81.5
Share of food spending	100.0	4.1	9.0	11.4	79.6
Share of alcoholic beverages spending	100.0	2.2	5.2	6.8	87.8
FOOD AT HOME	**100.0**	**4.0**	**9.8**	**11.7**	**78.6**
Cereals and bakery products	**100.0**	**3.6**	**9.5**	**10.5**	**79.9**
Cereals and cereal products	100.0	4.8	10.7	12.8	76.7
Flour	100.0	9.6	9.3	16.4	74.7
Prepared flour mixes	100.0	1.6	9.1	9.5	81.3
Ready-to-eat and cooked cereals	100.0	3.0	11.2	11.6	77.3
Rice	100.0	14.8	12.2	21.2	67.5
Pasta, cornmeal, and other cereal products	100.0	4.9	9.1	11.8	79.2
Bakery products	100.0	3.1	9.0	9.5	81.4
Bread	100.0	3.4	9.7	11.5	78.8
White bread	100.0	3.4	11.2	13.5	75.5
Bread, other than white	100.0	3.3	8.8	10.2	80.9
Cookies and crackers	100.0	2.4	9.0	8.1	82.7
Cookies	100.0	2.7	9.7	8.9	81.2
Crackers	100.0	1.9	7.9	7.0	84.7
Frozen and refrigerated bakery products	100.0	2.9	10.3	8.7	80.8
Other bakery products	100.0	3.3	8.2	9.1	82.5
Biscuits and rolls	100.0	4.0	7.3	8.7	83.8
Cakes and cupcakes	100.0	3.0	9.8	8.4	81.6
Bread and cracker products	100.0	1.2	4.7	5.7	89.2
Sweetrolls, coffee cakes, doughnuts	100.0	3.7	7.3	13.3	79.5
Pies, tarts, turnovers	100.0	2.0	9.1	7.4	83.1
Meats, poultry, fish, and eggs	**100.0**	**4.7**	**12.9**	**13.5**	**73.9**
Beef	100.0	3.6	10.3	13.9	76.0
Ground beef	100.0	2.4	12.3	13.2	74.7
Roast	100.0	5.8	9.7	11.2	79.0
Chuck roast	100.0	6.7	10.9	13.1	76.2
Round roast	100.0	–	9.1	10.4	80.4
Other roast	100.0	3.3	9.3	10.5	80.1
Steak	100.0	3.2	8.0	14.6	77.7
Round steak	100.0	3.8	6.5	22.4	71.9
Sirloin steak	100.0	2.2	6.5	12.6	80.9
Other steak	100.0	3.5	9.2	13.3	77.7
Other beef	100.0	7.5	10.6	20.8	69.5
Pork	100.0	3.8	14.9	12.8	72.7
Bacon	100.0	3.1	12.9	9.6	77.5
Pork chops	100.0	1.9	20.8	12.2	67.2
Ham	100.0	2.9	11.9	15.3	73.4
Ham, not canned	100.0	2.9	12.1	15.2	73.3
Canned ham	100.0	4.4	4.5	18.4	77.4
Sausage	100.0	4.0	16.5	10.4	73.2
Other pork	100.0	6.3	13.1	15.2	72.3

	total consumer units	Asian	black	Hispanic	non-Hispanic white and other
Other meats	100.0%	3.6%	10.9%	11.4%	78.0%
Frankfurters	100.0	3.5	14.2	13.3	72.8
Lunch meats (cold cuts)	100.0	2.5	9.9	9.8	80.2
Bologna, liverwurst, salami	100.0	2.8	11.6	10.7	77.7
Other lunch meats	100.0	2.4	9.3	9.5	81.1
Lamb, organ meats, and others	100.0	–	12.9	19.8	70.6
Poultry	100.0	3.9	15.9	16.1	68.5
Fresh and frozen chicken	100.0	4.1	15.8	18.3	66.7
Fresh and frozen whole chicken	100.0	5.9	14.4	22.2	64.4
Fresh and frozen chicken parts	100.0	3.4	16.3	16.9	67.5
Other poultry	100.0	3.4	16.4	7.4	76.0
Fish and seafood	100.0	9.3	13.6	11.5	75.0
Canned fish and seafood	100.0	3.0	10.7	9.7	79.4
Fresh fish and shellfish	100.0	12.2	14.6	12.3	73.3
Frozen fish and shellfish	100.0	7.3	13.1	11.0	75.9
Eggs	100.0	5.0	11.6	16.6	72.3
Dairy products	**100.0**	**3.2**	**8.0**	**11.2**	**80.8**
Fresh milk and cream	100.0	3.5	8.7	12.9	78.5
Fresh milk, all types	100.0	3.7	9.1	13.3	77.8
Cream	100.0	1.9	5.3	9.9	84.6
Other dairy products	100.0	3.0	7.6	10.1	82.3
Butter	100.0	3.0	7.6	6.7	85.4
Cheese	100.0	2.1	7.0	10.7	82.4
Ice cream and related products	100.0	4.2	8.0	8.9	82.9
Miscellaneous dairy products	100.0	3.6	8.7	11.9	79.6
Fruits and vegetables	**100.0**	**5.2**	**9.1**	**12.8**	**78.2**
Fresh fruits	100.0	5.4	7.8	13.3	79.1
Apples	100.0	5.3	8.4	11.5	80.2
Bananas	100.0	5.0	9.7	15.2	75.5
Oranges	100.0	7.0	9.0	17.0	74.5
Citrus fruits, excluding oranges	100.0	6.4	6.6	19.0	75.0
Other fresh fruits	100.0	5.0	7.0	11.5	81.5
Fresh vegetables	100.0	6.8	8.4	14.2	77.7
Potatoes	100.0	5.1	9.6	12.0	78.5
Lettuce	100.0	5.8	8.8	12.7	78.7
Tomatoes	100.0	5.0	9.3	18.4	72.9
Other fresh vegetables	100.0	8.3	7.6	13.8	78.8
Processed fruits	100.0	3.6	11.5	11.1	77.5
Frozen fruits and fruit juices	100.0	1.6	8.3	7.9	83.6
Frozen orange juice	100.0	1.9	8.4	10.0	81.8
Frozen fruits	100.0	1.4	6.7	4.7	88.0
Frozen fruit juices, excluding orange	100.0	1.7	11.8	11.2	77.0
Canned fruits	100.0	1.7	10.2	8.1	81.5
Dried fruits	100.0	5.3	6.2	8.1	85.3
Fresh fruit juice	100.0	4.7	11.8	12.3	76.0
Canned and bottled fruit juice	100.0	4.2	13.2	12.9	74.3
Processed vegetables	100.0	3.4	10.5	11.2	78.4
Frozen vegetables	100.0	3.5	10.6	6.7	82.3
Canned and dried vegetables and juices	100.0	3.4	10.4	13.4	76.5
Canned beans	100.0	2.6	12.2	14.2	73.9
Canned corn	100.0	2.1	13.9	14.0	72.4
Canned miscellaneous vegetables	100.0	2.3	9.4	9.0	81.4
Dried peas	100.0	2.4	16.5	8.9	76.3
Dried beans	100.0	5.4	11.3	35.2	55.4
Dried miscellaneous vegetables	100.0	3.5	11.9	13.6	74.7
Fresh and canned vegetable juices	100.0	2.8	8.5	14.2	77.7

	total consumer units	Asian	black	Hispanic	non-Hispanic white and other
Sugar and other sweets	100.0%	3.8%	8.5%	9.2%	82.2%
Candy and chewing gum	100.0	4.0	7.3	7.9	84.5
Sugar	100.0	4.2	15.0	17.0	68.5
Artificial sweeteners	100.0	1.8	8.2	5.4	86.0
Jams, preserves, other sweets	100.0	3.1	7.9	9.0	83.0
Fats and oils	100.0	3.6	10.7	11.6	77.9
Margarine	100.0	1.7	8.6	7.7	83.7
Fats and oils	100.0	6.1	14.4	18.2	68.0
Salad dressings	100.0	2.3	10.2	8.5	81.1
Nondairy cream and imitation milk	100.0	2.6	5.7	10.3	83.9
Peanut butter	100.0	2.6	9.0	6.0	84.8
Miscellaneous foods	100.0	3.0	8.4	9.9	81.5
Frozen prepared foods	100.0	3.0	8.5	7.3	83.9
Frozen meals	100.0	3.3	9.2	6.6	83.8
Other frozen prepared foods	100.0	2.6	7.7	8.1	83.9
Canned and packaged soups	100.0	3.6	8.6	8.2	82.9
Potato chips, nuts, and other snacks	100.0	2.7	7.9	8.8	83.0
Potato chips and other snacks	100.0	2.7	8.3	9.4	82.1
Nuts	100.0	2.8	6.8	7.2	85.7
Condiments and seasonings	100.0	3.5	8.7	9.0	82.1
Salt, spices, and other seasonings	100.0	4.8	10.2	11.8	78.0
Olives, pickles, relishes	100.0	1.9	7.3	7.5	85.0
Sauces and gravies	100.0	3.5	9.4	10.0	80.6
Baking needs and miscellaneous products	100.0	3.2	6.7	5.1	87.6
Other canned or packaged prepared foods	100.0	2.8	8.5	12.7	78.9
Prepared salads	100.0	2.2	7.3	6.2	86.0
Prepared desserts	100.0	2.1	7.4	9.8	82.6
Baby food	100.0	2.8	11.8	16.8	72.0
Miscellaneous prepared foods	100.0	3.0	8.0	13.3	78.9
Nonalcoholic beverages	100.0	3.6	10.0	12.2	77.9
Cola	100.0	2.5	8.9	13.8	77.6
Other carbonated drinks	100.0	2.0	8.9	14.0	77.4
Tea	100.0	6.2	10.5	9.3	80.1
Coffee	100.0	4.7	6.1	9.5	84.2
Roasted coffee	100.0	3.6	6.0	9.7	84.1
Instant and freeze-dried coffee	100.0	6.5	6.3	9.1	84.3
Noncarbonated fruit-flavored drinks	100.0	2.2	15.9	16.6	68.1
Other noncarbonated beverages and ice	100.0	4.4	12.7	10.3	76.9
Bottled water	100.0	4.5	11.7	12.0	76.3
Food prepared by consumer unit on trips	100.0	3.3	4.2	7.3	88.5
FOOD AWAY FROM HOME	100.0	4.3	8.0	11.1	81.0
Meals at restaurants, carry-outs, other	100.0	4.2	8.4	11.7	79.9
Lunch	100.0	4.6	8.6	13.0	78.5
At fast-food restaurants*	100.0	4.7	10.1	14.5	75.8
At full-service restaurants	100.0	4.5	6.2	11.3	82.5
At vending machines, mobile vendors	100.0	1.8	6.2	23.6	71.2
At employer and school cafeterias	100.0	5.1	11.9	11.8	76.3
Dinner	100.0	3.8	8.1	10.2	81.6
At fast-food restaurants*	100.0	3.6	12.1	13.5	74.6
At full-service restaurants	100.0	3.9	6.3	8.7	84.7
At vending machines, mobile vendors	100.0	2.7	6.1	16.1	78.0
At employer and school cafeterias	100.0	4.7	11.0	7.3	81.4
Snacks and nonalcoholic beverages	100.0	5.0	7.4	12.2	80.6
At fast-food restaurants*	100.0	4.7	6.6	11.8	81.8
At full-service restaurants	100.0	8.3	5.9	11.1	83.0
At vending machines, mobile vendors	100.0	3.2	11.6	15.4	73.4
At employer and school cafeterias	100.0	4.9	10.4	9.5	80.4

	total consumer units	Asian	black	Hispanic	non-Hispanic white and other
Breakfast and brunch	100.0%	4.3%	9.9%	14.0%	76.4%
At fast-food restaurants*	100.0	4.2	11.9	15.5	73.1
At full-service restaurants	100.0	3.9	6.6	11.8	81.6
At vending machines, mobile vendors	100.0	7.2	6.9	26.1	68.0
At employer and school cafeterias	100.0	7.0	17.4	12.1	70.6
Board (including at school)	**100.0**	**1.6**	**8.0**	**3.6**	**88.4**
Catered affairs	**100.0**	**7.5**	**2.3**	**8.3**	**89.5**
Food on trips	**100.0**	**4.7**	**4.4**	**6.8**	**88.9**
School lunches	**100.0**	**3.1**	**11.5**	**10.9**	**77.7**
Meals as pay	**100.0**	**4.3**	**9.7**	**14.9**	**75.9**
ALCOHOLIC BEVERAGES	**100.0**	**2.2**	**5.2**	**6.8**	**87.8**
At home	**100.0**	**2.4**	**6.9**	**8.2**	**84.9**
Beer and ale	100.0	2.2	8.4	12.3	80.1
Whiskey	100.0	3.7	8.2	0.7	90.2
Wine	100.0	2.1	4.2	5.0	90.1
Other alcoholic beverages	100.0	4.8	11.7	3.2	84.4
Away from home	**100.0**	**2.0**	**3.3**	**5.2**	**91.0**
Beer and ale	100.0	1.5	2.4	5.6	91.4
At fast-food restaurants*	100.0	1.1	3.4	6.7	89.5
At full-service restaurants	100.0	1.6	2.2	5.5	91.7
At vending machines, mobile vendors	100.0	–	5.9	–	92.9
Wine	100.0	1.6	4.0	6.4	89.1
At fast-food restaurants*	100.0	–	1.4	9.3	88.8
At full-service restaurants	100.0	1.6	4.1	6.3	89.1
Other alcoholic beverages	100.0	2.6	4.6	4.1	90.6
At fast-food restaurants*	100.0	2.2	6.5	1.7	91.1
At full-service restaurants	100.0	2.7	4.4	4.2	90.6
Alcoholic beverages purchased on trips	100.0	2.5	2.4	5.2	92.5

The category fast-food restaurants also includes take-out, delivery, concession stands, buffets, and cafeterias other than employer and school.

Note: "Asian" and "black" include Hispanics and non-Hispanics who identify themselves as being of the respective race alone. "Hispanic" includes people of any race who identify themselves as Hispanic. "Other" includes people who identify themselves as non-Hispanic and as Alaska Native, American Indian, Asian (who are also included in the "Asian" column), Native Hawaiian or other Pacific Islander, as well as non-Hispanics reporting more than one race. "–" means sample is too small to make a reliable estimate.

Source: Calculations by New Strategist based on the Bureau of Labor Statistics' 2007 Consumer Expenditure Survey

Spending on Gifts for People in Other Households, 2007

The average household spent $1,198 in 2007 on gifts for people in other households, 8 percent less than in 2000 after adjusting for inflation.

Asians spend more than other racial or ethnic groups on gifts for people in other households. In 2007, the average Asian household spent $1,454 on this item, 21 percent more than average. Non-Hispanic whites spend 13 percent more than the average household on gifts. In contrast, Hispanics spend 43 percent less than average on gifts for people in other households and blacks spend 42 percent less.

Although blacks and Hispanics spend less overall on gifts for people in other households, they spend more than average on some gift categories. Hispanics spend three times the average on gifts of babysitting services and over twice the average on gifts of men's and women's shoes. Blacks spend nearly three times the average on gifts of boys' shoes and 57 percent more than average on gifts of natural gas for a renter.

Table 22. Gifts for People in Other Households: Average spending by race and Hispanic origin, 2007

(average annual spending of consumer units on selected gifts of products and services for people in other households by race and Hispanic origin of consumer unit reference person, 2007)

	total consumer units	Asian	black	Hispanic	non-Hispanic white and other
Number of consumer units (in 000s)	120,171	4,240	14,422	14,185	91,734
Average number of persons per consumer unit	2.5	2.8	2.6	3.2	2.3
Average before-tax income of consumer units	$63,091.00	$80,487.00	$44,381.00	$48,330.00	$68,285.00
Average spending of consumer units, total	49,637.95	60,402.09	36,067.28	41,501.12	53,002.87
Gifts, average spending	1,198.19	1,454.57	697.52	679.07	1,354.74
Food	92.80	89.85	27.47	36.04	111.66
Cakes and cupcakes	2.82	0.76	2.49	1.31	3.08
Candy and chewing gum	10.10	7.99	3.16	4.23	12.00
Food or board at school	11.59	2.28	6.88	4.10	13.47
Catered affairs	27.30	50.13	2.02	1.55	35.20
Food on trips	2.21	4.60	1.53	0.78	2.53
Alcoholic beverages	11.16	9.97	3.30	2.73	13.57
Housing	224.62	221.98	117.11	131.84	255.00
Housekeeping supplies	29.97	11.80	11.37	23.60	33.82
Stationery, stationery supplies, giftwrap	14.12	7.25	2.27	9.39	16.60
Postage	4.45	–	2.51	10.20	3.93
Household textiles	12.96	0.90	0.88	6.04	15.85
Appliances and miscellaneous housewares	20.54	29.19	19.47	6.67	22.71
Major appliances	7.43	18.34	11.72	3.22	7.38
Small appliances and miscellaneous housewares	13.11	10.85	7.75	3.44	15.33
Miscellaneous household equipment	55.13	42.33	14.71	32.17	64.66
Infants' equipment	4.68	5.56	0.14	0.55	5.96
Household decorative items	13.94	8.22	0.87	5.08	17.20
Indoor plants, fresh flowers	14.82	2.28	1.73	4.34	18.32
Computers and computer hardware for nonbusiness use	7.64	13.94	6.83	2.71	8.52
Housing while attending school	41.83	82.34	35.70	15.17	46.84
Lodging on trips	5.20	6.17	1.88	1.19	6.33
Natural gas (renter)	2.70	1.36	4.23	1.57	2.63
Electricity (renter)	9.45	3.74	10.95	10.33	9.07
Babysitting	4.40	10.73	1.97	13.16	3.42
Day care centers, nurseries, and preschools	10.30	14.76	4.77	7.28	11.62
Apparel and services	240.74	265.75	196.79	251.02	246.34
Men and boys, aged 2 or older	57.15	50.02	62.89	66.19	55.17
Women and girls, aged 2 or older	87.01	113.77	48.06	66.02	96.09
Children under age 2	45.02	59.66	36.69	52.58	45.22
Watches	3.52	5.55	3.78	–	3.97
Jewelry	17.20	15.30	4.94	12.02	19.90
Men's footwear	8.33	6.53	15.37	18.69	5.75
Boys' footwear	5.48	–	15.35	8.02	3.58
Women's footwear	8.13	8.98	5.80	17.05	7.21
Girls' footwear	6.39	5.95	2.55	10.39	6.41
Transportation	108.83	230.48	59.63	66.54	123.22
Vehicle purchases	50.72	150.63	35.94	41.24	54.41
Gasoline on trips	17.05	18.88	6.37	7.94	20.11
Airline fares	14.17	19.33	7.63	7.38	16.39
Intercity train fares	2.54	8.86	1.41	1.59	2.89
Ship fares	5.57	13.44	3.92	4.02	6.29
Health care	22.98	42.97	5.83	18.79	26.27

	total consumer units	Asian	black	Hispanic	non-Hispanic white and other
Entertainment	**$102.71**	**$169.14**	**$24.30**	**$36.78**	**$124.47**
Toys, games, hobbies, and tricycles	34.94	33.14	9.37	13.59	41.89
Personal care products and services	**17.52**	**26.39**	**6.96**	**12.79**	**19.80**
Cosmetics, perfume, bath preparations	13.04	23.18	5.74	7.27	14.97
Reading	**1.03**	**0.33**	**0.02**	**0.15**	**1.32**
Education	**282.92**	**334.98**	**213.17**	**63.86**	**327.25**
College tuition	234.64	304.36	188.11	37.74	271.97
All other gifts	**92.87**	**62.71**	**42.94**	**58.54**	**105.83**
Gifts of out-of-town trip expenses	64.96	53.75	20.62	18.78	78.95

Note: "Asian" and "black" include Hispanics and non-Hispanics who identify themselves as being of the respective race alone. "Hispanic" includes people of any race who identify themselves as Hispanic. "Other" includes people who identify themselves as non-Hispanic and as Alaska Native, American Indian, Asian (who are also included in the "Asian" column), Native Hawaiian or other Pacific Islander, as well as non-Hispanics reporting more than one race. "–" means sample is too small to make a reliable estimate. Numbers may not add to total because not all categories are shown. Spending on gifts is also included in the product and service categories in other chapters.
Source: Bureau of Labor Statistics, unpublished tables from the 2007 Consumer Expenditure Survey

Table 23. Gifts for People in Other Households: Indexed spending by race and Hispanic origin, 2007

(indexed average annual spending of consumer units on selected gifts of products and services for people in other households by race and Hispanic origin of consumer unit reference person, 2007; index definition: an index of 100 is the average for all consumer units; an index of 132 means that spending by consumer units in that group is 32 percent above the average for all consumer units; an index of 68 indicates spending that is 32 percent below the average for all consumer units)

	total consumer units	Asian	black	Hispanic	non-Hispanic white and other
Average spending of consumer units, total	$49,638	$60,402	$36,067	$41,501	$53,003
Average spending of consumer units, index	100	122	73	84	107
Gifts, spending index	100	121	58	57	113
Food	**100**	**97**	**30**	**39**	**120**
Cakes and cupcakes	100	27	88	46	109
Candy and chewing gum	100	79	31	42	119
Food or board at school	100	20	59	35	116
Catered affairs	100	184	7	6	129
Food on trips	100	208	69	35	114
Alcoholic beverages	**100**	**89**	**30**	**24**	**122**
Housing	**100**	**99**	**52**	**59**	**114**
Housekeeping supplies	100	39	38	79	113
Stationery, stationery supplies, giftwrap	100	51	16	67	118
Postage	100	–	56	229	88
Household textiles	100	7	7	47	122
Appliances and miscellaneous housewares	100	142	95	32	111
Major appliances	100	247	158	43	99
Small appliances and miscellaneous housewares	100	83	59	26	117
Miscellaneous household equipment	100	77	27	58	117
Infants' equipment	100	119	3	12	127
Household decorative items	100	59	6	36	123
Indoor plants, fresh flowers	100	15	12	29	124
Computers and computer hardware for nonbusiness use	100	182	89	35	112
Housing while attending school	100	197	85	36	112
Lodging on trips	100	119	36	23	122
Natural gas (renter)	100	50	157	58	97
Electricity (renter)	100	40	116	109	96
Babysitting	100	244	45	299	78
Day care centers, nurseries, and preschools	100	143	46	71	113
Apparel and services	**100**	**110**	**82**	**104**	**102**
Men and boys, aged 2 or older	100	88	110	116	97
Women and girls, aged 2 or older	100	131	55	76	110
Children under age 2	100	133	81	117	100
Watches	100	158	107	–	113
Jewelry	100	89	29	70	116
Men's footwear	100	78	185	224	69
Boys' footwear	100	–	280	146	65
Women's footwear	100	110	71	210	89
Girls' footwear	100	93	40	163	100
Transportation	**100**	**212**	**55**	**61**	**113**
Vehicle purchases	100	297	71	81	107
Gasoline on trips	100	111	37	47	118
Airline fares	100	136	54	52	116
Intercity train fares	100	349	56	63	114
Ship fares	100	241	70	72	113
Health care	**100**	**187**	**25**	**82**	**114**

	total consumer units	Asian	black	Hispanic	non-Hispanic white and other
Entertainment	100	165	24	36	121
Toys, games, hobbies, and tricycles	100	95	27	39	120
Personal care products and services	100	151	40	73	113
Cosmetics, perfume, bath preparations	100	178	44	56	115
Reading	100	32	2	15	128
Education	100	118	75	23	116
College tuition	100	130	80	16	116
All other gifts	100	68	46	63	114
Gifts of out-of-town trip expenses	100	83	32	29	122

Note: "Asian" and "black" include Hispanics and non-Hispanics who identify themselves as being of the respective race alone. "Hispanic" includes people of any race who identify themselves as Hispanic. "Other" includes people who identify themselves as non-Hispanic and as Alaska Native, American Indian, Asian (who are also included in the "Asian" column), Native Hawaiian or other Pacific Islander, as well as non-Hispanics reporting more than one race. "–" means sample is too small to make a reliable estimate. Spending on gifts is also included in the product and service categories in other chapters.
Source: Calculations by New Strategist based on the Bureau of Labor Statistics' 2007 Consumer Expenditure Survey

Table 24. Gifts for People in Other Households: Total spending by race and Hispanic origin, 2007

(total annual spending on selected gifts of products and services for people in other households by consumer unit race and Hispanic origin groups, 2007; consumer units and dollars in thousands)

	total consumer units	Asian	black	Hispanic	non-Hispanic white and other
Number of consumer units	120,171	4,240	14,422	14,185	91,734
Total spending of all consumer units	$5,965,042,089	$256,104,862	$520,162,312	$588,693,387	$4,862,165,277
Gifts, total spending	**143,987,690**	**6,167,377**	**10,059,633**	**9,632,608**	**124,275,719**
Food	**11,151,869**	**380,964**	**396,172**	**511,227**	**10,243,018**
Cakes and cupcakes	338,882	3,222	35,911	18,582	282,541
Candy and chewing gum	1,213,727	33,878	45,574	60,003	1,100,808
Food or board at school	1,392,782	9,667	99,223	58,159	1,235,657
Catered affairs	3,280,668	212,551	29,132	21,987	3,229,037
Food on trips	265,578	19,504	22,066	11,064	232,087
Alcoholic beverages	**1,341,108**	**42,273**	**47,593**	**38,725**	**1,244,830**
Housing	**26,992,810**	**941,195**	**1,688,960**	**1,870,150**	**23,392,170**
Housekeeping supplies	3,601,525	50,032	163,978	334,766	3,102,444
Stationery, stationery supplies, giftwrap	1,696,815	30,740	32,738	133,197	1,522,784
Postage	534,761	–	36,199	144,687	360,515
Household textiles	1,557,416	3,816	12,691	85,677	1,453,984
Appliances and miscellaneous housewares	2,468,312	123,766	280,796	94,614	2,083,279
Major appliances	892,871	77,762	169,026	45,676	676,997
Small appliances and miscellaneous housewares	1,575,442	46,004	111,771	48,796	1,406,282
Miscellaneous household equipment	6,625,027	179,479	212,148	456,331	5,931,520
Infants' equipment	562,400	23,574	2,019	7,802	546,735
Household decorative items	1,675,184	34,853	12,547	72,060	1,577,825
Indoor plants, fresh flowers	1,780,934	9,667	24,950	61,563	1,680,567
Computers and computer hardware for nonbusiness use	918,106	59,106	98,502	38,441	781,574
Housing while attending school	5,026,753	349,122	514,865	215,186	4,296,821
Lodging on trips	624,889	26,161	27,113	16,880	580,676
Natural gas (renter)	324,462	5,766	61,005	22,270	241,260
Electricity (renter)	1,135,616	15,858	157,921	146,531	832,027
Babysitting	528,752	45,495	28,411	186,675	313,730
Day care centers, nurseries, and preschools	1,237,761	62,582	68,793	103,267	1,065,949
Apparel and services	**28,929,967**	**1,126,780**	**2,838,105**	**3,560,719**	**22,597,754**
Men and boys, aged 2 or older	6,867,773	212,085	907,000	938,905	5,060,965
Women and girls, aged 2 or older	10,456,079	482,385	693,121	936,494	8,814,720
Children under age 2	5,410,098	252,958	529,143	745,847	4,148,211
Watches	423,002	23,532	54,515	–	364,184
Jewelry	2,066,941	64,872	71,245	170,504	1,825,507
Men's footwear	1,001,024	27,687	221,666	265,118	527,471
Boys' footwear	658,537	–	221,378	113,764	328,408
Women's footwear	976,990	38,075	83,648	241,854	661,402
Girls' footwear	767,893	25,228	36,776	147,382	588,015
Transportation	**13,078,210**	**977,235**	**859,984**	**943,870**	**11,303,463**
Vehicle purchases	6,095,073	638,671	518,327	584,989	4,991,247
Gasoline on trips	2,048,916	80,051	91,868	112,629	1,844,771
Airline fares	1,702,823	81,959	110,040	104,685	1,503,520
Intercity train fares	305,234	37,566	20,335	22,554	265,111
Ship fares	669,352	56,986	56,534	57,024	577,007
Health care	**2,761,530**	**182,193**	**84,080**	**266,536**	**2,409,852**

	total consumer units	Asian	black	Hispanic	non-Hispanic white and other
Entertainment	$12,342,763	$717,154	$350,455	$521,724	$11,418,131
Toys, games, hobbies, and tricycles	4,198,775	140,514	135,134	192,774	3,842,737
Personal care products and services	2,105,396	111,894	100,377	181,426	1,816,333
Cosmetics, perfume, bath preparations	1,567,030	98,283	82,782	103,125	1,373,258
Reading	123,776	1,399	288	2,128	121,089
Education	33,998,779	1,420,315	3,074,338	905,854	30,019,952
College tuition	28,196,923	1,290,486	2,712,922	535,342	24,948,896
All other gifts	11,160,281	265,890	619,281	830,390	9,708,209
Gifts of out-of-town trip expenses	7,806,308	227,900	297,382	266,394	7,242,399

Note: "Asian" and "black" include Hispanics and non-Hispanics who identify themselves as being of the respective race alone. "Hispanic" includes people of any race who identify themselves as Hispanic. "Other" includes people who identify themselves as non-Hispanic and as Alaska Native, American Indian, Asian (who are also included in the "Asian" column), Native Hawaiian or other Pacific Islander, as well as non-Hispanics reporting more than one race. Numbers may not add to total because of rounding. "–" means sample is too small to make a reliable estimate. Spending on gifts is also included in the product and service categories in other chapters.
Source: Calculations by New Strategist based on the Bureau of Labor Statistics' 2007 Consumer Expenditure Survey

Table 25. Gifts for People in Other Households: Market shares by race and Hispanic origin, 2007

(percentage of total annual spending on selected gifts of products and services for people in other households accounted for by consumer unit race and Hispanic origin groups, 2007)

	total consumer units	Asian	black	Hispanic	non-Hispanic white and other
Share of total consumer units	100.0%	3.5%	12.0%	11.8%	76.3%
Share of total before-tax income	100.0	4.5	8.4	9.0	82.6
Share of total spending	100.0	4.3	8.7	9.9	81.5
Share of gifts spending	100.0	4.3	7.0	6.7	86.3
Food	100.0	3.4	3.6	4.6	91.9
Cakes and cupcakes	100.0	1.0	10.6	5.5	83.4
Candy and chewing gum	100.0	2.8	3.8	4.9	90.7
Food or board at school	100.0	0.7	7.1	4.2	88.7
Catered affairs	100.0	6.5	0.9	0.7	98.4
Food on trips	100.0	7.3	8.3	4.2	87.4
Alcoholic beverages	100.0	3.2	3.5	2.9	92.8
Housing	100.0	3.5	6.3	6.9	86.7
Housekeeping supplies	100.0	1.4	4.6	9.3	86.1
Stationery, stationery supplies, giftwrap	100.0	1.8	1.9	7.8	89.7
Postage	100.0	–	6.8	27.1	67.4
Household textiles	100.0	0.2	0.8	5.5	93.4
Appliances and miscellaneous housewares	100.0	5.0	11.4	3.8	84.4
Major appliances	100.0	8.7	18.9	5.1	75.8
Small appliances and miscellaneous housewares	100.0	2.9	7.1	3.1	89.3
Miscellaneous household equipment	100.0	2.7	3.2	6.9	89.5
Infants' equipment	100.0	4.2	0.4	1.4	97.2
Household decorative items	100.0	2.1	0.7	4.3	94.2
Indoor plants, fresh flowers	100.0	0.5	1.4	3.5	94.4
Computers and computer hardware for nonbusiness use	100.0	6.4	10.7	4.2	85.1
Housing while attending school	100.0	6.9	10.2	4.3	85.5
Lodging on trips	100.0	4.2	4.3	2.7	92.9
Natural gas (renter)	100.0	1.8	18.8	6.9	74.4
Electricity (renter)	100.0	1.4	13.9	12.9	73.3
Babysitting	100.0	8.6	5.4	35.3	59.3
Day care centers, nurseries, and preschools	100.0	5.1	5.6	8.3	86.1
Apparel and services	100.0	3.9	9.8	12.3	78.1
Men and boys, aged 2 or older	100.0	3.1	13.2	13.7	73.7
Women and girls, aged 2 or older	100.0	4.6	6.6	9.0	84.3
Children under age 2	100.0	4.7	9.8	13.8	76.7
Watches	100.0	5.6	12.9	–	86.1
Jewelry	100.0	3.1	3.4	8.2	88.3
Men's footwear	100.0	2.8	22.1	26.5	52.7
Boys' footwear	100.0	–	33.6	17.3	49.9
Women's footwear	100.0	3.9	8.6	24.8	67.7
Girls' footwear	100.0	3.3	4.8	19.2	76.6
Transportation	100.0	7.5	6.6	7.2	86.4
Vehicle purchases	100.0	10.5	8.5	9.6	81.9
Gasoline on trips	100.0	3.9	4.5	5.5	90.0
Airline fares	100.0	4.8	6.5	6.1	88.3
Intercity train fares	100.0	12.3	6.7	7.4	86.9
Ship fares	100.0	8.5	8.4	8.5	86.2
Health care	100.0	6.6	3.0	9.7	87.3

	total consumer units	Asian	black	Hispanic	non-Hispanic white and other
Entertainment	**100.0%**	**5.8%**	**2.8%**	**4.2%**	**92.5%**
Toys, games, hobbies, and tricycles	100.0	3.3	3.2	4.6	91.5
Personal care products and services	**100.0**	**5.3**	**4.8**	**8.6**	**86.3**
Cosmetics, perfume, bath preparations	100.0	6.3	5.3	6.6	87.6
Reading	**100.0**	**1.1**	**0.2**	**1.7**	**97.8**
Education	**100.0**	**4.2**	**9.0**	**2.7**	**88.3**
College tuition	100.0	4.6	9.6	1.9	88.5
All other gifts	**100.0**	**2.4**	**5.5**	**7.4**	**87.0**
Gifts of out-of-town trip expenses	100.0	2.9	3.8	3.4	92.8

Note: "Asian" and "black" include Hispanics and non-Hispanics who identify themselves as being of the respective race alone. "Hispanic" includes people of any race who identify themselves as Hispanic. "Other" includes people who identify themselves as non-Hispanic and as Alaska Native, American Indian, Asian (who are also included in the "Asian" column), Native Hawaiian or other Pacific Islander, as well as non-Hispanics reporting more than one race. "–" means sample is too small to make a reliable estimate. Numbers may not add to total because of rounding and because not all categories are shown. Spending on gifts is also included in the product and service categories in other chapters.
Source: Calculations by New Strategist based on the Bureau of Labor Statistics' 2007 Consumer Expenditure Survey

Spending on Health Care (Out-of-Pocket Expenses), 2007

The average American household spent $2,853 on out-of-pocket health care expenses in 2007, up 15 percent from the inflation-adjusted $2,488 it spent in 2000. Out-of-pocket spending on health insurance rose by a substantial 31 percent during those years, while prescription and nonprescription drug spending decreased 4 percent. Out-of-pocket health care costs absorbed 5.7 percent of the household budget in 2007, up from 5.4 percent in 2000.

Minority households spend less than the average household on out-of-pocket health care costs. Asians spend 24 percent less on health care than the average household. Hispanics spend an even larger 48 percent less than the average household on health care, and blacks spend 41 percent less. One reason for the lower out-of-pocket spending of Asians, blacks, and Hispanics is their younger age, which reduces the need for health care services. Non-Hispanic whites spend 14 percent more than the average household on out-of-pocket health care costs.

Table 26. Health Care: Average spending by race and Hispanic origin, 2007

(average annual out-of-pocket spending of consumer units on health care, by race and Hispanic origin of consumer unit reference person, 2007)

	total consumer units	Asian	black	Hispanic	non-Hispanic white and other
Number of consumer units (in 000s)	120,171	4,240	14,422	14,185	91,734
Average number of persons per consumer unit	2.5	2.8	2.6	3.2	2.3
Average before-tax income of consumer units	$63,091.00	$80,487.00	$44,381.00	$48,330.00	$68,285.00
Average spending of consumer units, total	49,637.95	60,402.09	36,067.28	41,501.12	53,002.87
Health care, average spending	2,852.77	2,170.36	1,689.46	1,486.10	3,243.54
HEALTH INSURANCE	1,544.83	1,377.90	1,000.99	743.57	1,752.45
Commercial health insurance	292.41	260.17	190.17	135.96	332.47
Traditional fee-for-service health plan (not BCBS)	88.51	84.91	44.66	38.95	102.97
Preferred-provider health plan (not BCBS)	203.89	175.26	145.51	97.01	229.50
Blue Cross, Blue Shield	435.80	399.76	260.55	158.95	505.46
Traditional fee-for-service health plan	77.16	49.95	49.01	12.41	91.51
Preferred-provider health plan	194.30	173.62	78.29	67.31	231.81
Health maintenance organization	125.30	142.34	110.46	73.03	135.53
Commercial Medicare supplement	34.90	30.35	22.17	5.32	41.41
Other BCBS health insurance	4.15	3.50	0.63	0.89	5.20
Health maintenance plans (HMOs)	250.49	329.08	210.01	197.87	264.64
Medicare payments	323.35	204.79	240.59	175.20	359.02
Medicare prescription drug premium	48.36	27.67	41.71	25.91	52.94
Commercial Medicare supplements, other health insurance	126.93	64.34	43.03	39.88	153.35
Commercial Medicare supplement (not BCBS)	90.44	36.62	28.23	23.41	110.42
Other health insurance (not BCBS)	36.49	27.73	14.80	16.47	42.93
Long-term care insurance	67.49	92.08	14.92	9.80	84.56
MEDICAL SERVICES	709.29	486.73	370.14	468.15	799.39
Physician's services	171.10	103.99	75.52	103.45	196.65
Dental services	244.67	228.46	105.67	171.66	277.61
Eye care services	37.88	18.90	15.00	24.71	43.48
Service by professionals other than physician	72.44	14.51	15.77	43.79	85.64
Lab tests, X-rays	39.08	17.46	13.01	23.83	45.47
Hospital room and services	113.93	38.25	150.66	70.15	114.85
Care in convalescent or nursing home	15.62	–	–	–	20.37
Other medical services	13.72	16.29	9.61	14.63	14.20
DRUGS	480.90	219.50	261.59	212.87	555.63
Nonprescription drugs	75.40	61.80	47.33	48.88	83.41
Nonprescription vitamins	46.18	27.75	11.20	15.05	55.98
Prescription drugs	359.32	129.95	203.07	148.94	416.25
MEDICAL SUPPLIES	117.75	86.22	56.74	61.51	136.06
Eyeglasses and contact lenses	61.01	51.68	40.10	37.10	68.24
Hearing aids	15.19	6.83	0.24	1.98	19.55
Topicals and dressings	31.81	26.47	13.54	21.16	36.14
Medical equipment for general use	4.45	0.53	1.38	0.32	5.57
Supportive and convalescent medical equipment	3.18	0.71	1.00	0.43	3.95
Rental of medical equipment	1.43	–	0.18	0.08	1.84
Rental of supportive and convalescent medical equipment	0.68	–	0.31	0.43	0.78

Note: "Asian" and "black" include Hispanics and non-Hispanics who identify themselves as being of the respective race alone. "Hispanic" includes people of any race who identify themselves as Hispanic. "Other" includes people who identify themselves as non-Hispanic and as Alaska Native, American Indian, Asian (who are also included in the "Asian" column), Native Hawaiian or other Pacific Islander, as well as non-Hispanics reporting more than one race. Subcategories may not add to total because some are not shown. "–" means sample is too small to make a reliable estimate.
Source: Bureau of Labor Statistics, unpublished tables from the 2007 Consumer Expenditure Survey

Table 27. Health Care: Indexed spending by race and Hispanic origin, 2007

(indexed average annual out-of-pocket spending of consumer units on health care, by race and Hispanic origin of consumer unit reference person, 2007; index definition: an index of 100 is the average for all consumer units; an index of 132 means that spending by consumer units in that group is 32 percent above the average for all consumer units; an index of 68 indicates spending that is 32 percent below the average for all consumer units)

	total consumer units	Asian	black	Hispanic	non-Hispanic white and other
Average spending of consumer units, total	$49,638	$60,402	$36,067	$41,501	$53,003
Average spending of consumer units, index	100	122	73	84	107
Health care, spending index	100	76	59	52	114
HEALTH INSURANCE	100	89	65	48	113
Commercial health insurance	100	89	65	46	114
Traditional fee-for-service health plan (not BCBS)	100	96	50	44	116
Preferred-provider health plan (not BCBS)	100	86	71	48	113
Blue Cross, Blue Shield	100	92	60	36	116
Traditional fee-for-service health plan	100	65	64	16	119
Preferred-provider health plan	100	89	40	35	119
Health maintenance organization	100	114	88	58	108
Commercial Medicare supplement	100	87	64	15	119
Other BCBS health insurance	100	84	15	21	125
Health maintenance plans (HMOs)	100	131	84	79	106
Medicare payments	100	63	74	54	111
Medicare prescription drug premium	100	57	86	54	109
Commercial Medicare supplements, other health insurance	100	51	34	31	121
Commercial Medicare supplement (not BCBS)	100	40	31	26	122
Other health insurance (not BCBS)	100	76	41	45	118
Long-term care insurance	100	136	22	15	125
MEDICAL SERVICES	100	69	52	66	113
Physician's services	100	61	44	60	115
Dental services	100	93	43	70	113
Eye care services	100	50	40	65	115
Service by professionals other than physician	100	20	22	60	118
Lab tests, X-rays	100	45	33	61	116
Hospital room and services	100	34	132	62	101
Care in convalescent or nursing home	100	–	–	–	130
Other medical services	100	119	70	107	103
DRUGS	100	46	54	44	116
Nonprescription drugs	100	82	63	65	111
Nonprescription vitamins	100	60	24	33	121
Prescription drugs	100	36	57	41	116
MEDICAL SUPPLIES	100	73	48	52	116
Eyeglasses and contact lenses	100	85	66	61	112
Hearing aids	100	45	2	13	129
Topicals and dressings	100	83	43	67	114
Medical equipment for general use	100	12	31	7	125
Supportive and convalescent medical equipment	100	22	31	14	124
Rental of medical equipment	100	–	13	6	129
Rental of supportive and convalescent medical equipment	100	–	46	63	115

Note: "Asian" and "black" include Hispanics and non-Hispanics who identify themselves as being of the respective race alone. "Hispanic" includes people of any race who identify themselves as Hispanic. "Other" includes people who identify themselves as non-Hispanic and as Alaska Native, American Indian, Asian (who are also included in the "Asian" column), Native Hawaiian or other Pacific Islander, as well as non-Hispanics reporting more than one race. "–" means sample is too small to make a reliable estimate.
Source: Calculations by New Strategist based on the Bureau of Labor Statistics' 2007 Consumer Expenditure Survey

Table 28. Health Care: Total spending by race and Hispanic origin, 2007

(total annual out-of-pocket spending on health care, by consumer unit race and Hispanic origin groups, 2007; consumer units and dollars in thousands)

	total consumer units	Asian	black	Hispanic	non-Hispanic white and other
Number of consumer units	120,171	4,240	14,422	14,185	91,734
Total spending of all consumer units	$5,965,042,089	$256,104,862	$520,162,312	$588,693,387	$4,862,165,277
Health care, total spending	342,820,224	9,202,326	24,365,392	21,080,329	297,542,898
HEALTH INSURANCE	185,643,766	5,842,296	14,436,278	10,547,540	160,759,248
Commercial health insurance	35,139,202	1,103,121	2,742,632	1,928,593	30,498,803
Traditional fee-for-service health plan (not BCBS)	10,636,335	360,018	644,087	552,506	9,445,850
Preferred-provider health plan (not BCBS)	24,501,665	743,102	2,098,545	1,376,087	21,052,953
Blue Cross, Blue Shield	52,370,522	1,694,982	3,757,652	2,254,706	46,367,868
Traditional fee-for-service health plan	9,272,394	211,788	706,822	176,036	8,394,578
Preferred-provider health plan	23,349,225	736,149	1,129,098	954,792	21,264,859
Health maintenance organization	15,057,426	603,522	1,593,054	1,035,931	12,432,709
Commercial Medicare supplement	4,193,968	128,684	319,736	75,464	3,798,705
Other BCBS health insurance	498,710	14,840	9,086	12,625	477,017
Health maintenance plans (HMOs)	30,101,634	1,395,299	3,028,764	2,806,786	24,276,486
Medicare payments	38,857,293	868,310	3,469,789	2,485,212	32,934,341
Medicare prescription drug premium	5,811,470	117,321	601,542	367,533	4,856,398
Commercial Medicare supplements and other health insurance	15,253,305	272,802	620,579	565,698	14,067,409
Commercial Medicare supplement (not BCBS)	10,868,265	155,269	407,133	332,071	10,129,268
Other health insurance (not BCBS)	4,385,040	117,575	213,446	233,627	3,938,141
Long-term care insurance	8,110,341	390,419	215,176	139,013	7,757,027
MEDICAL SERVICES	85,236,089	2,063,735	5,338,159	6,640,708	73,331,242
Physician's services	20,561,258	440,918	1,089,149	1,467,438	18,039,491
Dental services	29,402,239	968,670	1,523,973	2,434,997	25,466,276
Eye care services	4,552,077	80,136	216,330	350,511	3,988,594
Service by professionals other than physician	8,705,187	61,522	227,435	621,161	7,856,100
Lab tests, X-rays	4,696,283	74,030	187,630	338,029	4,171,145
Hospital room and services	13,691,082	162,180	2,172,819	995,078	10,535,650
Care in convalescent or nursing home	1,877,071	–	–	–	1,868,622
Other medical services	1,648,746	69,070	138,595	207,527	1,302,623
DRUGS	57,790,234	930,680	3,772,651	3,019,561	50,970,162
Nonprescription drugs	9,060,893	262,032	682,593	693,363	7,651,533
Nonprescription vitamins	5,549,497	117,660	161,526	213,484	5,135,269
Prescription drugs	43,179,844	550,988	2,928,676	2,112,714	38,184,278
MEDICAL SUPPLIES	14,150,135	365,573	818,304	872,519	12,481,328
Eyeglasses and contact lenses	7,331,633	219,123	578,322	526,264	6,259,928
Hearing aids	1,825,397	28,959	3,461	28,086	1,793,400
Topicals and dressings	3,822,640	112,233	195,274	300,155	3,315,267
Medical equipment for general use	534,761	2,247	19,902	4,539	510,958
Supportive and convalescent medical equipment	382,144	3,010	14,422	6,100	362,349
Rental of medical equipment	171,845	–	2,596	1,135	168,791
Rental of supportive and convalescent medical equipment	81,716	–	4,471	6,100	71,553

Note: "Asian" and "black" include Hispanics and non-Hispanics who identify themselves as being of the respective race alone. "Hispanic" includes people of any race who identify themselves as Hispanic. "Other" includes people who identify themselves as non-Hispanic and as Alaska Native, American Indian, Asian (who are also included in the "Asian" column), Native Hawaiian or other Pacific Islander, as well as non-Hispanics reporting more than one race. Numbers may not add to total because of rounding and missing subcategories. "–" means sample is too small to make a reliable estimate.
Source: Calculations by New Strategist based on the Bureau of Labor Statistics' 2007 Consumer Expenditure Survey

Table 29. Health Care: Market shares by race and Hispanic origin, 2007

(percentage of total annual out-of-pocket spending on health care accounted for by consumer unit race and Hispanic origin groups, 2007)

	total consumer units	Asian	black	Hispanic	non-Hispanic white and other
Share of total consumer units	100.0%	3.5%	12.0%	11.8%	76.3%
Share of total before-tax income	100.0	4.5	8.4	9.0	82.6
Share of total spending	100.0	4.3	8.7	9.9	81.5
Share of health care spending	100.0	2.7	7.1	6.1	86.8
HEALTH INSURANCE	100.0	3.1	7.8	5.7	86.6
Commercial health insurance	100.0	3.1	7.8	5.5	86.8
Traditional fee-for-service health plan (not BCBS)	100.0	3.4	6.1	5.2	88.8
Preferred-provider health plan (not BCBS)	100.0	3.0	8.6	5.6	85.9
Blue Cross, Blue Shield	100.0	3.2	7.2	4.3	88.5
Traditional fee-for-service health plan	100.0	2.3	7.6	1.9	90.5
Preferred-provider health plan	100.0	3.2	4.8	4.1	91.1
Health maintenance organization	100.0	4.0	10.6	6.9	82.6
Commercial Medicare supplement	100.0	3.1	7.6	1.8	90.6
Other BCBS health insurance	100.0	3.0	1.8	2.5	95.7
Health maintenance plans (HMOs)	100.0	4.6	10.1	9.3	80.6
Medicare payments	100.0	2.2	8.9	6.4	84.8
Medicare prescription drug premium	100.0	2.0	10.4	6.3	83.6
Commercial Medicare supplements, other health insurance	100.0	1.8	4.1	3.7	92.2
Commercial Medicare supplement (not BCBS)	100.0	1.4	3.7	3.1	93.2
Other health insurance (not BCBS)	100.0	2.7	4.9	5.3	89.8
Long-term care insurance	100.0	4.8	2.7	1.7	95.6
MEDICAL SERVICES	100.0	2.4	6.3	7.8	86.0
Physician's services	100.0	2.1	5.3	7.1	87.7
Dental services	100.0	3.3	5.2	8.3	86.6
Eye care services	100.0	1.8	4.8	7.7	87.6
Service by professionals other than physician	100.0	0.7	2.6	7.1	90.2
Lab tests, X-rays	100.0	1.6	4.0	7.2	88.8
Hospital room and services	100.0	1.2	15.9	7.3	77.0
Care in convalescent or nursing home	100.0	–	–	–	99.5
Other medical services	100.0	4.2	8.4	12.6	79.0
DRUGS	100.0	1.6	6.5	5.2	88.2
Nonprescription drugs	100.0	2.9	7.5	7.7	84.4
Nonprescription vitamins	100.0	2.1	2.9	3.8	92.5
Prescription drugs	100.0	1.3	6.8	4.9	88.4
MEDICAL SUPPLIES	100.0	2.6	5.8	6.2	88.2
Eyeglasses and contact lenses	100.0	3.0	7.9	7.2	85.4
Hearing aids	100.0	1.6	0.2	1.5	98.2
Topicals and dressings	100.0	2.9	5.1	7.9	86.7
Medical equipment for general use	100.0	0.4	3.7	0.8	95.5
Supportive and convalescent medical equipment	100.0	0.8	3.8	1.6	94.8
Rental of medical equipment	100.0	–	1.5	0.7	98.2
Rental of supportive and convalescent medical equipment	100.0	–	5.5	7.5	87.6

Note: "Asian" and "black" include Hispanics and non-Hispanics who identify themselves as being of the respective race alone. "Hispanic" includes people of any race who identify themselves as Hispanic. "Other" includes people who identify themselves as non-Hispanic and as Alaska Native, American Indian, Asian (who are also included in the "Asian" column), Native Hawaiian or other Pacific Islander, as well as non-Hispanics reporting more than one race. "–" means sample is too small to make a reliable estimate.
Source: Calculations by New Strategist based on the Bureau of Labor Statistics' 2007 Consumer Expenditure Survey

Spending on Housing: Household Operations, 2007

For the average household, housing is biggest expense. In 2007, housing costs—including shelter, utilities, and all household operations (household services, housekeeping supplies, furniture, and equipment)—absorbed 34.0 percent of average household expenditures. That figure has increased slightly from the 32.4 percent of 2000. Spending on household furnishings and equipment fell 4 percent between 2000 and 2007, after adjusting for inflation, but spending on housekeeping supplies rose 10 percent during those years, and spending on household services increased 19 percent.

Asians spend 33 percent more than the average household on housing—$22,554 in 2007. Hispanics spend 8 percent less than average on housing ($15,573), while blacks spend 20 percent less ($13,494). Two factors are behind the higher spending of Asians on housing—their higher incomes and the fact that many live in California, where housing costs are well above average. Asian households spend 60 percent more than the average household on day care centers. Hispanics spend twice the average on babysitting services in someone else's home. Black householders outspend the average on water-softening service, home security system service fees, appliance rental, and computer installation among others.

Because of their relatively large families, Hispanics spend 21 percent more than average on laundry and cleaning supplies (blacks spend an average amount on this item, Asians spend 26 percent less than average) and 50 percent more than average on bathroom linens. Asians spend 59 percent more than average on gardening and lawn care service, 39 percent more than average on home security system service fees, and almost twice the average on furniture.

Table 30. Housing: Household Operations: Average spending by race and Hispanic origin, 2007

(average annual spending of consumer units on household services, supplies, furnishings, and equipment, by race and Hispanic origin of consumer unit reference person, 2007)

	total consumer units	Asian	black	Hispanic	non-Hispanic white and other
Number of consumer units (in 000s)	120,171	4,240	14,422	14,185	91,734
Average number of persons per consumer unit	2.5	2.8	2.6	3.2	2.3
Average before-tax income of consumer units	$63,091.00	$80,487.00	$44,381.00	$48,330.00	$68,285.00
Average spending of consumer units, total	49,637.95	60,402.09	36,067.28	41,501.12	53,002.87
Housing, average spending	16,919.99	22,553.92	13,493.74	15,573.45	17,662.03
HOUSEHOLD SERVICES	**984.17**	**1,156.98**	**616.29**	**681.43**	**1,087.94**
Personal services	**415.46**	**529.49**	**296.80**	**347.94**	**444.29**
Babysitting and child care in own home	51.96	40.18	28.59	41.48	57.16
Babysitting and child care in someone else's home	33.95	35.65	25.00	67.43	30.21
Care for elderly, invalids, handicapped, etc.	57.52	23.79	17.63	12.55	70.75
Day care centers, nurseries, and preschools	267.66	427.91	225.54	213.67	282.44
Other household services	**568.71**	**627.48**	**319.49**	**333.48**	**643.65**
Housekeeping services	118.26	137.19	26.96	57.78	141.74
Gardening, lawn care service	106.94	169.95	62.81	57.84	121.42
Water-softening service	4.49	3.68	6.10	3.06	4.44
Nonclothing laundry and dry cleaning, sent out	1.05	0.41	0.82	0.30	1.21
Nonclothing laundry and dry cleaning, coin-operated	3.26	3.70	4.53	8.17	2.33
Termite and pest control services	15.94	12.17	6.65	7.49	18.68
Home security system service fee	19.89	27.60	23.30	12.89	20.45
Other home services	14.64	7.88	11.17	6.96	16.34
Termite and pest control products	2.55	1.89	0.81	1.35	3.00
Moving, storage, and freight express	50.22	13.61	16.89	20.87	59.90
Appliance repair, including at service center	15.93	13.11	7.24	10.83	18.05
Reupholstering and furniture repair	4.80	–	2.06	2.73	5.55
Repairs and rentals of lawn and garden equipment, hand and power tools, etc.	6.69	2.87	3.35	5.03	7.45
Appliance rental	1.33	1.36	2.86	1.01	1.13
Repair of computer systems for nonbusiness use	6.99	2.83	3.19	4.22	8.00
Computer information services	194.11	226.36	138.49	132.78	212.20
Installation of computer	0.41	1.23	0.57	0.18	0.42
HOUSEKEEPING SUPPLIES	**638.78**	**496.24**	**383.26**	**570.97**	**687.88**
Laundry and cleaning supplies	**139.99**	**103.17**	**141.54**	**169.79**	**135.53**
Soaps and detergents	75.68	59.03	82.33	102.72	70.83
Other laundry cleaning products	64.30	44.14	59.21	67.08	64.69
Other household products	**346.60**	**237.83**	**184.07**	**244.64**	**386.34**
Cleansing and toilet tissue, paper towels, and napkins	98.65	82.68	91.05	108.99	98.40
Miscellaneous household products	132.92	96.51	75.51	102.04	146.22
Lawn and garden supplies	115.03	58.64	17.51	33.62	141.72
Postage and stationery	**152.19**	**155.24**	**57.65**	**156.54**	**166.01**
Stationery, stationery supplies, giftwrap	75.19	65.98	24.59	42.51	87.57
Postage	74.12	86.66	32.90	113.56	74.80
Delivery services	2.88	2.60	0.16	0.47	3.64
HOUSEHOLD FURNISHINGS AND EQUIPMENT	**1,797.15**	**2,081.18**	**910.14**	**1,253.23**	**2,014.46**
Household textiles	**133.10**	**124.93**	**51.42**	**112.29**	**148.93**
Bathroom linens	24.80	22.63	10.77	37.27	25.21
Bedroom linens	67.07	47.12	26.13	55.05	75.02
Kitchen and dining room linens	6.63	2.95	2.08	5.35	7.50
Curtains and draperies	18.98	43.25	6.50	6.62	22.83
Slipcovers and decorative pillows	3.39	3.78	2.47	3.51	3.56
Sewing materials for household items	11.21	3.79	2.91	3.10	13.77
Other linens	1.02	1.41	0.55	1.40	1.04
Furniture	**445.69**	**857.97**	**312.66**	**364.01**	**478.24**
Mattresses and springs	55.53	82.31	27.12	68.88	57.83
Other bedroom furniture	76.91	104.29	71.95	78.08	77.38
Sofas	112.62	201.97	56.88	113.41	121.06
Living room chairs	45.85	61.39	25.09	18.87	53.20

	total consumer units	Asian	black	Hispanic	non-Hispanic white and other
Living room tables	$15.78	–	$12.71	$11.80	$16.85
Kitchen and dining room furniture	47.05	–	19.42	26.91	54.49
Infants' furniture	9.09	$3.17	7.23	16.60	8.21
Outdoor furniture	26.06	–	–	–	26.48
Wall units, cabinets, and other furniture	56.79	120.37	46.02	28.65	62.75
Floor coverings	46.47	35.01	32.15	15.41	53.54
Wall-to-wall carpeting	25.51	23.67	18.41	5.45	29.69
Floor coverings, nonpermanent	20.96	11.34	13.74	9.96	23.86
Major appliances	**231.32**	**195.64**	**119.23**	**136.17**	**263.35**
Dishwashers (built-in), garbage disposals, range hoods	20.88	16.53	6.29	8.20	25.10
Refrigerators and freezers	61.24	71.10	35.16	38.80	68.70
Washing machines	37.55	32.28	17.84	22.31	42.92
Clothes dryers	29.60	10.14	14.20	11.48	34.78
Cooking stoves, ovens	38.00	21.52	24.47	23.39	42.33
Microwave ovens	9.66	5.26	7.05	5.79	10.69
Portable dishwashers	0.57	–	–	–	0.74
Window air conditioners	5.06	11.34	5.90	7.66	4.56
Electric floor-cleaning equipment	16.74	23.54	6.75	15.53	18.55
Sewing machines	6.25	3.93	0.66	0.87	7.95
Miscellaneous household appliances	5.75	–	0.92	2.15	7.00
Small appliances and miscellaneous housewares	**101.07**	**102.92**	**58.20**	**97.82**	**108.21**
Housewares	70.44	82.14	40.41	60.66	76.44
Plastic dinnerware	2.48	1.44	3.60	2.42	2.30
China and other dinnerware	8.56	11.07	5.02	3.14	9.86
Flatware	4.06	–	2.36	4.54	4.25
Glassware	13.80	8.48	3.07	10.99	15.85
Other serving pieces	1.42	2.04	1.20	0.96	1.52
Nonelectric cookware	14.47	23.70	14.25	7.97	15.43
Tableware, nonelectric kitchenware	25.66	17.55	10.91	30.63	27.22
Small appliances	30.63	20.78	17.79	37.16	31.77
Small electric kitchen appliances	19.17	14.19	10.98	15.82	21.00
Portable heating and cooling equipment	11.46	6.58	6.81	21.34	10.76
Miscellaneous household equipment	**839.50**	**764.71**	**336.48**	**527.52**	**962.20**
Window coverings	32.03	87.50	5.92	5.51	40.20
Infants' equipment	14.07	24.02	1.66	13.44	16.07
Laundry and cleaning equipment	18.62	18.30	14.38	17.94	19.36
Outdoor equipment	39.82	17.76	3.36	8.82	49.84
Lamps and lighting fixtures	36.69	21.45	10.10	22.37	42.80
Household decorative items	154.92	87.82	40.47	105.09	179.57
Telephones and accessories	30.38	7.56	14.23	32.24	32.58
Lawn and garden equipment	114.63	47.49	36.14	28.68	138.84
Power tools	24.41	26.54	3.65	55.35	23.20
Office furniture for home use	10.70	19.24	2.96	1.68	13.30
Hand tools	16.77	24.43	5.92	27.52	16.91
Indoor plants and fresh flowers	56.78	25.50	24.96	17.68	67.32
Closet and storage items	20.32	13.95	9.36	9.84	23.47
Rental of furniture	3.99	0.11	10.14	8.00	2.39
Luggage	12.06	24.72	6.21	2.47	14.31
Computers and computer hardware for nonbusiness use	148.08	246.12	86.29	106.75	163.96
Computer software and accessories for nonbusiness use	21.28	18.62	11.45	14.17	23.88
Personal digital assistants	3.68	3.31	2.54	3.39	3.90
Internet services away from home	2.43	2.77	1.82	1.97	2.60
Telephone answering devices	0.59	0.78	0.26	0.69	0.63
Business equipment for home use	2.26	1.35	2.08	1.28	2.45
Other hardware	30.36	1.70	15.27	21.70	33.88
Smoke alarms	2.09	1.92	0.87	0.87	2.46
Other household appliances	6.26	7.36	3.01	3.96	7.11
Miscellaneous household equipment and parts	36.28	34.41	23.44	16.11	41.17

Note: "Asian" and "black" include Hispanics and non-Hispanics who identify themselves as being of the respective race alone. "Hispanic" includes people of any race who identify themselves as Hispanic. "Other" includes people who identify themselves as non-Hispanic and as Alaska Native, American Indian, Asian (who are also included in the "Asian" column), Native Hawaiian or other Pacific Islander, as well as non-Hispanics reporting more than one race. Subcategories may not add to total because some are not shown. "–" means sample is too small to make a reliable estimate.
Source: Bureau of Labor Statistics, unpublished tables from the 2007 Consumer Expenditure Survey

Table 31. Housing: Household Operations: Indexed spending by race and Hispanic origin, 2007

(indexed average annual spending of consumer units on household services, supplies, furnishings, and equipment, by race and Hispanic origin of consumer unit reference person, 2007; index definition: an index of 100 is the average for all consumer units; an index of 132 means that spending by consumer units in that group is 32 percent above the average for all consumer units; an index of 68 indicates spending that is 32 percent below the average for all consumer units)

	total consumer units	Asian	black	Hispanic	non-Hispanic white and other
Average spending of consumer units, total	$49,638	$60,402	$36,067	$41,501	$53,003
Average spending of consumer units, index	100	122	73	84	107
Housing, spending index	**100**	**133**	**80**	**92**	**104**
HOUSEHOLD SERVICES	**100**	**118**	**63**	**69**	**111**
Personal services	**100**	**127**	**71**	**84**	**107**
Babysitting and child care in own home	100	77	55	80	110
Babysitting and child care in someone else's home	100	105	74	199	89
Care for elderly, invalids, handicapped, etc.	100	41	31	22	123
Day care centers, nurseries, and preschools	100	160	84	80	106
Other household services	**100**	**110**	**56**	**59**	**113**
Housekeeping services	100	116	23	49	120
Gardening, lawn care service	100	159	59	54	114
Water-softening service	100	82	136	68	99
Nonclothing laundry and dry cleaning, sent out	100	39	78	29	115
Nonclothing laundry and dry cleaning, coin-operated	100	113	139	251	71
Termite and pest control services	100	76	42	47	117
Home security system service fee	100	139	117	65	103
Other home services	100	54	76	48	112
Termite and pest control products	100	74	32	53	118
Moving, storage, and freight express	100	27	34	42	119
Appliance repair, including at service center	100	82	45	68	113
Reupholstering and furniture repair	100	–	43	57	116
Repairs and rentals of lawn and garden equipment, hand and power tools, etc.	100	43	50	75	111
Appliance rental	100	102	215	76	85
Repair of computer systems for nonbusiness use	100	40	46	60	114
Computer information services	100	117	71	68	109
Installation of computer	100	300	139	44	102
HOUSEKEEPING SUPPLIES	**100**	**78**	**60**	**89**	**108**
Laundry and cleaning supplies	**100**	**74**	**101**	**121**	**97**
Soaps and detergents	100	78	109	136	94
Other laundry cleaning products	100	69	92	104	101
Other household products	**100**	**69**	**53**	**71**	**111**
Cleansing and toilet tissue, paper towels, and napkins	100	84	92	110	100
Miscellaneous household products	100	73	57	77	110
Lawn and garden supplies	100	51	15	29	123
Postage and stationery	**100**	**102**	**38**	**103**	**109**
Stationery, stationery supplies, giftwrap	100	88	33	57	116
Postage	100	117	44	153	101
Delivery services	100	90	6	16	126
HOUSEHOLD FURNISHINGS AND EQUIPMENT	**100**	**116**	**51**	**70**	**112**
Household textiles	**100**	**94**	**39**	**84**	**112**
Bathroom linens	100	91	43	150	102
Bedroom linens	100	70	39	82	112
Kitchen and dining room linens	100	44	31	81	113
Curtains and draperies	100	228	34	35	120
Slipcovers and decorative pillows	100	112	73	104	105
Sewing materials for household items	100	34	26	28	123
Other linens	100	138	54	137	102
Furniture	**100**	**193**	**70**	**82**	**107**
Mattresses and springs	100	148	49	124	104
Other bedroom furniture	100	136	94	102	101
Sofas	100	179	51	101	107
Living room chairs	100	134	55	41	116

	total consumer units	Asian	black	Hispanic	non-Hispanic white and other
Living room tables	100	–	81	75	107
Kitchen and dining room furniture	100	–	41	57	116
Infants' furniture	100	35	80	183	90
Outdoor furniture	100	–	–	–	102
Wall units, cabinets, and other furniture	100	212	81	50	110
Floor coverings	**100**	**75**	**69**	**33**	**115**
Wall-to-wall carpeting	100	93	72	21	116
Floor coverings, nonpermanent	100	54	66	48	114
Major appliances	**100**	**85**	**52**	**59**	**114**
Dishwashers (built-in), garbage disposals, range hoods	100	79	30	39	120
Refrigerators and freezers	100	116	57	63	112
Washing machines	100	86	48	59	114
Clothes dryers	100	34	48	39	118
Cooking stoves, ovens	100	57	64	62	111
Microwave ovens	100	54	73	60	111
Portable dishwashers	100	–	–	–	130
Window air conditioners	100	224	117	151	90
Electric floor-cleaning equipment	100	141	40	93	111
Sewing machines	100	63	11	14	127
Miscellaneous household appliances	100	–	16	37	122
Small appliances and miscellaneous housewares	**100**	**102**	**58**	**97**	**107**
Housewares	100	117	57	86	109
Plastic dinnerware	100	58	145	98	93
China and other dinnerware	100	129	59	37	115
Flatware	100	–	58	112	105
Glassware	100	61	22	80	115
Other serving pieces	100	144	85	68	107
Nonelectric cookware	100	164	98	55	107
Tableware, nonelectric kitchenware	100	68	43	119	106
Small appliances	100	68	58	121	104
Small electric kitchen appliances	100	74	57	83	110
Portable heating and cooling equipment	100	57	59	186	94
Miscellaneous household equipment	**100**	**91**	**40**	**63**	**115**
Window coverings	100	273	18	17	126
Infants' equipment	100	171	12	96	114
Laundry and cleaning equipment	100	98	77	96	104
Outdoor equipment	100	45	8	22	125
Lamps and lighting fixtures	100	58	28	61	117
Household decorative items	100	57	26	68	116
Telephones and accessories	100	25	47	106	107
Lawn and garden equipment	100	41	32	25	121
Power tools	100	109	15	227	95
Office furniture for home use	100	180	28	16	124
Hand tools	100	146	35	164	101
Indoor plants and fresh flowers	100	45	44	31	119
Closet and storage items	100	69	46	48	116
Rental of furniture	100	3	254	201	60
Luggage	100	205	51	20	119
Computers and computer hardware for nonbusiness use	100	166	58	72	111
Computer software and accessories for nonbusiness use	100	88	54	67	112
Personal digital assistants	100	90	69	92	106
Internet services away from home	100	114	75	81	107
Telephone answering devices	100	132	44	117	107
Business equipment for home use	100	60	92	57	108
Other hardware	100	6	50	71	112
Smoke alarms	100	92	42	42	118
Other household appliances	100	118	48	63	114
Miscellaneous household equipment and parts	100	95	65	44	113

Note: "Asian" and "black" include Hispanics and non-Hispanics who identify themselves as being of the respective race alone. "Hispanic" includes people of any race who identify themselves as Hispanic. "Other" includes people who identify themselves as non-Hispanic and as Alaska Native, American Indian, Asian (who are also included in the "Asian" column), Native Hawaiian or other Pacific Islander, as well as non-Hispanics reporting more than one race. "–" means sample is too small to make a reliable estimate.
Source: Calculations by New Strategist based on the Bureau of Labor Statistics' 2007 Consumer Expenditure Survey

Table 32. Housing: Household Operations: Total spending by race and Hispanic origin, 2007

(total annual spending on household services, supplies, furnishings, and equipment, by consumer unit race and Hispanic origin groups, 2007; consumer units and dollars in thousands)

	total consumer units	Asian	black	Hispanic	non-Hispanic white and other
Number of consumer units	120,171	4,240	14,422	14,185	91,734
Total spending of all consumer units	$5,965,042,089	$256,104,862	$520,162,312	$588,693,387	$4,862,165,277
Housing, total spending	2,033,292,118	95,628,621	194,606,718	220,909,388	1,620,208,660
HOUSEHOLD SERVICES	**$118,268,693**	**$4,905,595**	**$8,888,134**	**$9,666,085**	**$99,801,088**
Personal services	**49,926,244**	**2,245,038**	**4,280,450**	**4,935,529**	**40,756,499**
Babysitting and child care in own home	6,244,085	170,363	412,325	588,394	5,243,515
Babysitting and child care in someone else's home	4,079,805	151,156	360,550	956,495	2,771,284
Care for elderly, invalids, handicapped, etc.	6,912,236	100,870	254,260	178,022	6,490,181
Day care centers, nurseries, and preschools	32,164,970	1,814,338	3,252,738	3,030,909	25,909,351
Other household services	**68,342,449**	**2,660,515**	**4,607,685**	**4,730,414**	**59,044,589**
Housekeeping services	14,211,422	581,686	388,817	819,609	13,002,377
Gardening, lawn care service	12,851,087	720,588	905,846	820,460	11,138,342
Water-softening service	539,568	15,603	87,974	43,406	407,299
Nonclothing laundry and dry cleaning, sent out	126,180	1,738	11,826	4,256	110,998
Nonclothing laundry and dry cleaning, coin-operated	391,757	15,688	65,332	115,891	213,740
Termite and pest control services	1,915,526	51,601	95,906	106,246	1,713,591
Home security system service fee	2,390,201	117,024	336,033	182,845	1,875,960
Other home services	1,759,303	33,411	161,094	98,728	1,498,934
Termite and pest control products	306,436	8,014	11,682	19,150	275,202
Moving, storage, and freight express	6,034,988	57,706	243,588	296,041	5,494,867
Appliance repair, including at service center	1,914,324	55,586	104,415	153,624	1,655,799
Reupholstering and furniture repair	576,821	–	29,709	38,725	509,124
Repairs and rentals of lawn and garden equipment, hand and power tools, etc.	803,944	12,169	48,314	71,351	683,418
Appliance rental	159,827	5,766	41,247	14,327	103,659
Repair of computer systems for nonbusiness use	839,995	11,999	46,006	59,861	733,872
Computer information services	23,326,393	959,766	1,997,303	1,883,484	19,465,955
Installation of computer	49,270	5,215	8,221	2,553	38,528
HOUSEKEEPING SUPPLIES	**76,762,831**	**2,104,058**	**5,527,376**	**8,099,209**	**63,101,984**
Laundry and cleaning supplies	**16,822,738**	**437,441**	**2,041,290**	**2,408,471**	**12,432,709**
Soaps and detergents	9,094,541	250,287	1,187,363	1,457,083	6,497,519
Other laundry cleaning products	7,726,995	187,154	853,927	951,530	5,934,272
Other household products	**41,651,269**	**1,008,399**	**2,654,658**	**3,470,218**	**35,440,514**
Cleansing and toilet tissue, paper towels, and napkins	11,854,869	350,563	1,313,123	1,546,023	9,026,626
Miscellaneous household products	15,973,129	409,202	1,089,005	1,447,437	13,413,345
Lawn and garden supplies	13,823,270	248,634	252,529	476,900	13,000,542
Postage and stationery	**18,288,824**	**658,218**	**831,428**	**2,220,520**	**15,228,761**
Stationery, stationery supplies, giftwrap	9,035,657	279,755	354,637	603,004	8,033,146
Postage	8,907,075	367,438	474,484	1,610,849	6,861,703
Delivery services	346,092	11,024	2,308	6,667	333,912
HOUSEHOLD FURNISHINGS AND EQUIPMENT	**215,965,313**	**8,824,203**	**13,126,039**	**17,777,068**	**184,794,474**
Household textiles	**15,994,760**	**529,703**	**741,579**	**1,592,834**	**13,661,945**
Bathroom linens	2,980,241	95,951	155,325	528,675	2,312,614
Bedroom linens	8,059,869	199,789	376,847	780,884	6,881,885
Kitchen and dining room linens	796,734	12,508	29,998	75,890	688,005
Curtains and draperies	2,280,846	183,380	93,743	93,905	2,094,287
Slipcovers and decorative pillows	407,380	16,027	35,622	49,789	326,573
Sewing materials for household items	1,347,117	16,070	41,968	43,974	1,263,177
Other linens	122,574	5,978	7,932	19,859	95,403
Furniture	**53,559,013**	**3,637,793**	**4,509,183**	**5,163,482**	**43,870,868**
Mattresses and springs	6,673,096	348,994	391,125	977,063	5,304,977
Other bedroom furniture	9,242,352	442,190	1,037,663	1,107,565	7,098,377
Sofas	13,533,658	856,353	820,323	1,608,721	11,105,318
Living room chairs	5,509,840	260,294	361,848	267,671	4,880,249

	total consumer units	Asian	black	Hispanic	non-Hispanic white and other
Living room tables	$1,896,298	–	$183,304	$167,383	$1,545,718
Kitchen and dining room furniture	5,654,046	–	280,075	381,718	4,998,586
Infants' furniture	1,092,354	$13,441	104,271	235,471	753,136
Outdoor furniture	3,131,656	–	–	–	2,429,116
Wall units, cabinets, and other furniture	6,824,511	510,369	663,700	406,400	5,756,309
Floor coverings	**5,584,346**	**148,442**	**463,667**	**218,591**	**4,911,438**
Wall-to-wall carpeting	3,065,562	100,361	265,509	77,308	2,723,582
Floor coverings, nonpermanent	2,518,784	48,082	198,158	141,283	2,188,773
Major appliances	**27,797,956**	**829,514**	**1,719,535**	**1,931,571**	**24,158,149**
Dishwashers (built-in), garbage disposals, range hoods	2,509,170	70,087	90,714	116,317	2,302,523
Refrigerators and freezers	7,359,272	301,464	507,078	550,378	6,302,126
Washing machines	4,512,421	136,867	257,288	316,467	3,937,223
Clothes dryers	3,557,062	42,994	204,792	162,844	3,190,509
Cooking stoves, ovens	4,566,498	91,245	352,906	331,787	3,883,100
Microwave ovens	1,160,852	22,302	101,675	82,131	980,636
Portable dishwashers	68,497	–	–	–	67,883
Window air conditioners	608,065	48,082	85,090	108,657	418,307
Electric floor-cleaning equipment	2,011,663	99,810	97,349	220,293	1,701,666
Sewing machines	751,069	16,663.20	9,519	12,341	729,285
Miscellaneous household appliances	690,983	–	13,268	30,498	642,138
Small appliances and miscellaneous housewares	**12,145,683**	**436,381**	**839,360**	**1,387,577**	**9,926,536**
Housewares	8,464,845	348,274	582,793	860,462	7,012,147
Plastic dinnerware	298,024	6,106	51,919	34,328	210,988
China and other dinnerware	1,028,664	46,937	72,398	44,541	904,497
Flatware	487,894	–	34,036	64,400	389,870
Glassware	1,658,360	35,955	44,276	155,893	1,453,984
Other serving pieces	170,643	8,650	17,306	13,618	139,436
Nonelectric cookware	1,738,874	100,488	205,514	113,054	1,415,456
Tableware, nonelectric kitchenware	3,083,588	74,412	157,344	434,487	2,496,999
Small appliances	3,680,838	88,107	256,567	527,115	2,914,389
Small electric kitchen appliances	2,303,678	60,166	158,354	224,407	1,926,414
Portable heating and cooling equipment	1,377,160	27,899	98,214	302,708	987,058
Miscellaneous household equipment	**100,883,555**	**3,242,370**	**4,852,715**	**7,482,871**	**88,266,455**
Window coverings	3,849,077	371,000	85,378	78,159	3,687,707
Infants' equipment	1,690,806	101,845	23,941	190,646	1,474,165
Laundry and cleaning equipment	2,237,584	77,592	207,388	254,479	1,775,970
Outdoor equipment	4,785,209	75,302	48,458	125,112	4,572,023
Lamps and lighting fixtures	4,409,074	90,948	145,662	317,318	3,926,215
Household decorative items	18,616,891	372,357	583,658	1,490,702	16,472,674
Telephones and accessories	3,650,795	32,054	205,225	457,324	2,988,694
Lawn and garden equipment	13,775,202	201,358	521,211	406,826	12,736,349
Power tools	2,933,374	112,530	52,640	785,140	2,128,229
Office furniture for home use	1,285,830	81,578	42,689	23,831	1,220,062
Hand tools	2,015,268	103,583	85,378	390,371	1,551,222
Indoor plants and fresh flowers	6,823,309	108,120	359,973	250,791	6,175,533
Closet and storage items	2,441,875	59,148	134,990	139,580	2,152,997
Rental of furniture	479,482	466	146,239	113,480	219,244
Luggage	1,449,262	104,813	89,561	35,037	1,312,714
Computers and computer hardware for nonbusiness use	17,794,922	1,043,549	1,244,474	1,514,249	15,040,707
Computer software and accessories for nonbusiness use	2,557,239	78,949	165,132	201,001	2,190,608
Personal digital assistants	442,229	14,034	36,632	48,087	357,763
Internet services away from home	292,016	11,745	26,248	27,944	238,508
Telephone answering devices	70,901	3,307	3,750	9,788	57,792
Business equipment for home use	271,586	5,724	29,998	18,157	224,748
Other hardware	3,648,392	7,208	220,224	307,815	3,107,948
Smoke alarms	251,157	8,141	12,547	12,341	225,666
Other household appliances	752,270	31,206	43,410	56,173	652,229
Miscellaneous household equipment and parts	4,359,804	145,898	338,052	228,520	3,776,689

Note: "Asian" and "black" include Hispanics and non-Hispanics who identify themselves as being of the respective race alone. "Hispanic" includes people of any race who identify themselves as Hispanic. "Other" includes people who identify themselves as non-Hispanic and as Alaska Native, American Indian, Asian (who are also included in the "Asian" column), Native Hawaiian or other Pacific Islander, as well as non-Hispanics reporting more than one race. Numbers may not add to total because of rounding and missing subcategories. "–" means sample is too small to make a reliable estimate.
Source: Calculations by New Strategist based on the Bureau of Labor Statistics' 2007 Consumer Expenditure Survey

Table 33. Housing: Household Operations: Market shares by race and Hispanic origin, 2007

(percentage of total annual spending on household services, supplies, furnishings, and equipment accounted for by consumer unit race and Hispanic origin groups, 2007)

	total consumer units	Asian	black	Hispanic	non-Hispanic white and other
Share of total consumer units	100.0%	3.5%	12.0%	11.8%	76.3%
Share of total before-tax income	100.0	4.5	8.4	9.0	82.6
Share of total spending	100.0	4.3	8.7	9.9	81.5
Share of housing spending	100.0	4.7	9.6	10.9	79.7
HOUSEHOLD SERVICES	100.0	4.1	7.5	8.2	84.4
Personal services	100.0	4.5	8.6	9.9	81.6
Babysitting and child care in own home	100.0	2.7	6.6	9.4	84.0
Babysitting and child care in someone else's home	100.0	3.7	8.8	23.4	67.9
Care for elderly, invalids, handicapped, etc.	100.0	1.5	3.7	2.6	93.9
Day care centers, nurseries, and preschools	100.0	5.6	10.1	9.4	80.6
Other household services	100.0	3.9	6.7	6.9	86.4
Housekeeping services	100.0	4.1	2.7	5.8	91.5
Gardening, lawn care service	100.0	5.6	7.0	6.4	86.7
Water-softening service	100.0	2.9	16.3	8.0	75.5
Nonclothing laundry and dry cleaning, sent out	100.0	1.4	9.4	3.4	88.0
Nonclothing laundry and dry cleaning, coin-operated	100.0	4.0	16.7	29.6	54.6
Termite and pest control services	100.0	2.7	5.0	5.5	89.5
Home security system service fee	100.0	4.9	14.1	7.6	78.5
Other home services	100.0	1.9	9.2	5.6	85.2
Termite and pest control products	100.0	2.6	3.8	6.2	89.8
Moving, storage, and freight express	100.0	1.0	4.0	4.9	91.1
Appliance repair, including at service center	100.0	2.9	5.5	8.0	86.5
Reupholstering and furniture repair	100.0	–	5.2	6.7	88.3
Repairs and rentals of lawn and garden equipment, hand and power tools, etc.	100.0	1.5	6.0	8.9	85.0
Appliance rental	100.0	3.6	25.8	9.0	64.9
Repair of computer systems for nonbusiness use	100.0	1.4	5.5	7.1	87.4
Computer information services	100.0	4.1	8.6	8.1	83.5
Installation of computer	100.0	10.6	16.7	5.2	78.2
HOUSEKEEPING SUPPLIES	100.0	2.7	7.2	10.6	82.2
Laundry and cleaning supplies	100.0	2.6	12.1	14.3	73.9
Soaps and detergents	100.0	2.8	13.1	16.0	71.4
Other laundry cleaning products	100.0	2.4	11.1	12.3	76.8
Other household products	100.0	2.4	6.4	8.3	85.1
Cleansing and toilet tissue, paper towels, and napkins	100.0	3.0	11.1	13.0	76.1
Miscellaneous household products	100.0	2.6	6.8	9.1	84.0
Lawn and garden supplies	100.0	1.8	1.8	3.4	94.0
Postage and stationery	100.0	3.6	4.5	12.1	83.3
Stationery, stationery supplies, giftwrap	100.0	3.1	3.9	6.7	88.9
Postage	100.0	4.1	5.3	18.1	77.0
Delivery services	100.0	3.2	0.7	1.9	96.5
HOUSEHOLD FURNISHINGS AND EQUIPMENT	100.0	4.1	6.1	8.2	85.6
Household textiles	100.0	3.3	4.6	10.0	85.4
Bathroom linens	100.0	3.2	5.2	17.7	77.6
Bedroom linens	100.0	2.5	4.7	9.7	85.4
Kitchen and dining room linens	100.0	1.6	3.8	9.5	86.4
Curtains and draperies	100.0	8.0	4.1	4.1	91.8
Slipcovers and decorative pillows	100.0	3.9	8.7	12.2	80.2
Sewing materials for household items	100.0	1.2	3.1	3.3	93.8
Other linens	100.0	4.9	6.5	16.2	77.8
Furniture	100.0	6.8	8.4	9.6	81.9
Mattresses and springs	100.0	5.2	5.9	14.6	79.5
Other bedroom furniture	100.0	4.8	11.2	12.0	76.8
Sofas	100.0	6.3	6.1	11.9	82.1
Living room chairs	100.0	4.7	6.6	4.9	88.6

	total consumer units	Asian	black	Hispanic	non-Hispanic white and other
Living room tables	100.0%	–	9.7%	8.8%	81.5%
Kitchen and dining room furniture	100.0	–	5.0	6.8	88.4
Infants' furniture	100.0	1.2%	9.5	21.6	68.9
Outdoor furniture	100.0	–	–	–	77.6
Wall units, cabinets, and other furniture	100.0	7.5	9.7	6.0	84.3
Floor coverings	**100.0**	**2.7**	**8.3**	**3.9**	**88.0**
Wall-to-wall carpeting	100.0	3.3	8.7	2.5	88.8
Floor coverings, nonpermanent	100.0	1.9	7.9	5.6	86.9
Major appliances	**100.0**	**3.0**	**6.2**	**6.9**	**86.9**
Dishwashers (built-in), garbage disposals, range hoods	100.0	2.8	3.6	4.6	91.8
Refrigerators and freezers	100.0	4.1	6.9	7.5	85.6
Washing machines	100.0	3.0	5.7	7.0	87.3
Clothes dryers	100.0	1.2	5.8	4.6	89.7
Cooking stoves, ovens	100.0	2.0	7.7	7.3	85.0
Microwave ovens	100.0	1.9	8.8	7.1	84.5
Portable dishwashers	100.0	–	–	–	99.1
Window air conditioners	100.0	7.9	14.0	17.9	68.8
Electric floor-cleaning equipment	100.0	5.0	4.8	11.0	84.6
Sewing machines	100.0	2.2	1.3	1.6	97.1
Miscellaneous household appliances	100.0	–	1.9	4.4	92.9
Small appliances and miscellaneous housewares	**100.0**	**3.6**	**6.9**	**11.4**	**81.7**
Housewares	100.0	4.1	6.9	10.2	82.8
Plastic dinnerware	100.0	2.0	17.4	11.5	70.8
China and other dinnerware	100.0	4.6	7.0	4.3	87.9
Flatware	100.0	–	7.0	13.2	79.9
Glassware	100.0	2.2	2.7	9.4	87.7
Other serving pieces	100.0	5.1	10.1	8.0	81.7
Nonelectric cookware	100.0	5.8	11.8	6.5	81.4
Tableware, nonelectric kitchenware	100.0	2.4	5.1	14.1	81.0
Small appliances	100.0	2.4	7.0	14.3	79.2
Small electric kitchen appliances	100.0	2.6	6.9	9.7	83.6
Portable heating and cooling equipment	100.0	2.0	7.1	22.0	71.7
Miscellaneous household equipment	**100.0**	**3.2**	**4.8**	**7.4**	**87.5**
Window coverings	100.0	9.6	2.2	2.0	95.8
Infants' equipment	100.0	6.0	1.4	11.3	87.2
Laundry and cleaning equipment	100.0	3.5	9.3	11.4	79.4
Outdoor equipment	100.0	1.6	1.0	2.6	95.5
Lamps and lighting fixtures	100.0	2.1	3.3	7.2	89.0
Household decorative items	100.0	2.0	3.1	8.0	88.5
Telephones and accessories	100.0	0.9	5.6	12.5	81.9
Lawn and garden equipment	100.0	1.5	3.8	3.0	92.5
Power tools	100.0	3.8	1.8	26.8	72.6
Office furniture for home use	100.0	6.3	3.3	1.9	94.9
Hand tools	100.0	5.1	4.2	19.4	77.0
Indoor plants and fresh flowers	100.0	1.6	5.3	3.7	90.5
Closet and storage items	100.0	2.4	5.5	5.7	88.2
Rental of furniture	100.0	0.1	30.5	23.7	45.7
Luggage	100.0	7.2	6.2	2.4	90.6
Computers and computer hardware for nonbusiness use	100.0	5.9	7.0	8.5	84.5
Computer software and accessories for nonbusiness use	100.0	3.1	6.5	7.9	85.7
Personal digital assistants	100.0	3.2	8.3	10.9	80.9
Internet services away from home	100.0	4.0	9.0	9.6	81.7
Telephone answering devices	100.0	4.7	5.3	13.8	81.5
Business equipment for home use	100.0	2.1	11.0	6.7	82.8
Other hardware	100.0	0.2	6.0	8.4	85.2
Smoke alarms	100.0	3.2	5.0	4.9	89.9
Other household appliances	100.0	4.1	5.8	7.5	86.7
Miscellaneous household equipment and parts	100.0	3.3	7.8	5.2	86.6

Note: "Asian" and "black" include Hispanics and non-Hispanics who identify themselves as being of the respective race alone. "Hispanic" includes people of any race who identify themselves as Hispanic. "Other" includes people who identify themselves as non-Hispanic and as Alaska Native, American Indian, Asian (who are also included in the "Asian" column), Native Hawaiian or other Pacific Islander, as well as non-Hispanics reporting more than one race. "–" means sample is too small to make a reliable estimate.
Source: Calculations by New Strategist based on the Bureau of Labor Statistics' 2007 Consumer Expenditure Survey

Spending on Housing: Shelter and Utilities, 2007

Housing is by far Americans' biggest expense. In 2007, housing costs—including shelter, utilities, and household operations—absorbed 34.0 percent of average household expenditures. That figure has increased slightly from the 32.4 percent of 2000. Spending on shelter rose 17 percent between 2000 and 2007, after adjusting for inflation. Spending on owned homes climbed 21 percent, while spending on rented homes increased by a smaller 6 percent. Spending on other lodging, which includes college dorms as well as hotels and motels, grew 20 percent. Spending on utilities and fuels increased 16 percent because of rising energy prices.

Asians spend 33 percent more than the average household on housing—$22,554 in 2007. Hispanics spend 8 percent less than average on housing ($15,573), while blacks spend 20 percent less ($13,494). Asians spend 69 percent more than average on mortgage interest, in part because many live in California, where housing costs are relatively high. Blacks spend 42 percent more than the average household on rent. Asians spend 59 percent more and Hispanics 60 percent more. Together, the three groups account for 42 percent of the rental market.

Asians spend twice the average on housing while attending school and 33 percent more than average on lodging while on trips. The spending of blacks and Hispanics on these categories is well below average.

Blacks spend 15 percent more than average on residential telephone service. Asians spend almost three times the average on phone cards, Hispanics spend almost four times the average on this item. Many are using phone cards to call family members abroad. Asians also spend twice the average on voice over IP services.

Table 34. Housing: Shelter and Utilities: Average spending by race and Hispanic origin, 2007

(average annual spending of consumer units on shelter and utilities, by race and Hispanic origin of consumer unit reference person, 2007)

	total consumer units	Asian	black	Hispanic	non-Hispanic white and other
Number of consumer units (in 000s)	120,171	4,240	14,422	14,185	91,734
Average number of persons per consumer unit	2.5	2.8	2.6	3.2	2.3
Average before-tax income of consumer units	$63,091.00	$80,487.00	$44,381.00	$48,330.00	$68,285.00
Average spending of consumer units, total	49,637.95	60,402.09	36,067.28	41,501.12	53,002.87
Housing, average spending	**16,919.99**	**22,553.92**	**13,493.74**	**15,573.45**	**17,662.03**
SHELTER	**10,022.69**	**15,383.12**	**8,083.95**	**9,793.72**	**10,366.99**
Owned dwellings*	**6,730.18**	**10,386.64**	**4,109.71**	**5,418.99**	**7,346.16**
Mortgage interest and charges	3,890.03	6,383.11	2,723.45	3,609.04	4,117.56
Mortgage interest	3,583.53	6,058.81	2,625.16	3,471.63	3,752.75
Interest paid, home equity loan	94.49	130.40	54.44	71.87	104.11
Interest paid, home equity line of credit	212.00	193.90	43.84	65.55	260.70
Property taxes	1,708.86	2,754.41	892.66	1,217.78	1,912.05
Maintenance, repairs, insurance, other expenses	1,131.29	1,249.12	493.60	592.17	1,316.56
Homeowner's insurance	340.31	310.69	217.00	195.24	381.95
Ground rent	61.77	–	24.00	45.59	70.16
Maintenance and repair services	574.87	408.04	205.36	258.26	683.75
Painting and papering	77.47	63.71	23.16	18.36	95.01
Plumbing and water heating	46.12	28.05	29.58	33.61	50.78
Heat, air conditioning, electrical work	87.13	82.86	34.88	39.34	103.52
Roofing and gutters	98.65	80.04	28.97	28.12	120.33
Other repair and maintenance services	216.38	123.22	63.59	118.09	256.92
Repair, replacement of hard-surface flooring	41.28	20.04	20.42	17.55	48.15
Repair of built-in appliances	7.84	10.13	4.76	3.18	9.04
Maintenance and repair materials	90.20	30.20	24.40	55.22	105.79
Paints, wallpaper, and supplies	15.39	6.20	5.21	12.63	17.38
Tools, equipment for painting, wallpapering	1.65	0.67	0.56	1.36	1.87
Plumbing supplies and equipment	4.10	4.36	1.52	4.12	4.49
Electrical supplies, heating and cooling equipment	3.46	0.12	0.55	2.68	4.03
Hard-surface flooring, repair and replacement	12.64	7.24	3.65	7.67	14.80
Roofing and gutters	5.98	2.67	0.07	8.95	6.44
Plaster, paneling, siding, windows, doors, screens, awnings	15.20	7.90	3.33	10.10	17.83
Patio, walk, fence, driveway, masonry, brick, stucco materials	1.29	–	1.74	2.57	1.02
Miscellaneous supplies and equipment	30.49	1.04	7.78	5.13	37.92
Property management and security	54.65	100.84	17.79	28.00	64.73
Property management	45.22	84.78	14.18	19.50	54.23
Management and upkeep services for security	9.42	16.07	3.61	8.50	10.50
Parking	9.50	–	5.06	9.86	10.19
Rented dwellings	**2,601.86**	**4,073.23**	**3,669.08**	**4,135.46**	**2,200.44**
Rent	2,491.52	3,955.16	3,544.21	3,978.69	2,099.62
Rent as pay	69.63	107.83	100.81	122.57	56.56
Maintenance, insurance, and other expenses	40.71	10.24	24.07	34.20	44.26
Tenant's insurance	10.30	6.43	9.13	4.30	11.39
Maintenance and repair services	17.55	1.89	9.34	9.58	20.04
Maintenance and repair materials	12.86	1.91	5.59	20.32	12.83
Other lodging	**690.65**	**923.25**	**305.15**	**239.27**	**820.39**
Owned vacation homes	286.81	346.60	161.33	89.77	336.50
Mortgage interest and charges	128.78	193.15	108.62	48.21	144.17
Property taxes	95.39	127.18	27.46	35.25	115.19
Maintenance, insurance, and other expenses	62.65	26.27	25.24	6.31	77.13
Housing while attending school	61.27	120.97	40.68	16.78	71.27
Lodging on trips	342.57	455.68	103.15	132.72	412.62

	total consumer units	Asian	black	Hispanic	non-Hispanic white and other
UTILITIES, FUELS, AND PUBLIC SERVICES	**$3,477.21**	**$3,436.40**	**$3,500.11**	**$3,274.11**	**$3,504.76**
Natural gas	**480.39**	**576.72**	**475.20**	**377.58**	**497.05**
Electricity	**1,302.85**	**1,168.75**	**1,354.93**	**1,258.10**	**1,300.96**
Fuel oil and other fuels	**150.62**	**44.10**	**56.25**	**61.93**	**179.36**
Fuel oil	88.18	24.86	42.39	44.70	102.39
Coal, wood, and other fuels	7.18	–	2.27	2.01	8.76
Bottled gas	55.25	19.25	11.59	15.21	68.21
Telephone services	**1,109.69**	**1,171.68**	**1,196.16**	**1,167.03**	**1,087.54**
Residential telephone and pay phones	482.12	443.75	554.90	430.35	478.71
Cellular phone service	607.58	675.44	625.25	678.95	593.99
Phone cards	14.88	42.36	12.59	53.84	9.28
Voice over IP	5.12	10.13	3.43	3.90	5.57
Water and other public services	**433.66**	**475.14**	**417.57**	**409.47**	**439.85**
Water and sewerage maintenance	317.25	373.94	339.44	307.44	315.32
Trash and garbage collection	113.33	101.20	76.32	101.45	120.87
Septic tank cleaning	3.08	–	1.80	0.58	3.66

* See Appendix B for information about mortgage principal reduction.

Note: "Asian" and "black" include Hispanics and non-Hispanics who identify themselves as being of the respective race alone. "Hispanic" includes people of any race who identify themselves as Hispanic. "Other" includes people who identify themselves as non-Hispanic and as Alaska Native, American Indian, Asian (who are also included in the "Asian" column), Native Hawaiian or other Pacific Islander, as well as non-Hispanics reporting more than one race. Subcategories may not add to total because some are not shown. "–" means sample is too small to make a reliable estimate.

Source: Bureau of Labor Statistics, unpublished tables from the 2007 Consumer Expenditure Survey

Table 35. Housing: Shelter and Utilities: Indexed spending by race and Hispanic origin, 2007

(indexed average annual spending of consumer units on shelter and utilities, by race and Hispanic origin of consumer unit reference person, 2007; index definition: an index of 100 is the average for all consumer units; an index of 132 means that spending by consumer units in that group is 32 percent above the average for all consumer units; an index of 68 indicates spending that is 32 percent below the average for all consumer units)

	total consumer units	Asian	black	Hispanic	non-Hispanic white and other
Average spending of consumer units, total	$49,638	$60,402	$36,067	$41,501	$53,003
Average spending of consumer units, index	100	122	73	84	107
Housing, spending index	100	133	80	92	104
SHELTER	100	153	81	98	103
Owned dwellings*	100	154	61	81	109
Mortgage interest and charges	100	164	70	93	106
Mortgage interest	100	169	73	97	105
Interest paid, home equity loan	100	138	58	76	110
Interest paid, home equity line of credit	100	91	21	31	123
Property taxes	100	161	52	71	112
Maintenance, repairs, insurance, other expenses	100	110	44	52	116
Homeowner's insurance	100	91	64	57	112
Ground rent	100	–	39	74	114
Maintenance and repair services	100	71	36	45	119
Painting and papering	100	82	30	24	123
Plumbing and water heating	100	61	64	73	110
Heat, air conditioning, electrical work	100	95	40	45	119
Roofing and gutters	100	81	29	29	122
Other repair and maintenance services	100	57	29	55	119
Repair, replacement of hard-surface flooring	100	49	49	43	117
Repair of built-in appliances	100	129	61	41	115
Maintenance and repair materials	100	33	27	61	117
Paints, wallpaper, and supplies	100	40	34	82	113
Tools, equipment for painting, wallpapering	100	41	34	82	113
Plumbing supplies and equipment	100	106	37	100	110
Electrical supplies, heating and cooling equipment	100	3	16	77	116
Hard-surface flooring, repair and replacement	100	57	29	61	117
Roofing and gutters	100	45	1	150	108
Plaster, paneling, siding, windows, doors, screens, awnings	100	52	22	66	117
Patio, walk, fence, driveway, masonry, brick, stucco materials	100	–	135	199	79
Miscellaneous supplies and equipment	100	3	26	17	124
Property management and security	100	185	33	51	118
Property management	100	187	31	43	120
Management and upkeep services for security	100	171	38	90	111
Parking	100	–	53	104	107
Rented dwellings	100	157	141	159	85
Rent	100	159	142	160	84
Rent as pay	100	155	145	176	81
Maintenance, insurance, and other expenses	100	25	59	84	109
Tenant's insurance	100	62	89	42	111
Maintenance and repair services	100	11	53	55	114
Maintenance and repair materials	100	15	43	158	100
Other lodging	100	134	44	35	119
Owned vacation homes	100	121	56	31	117
Mortgage interest and charges	100	150	84	37	112
Property taxes	100	133	29	37	121
Maintenance, insurance, and other expenses	100	42	40	10	123
Housing while attending school	100	197	66	27	116
Lodging on trips	100	133	30	39	120

	total consumer units	Asian	black	Hispanic	non-Hispanic white and other
UTILITIES, FUELS, AND PUBLIC SERVICES	**100**	**99**	**101**	**94**	**101**
Natural gas	**100**	**120**	**99**	**79**	**103**
Electricity	**100**	**90**	**104**	**97**	**100**
Fuel oil and other fuels	**100**	**29**	**37**	**41**	**119**
Fuel oil	100	28	48	51	116
Coal, wood, and other fuels	100	–	32	28	122
Bottled gas	100	35	21	28	123
Telephone services	**100**	**106**	**108**	**105**	**98**
Residential telephone and pay phones	100	92	115	89	99
Cellular phone service	100	111	103	112	98
Phone cards	100	285	85	362	62
Voice over IP	100	198	67	76	109
Water and other public services	**100**	**110**	**96**	**94**	**101**
Water and sewerage maintenance	100	118	107	97	99
Trash and garbage collection	100	89	67	90	107
Septic tank cleaning	100	–	58	19	119

* See Appendix B for information about mortgage principal reduction.

Note: "Asian" and "black" include Hispanics and non-Hispanics who identify themselves as being of the respective race alone. "Hispanic" includes people of any race who identify themselves as Hispanic. "Other" includes people who identify themselves as non-Hispanic and as Alaska Native, American Indian, Asian (who are also included in the "Asian" column), Native Hawaiian or other Pacific Islander, as well as non-Hispanics reporting more than one race. "–" means sample is too small to make a reliable estimate.

Source: Calculations by New Strategist based on the Bureau of Labor Statistics' 2007 Consumer Expenditure Survey

Table 36. Housing: Shelter and Utilities: Total spending by race and Hispanic origin, 2007

(total annual spending on shelter and utilities, by consumer unit race and Hispanic origin groups, 2007; consumer units and dollars in thousands)

	total consumer units	Asian	black	Hispanic	non-Hispanic white and other
Number of consumer units	120,171	4,240	14,422	14,185	91,734
Total spending of all consumer units	$5,965,042,089	$256,104,862	$520,162,312	$588,693,387	$4,862,165,277
Housing, total spending	2,033,292,118	95,628,621	194,606,718	220,909,388	1,620,208,660
SHELTER	**1,204,436,680**	**65,224,429**	**116,586,727**	**138,923,918**	**951,005,461**
Owned dwellings*	**808,772,461**	**44,039,354**	**59,270,238**	**76,868,373**	**673,892,641**
Mortgage interest and charges	467,468,795	27,064,386	39,277,596	51,194,232	377,720,249
Mortgage interest	430,636,384	25,689,354	37,860,058	49,245,072	344,254,769
Interest paid, home equity loan	11,354,958	552,896	785,134	1,019,476	9,550,427
Interest paid, home equity line of credit	25,476,252	822,136	632,260	929,827	23,915,054
Property taxes	205,355,415	11,678,698	12,873,943	17,274,209	175,399,995
Maintenance, repairs, insurance, other expenses	135,948,251	5,296,269	7,118,699	8,399,931	120,773,315
Homeowner's insurance	40,895,393	1,317,326	3,129,574	2,769,479	35,037,801
Ground rent	7,422,963	–	346,128	646,694	6,436,057
Maintenance and repair services	69,082,703	1,730,090	2,961,702	3,663,418	62,723,123
Painting and papering	9,309,647	270,130	334,014	260,437	8,715,647
Plumbing and water heating	5,542,287	118,932	426,603	476,758	4,658,253
Heat, air conditioning, electrical work	10,470,499	351,326	503,039	558,038	9,496,304
Roofing and gutters	11,854,869	339,370	417,805	398,882	11,038,352
Other repair and maintenance services	26,002,601	522,453	917,095	1,675,107	23,568,299
Repair, replacement of hard-surface flooring	4,960,659	84,970	294,497	248,947	4,416,992
Repair of built-in appliances	942,141	42,951	68,649	45,108	829,275
Maintenance and repair materials	10,839,424	128,048	351,897	783,296	9,704,540
Paints, wallpaper, and supplies	1,849,432	26,288	75,139	179,157	1,594,337
Tools, equipment for painting, wallpapering	198,282	2,841	8,076	19,292	171,543
Plumbing supplies and equipment	492,701	18,486	21,921	58,442	411,886
Electrical supplies, heating and cooling equipment	415,792	509	7,932	38,016	369,688
Hard-surface flooring, repair and replacement	1,518,961	30,698	52,640	108,799	1,357,663
Roofing and gutters	718,623	11,321	1,010	126,956	590,767
Plaster, paneling, siding, windows, doors, screens, awnings	1,826,599	33,496	48,025	143,269	1,635,617
Patio, walk, fence, driveway, masonry, brick, and stucco materials	155,021	–	25,094	36,455	93,569
Miscellaneous supplies and equipment	3,664,014	4,410	112,203	72,769	3,478,553
Property management and security	6,567,345	427,562	256,567	397,180	5,937,942
Property management	5,434,133	359,467	204,504	276,608	4,974,735
Management and upkeep services for security	1,132,011	68,137	52,063	120,573	963,207
Parking	1,141,625	–	72,975	139,864	934,769
Rented dwellings	**312,668,118**	**17,270,495**	**52,915,472**	**58,661,500**	**201,855,163**
Rent	299,408,450	16,769,878	51,114,597	56,437,718	192,606,541
Rent as pay	8,367,507	457,199	1,453,882	1,738,655	5,188,475
Maintenance, insurance, and other expenses	4,892,161	43,418	347,138	485,127	4,060,147
Tenant's insurance	1,237,761	27,263	131,673	60,996	1,044,850
Maintenance and repair services	2,109,001	8,014	134,701	135,892	1,838,349
Maintenance and repair materials	1,545,399	8,098	80,619	288,239	1,176,947
Other lodging	**82,996,101**	**3,914,580**	**4,400,873**	**3,394,045**	**75,257,656**
Owned vacation homes	34,466,245	1,469,584	2,326,701	1,273,387	30,868,491
Mortgage interest and charges	15,475,621	818,956	1,566,518	683,859	13,225,291
Property taxes	11,463,112	539,243	396,028	500,021	10,566,839
Maintenance, insurance, and other expenses	7,528,713	111,385	364,011	89,507	7,075,443
Housing while attending school	7,362,877	512,913	586,687	238,024	6,537,882
Lodging on trips	41,166,979	1,932,083	1,487,629	1,882,633	37,851,283

	total consumer units	Asian	black	Hispanic	non-Hispanic white and other
UTILITIES, FUELS, AND PUBLIC SERVICES	**$417,859,803**	**$14,570,336**	**$50,478,586**	**$46,443,250**	**$321,505,654**
Natural gas	**57,728,947**	**2,445,293**	**6,853,334**	**5,355,972**	**45,596,385**
Electricity	**156,564,787**	**4,955,500**	**19,540,800**	**17,846,149**	**119,342,265**
Fuel oil and other fuels	**18,100,156**	**186,984**	**811,238**	**878,477**	**16,453,410**
Fuel oil	10,596,679	105,406	611,349	634,070	9,392,644
Coal, wood, and other fuels	862,828	–	32,738	28,512	803,590
Bottled gas	6,639,448	81,620	167,151	215,754	6,257,176
Telephone services	**133,352,557**	**4,967,923**	**17,251,020**	**16,554,321**	**99,764,394**
Residential telephone and pay phones	57,936,843	1,881,500	8,002,768	6,104,515	43,913,983
Cellular phone service	73,013,496	2,863,866	9,017,356	9,630,906	54,489,079
Phone cards	1,788,144	179,606	181,573	763,720	851,292
Voice over IP	615,276	42,951	49,467	55,322	510,958
Water and other public services	**52,113,356**	**2,014,594**	**6,022,195**	**5,808,332**	**40,349,200**
Water and sewerage maintenance	38,124,250	1,585,506	4,895,404	4,361,036	28,925,565
Trash and garbage collection	13,618,979	429,088	1,100,687	1,439,068	11,087,889
Septic tank cleaning	370,127	–	25,960	8,227	335,746

* See Appendix B for information about mortgage principal reduction.
Note: "Asian" and "black" include Hispanics and non-Hispanics who identify themselves as being of the respective race alone. "Hispanic" includes people of any race who identify themselves as Hispanic. "Other" includes people who identify themselves as non-Hispanic and as Alaska Native, American Indian, Asian (who are also included in the "Asian" column), Native Hawaiian or other Pacific Islander, as well as non-Hispanics reporting more than one race. "–" means sample is too small to make a reliable estimate.
Source: Calculations by New Strategist based on the Bureau of Labor Statistics' 2007 Consumer Expenditure Survey

Table 37. Housing: Shelter and Utilities: Market shares by race and Hispanic origin, 2007

(percentage of total annual spending on shelter and utilities accounted for by consumer unit race and Hispanic origin groups, 2007)

	total consumer units	Asian	black	Hispanic	non-Hispanic white and other
Share of total consumer units	100.0%	3.5%	12.0%	11.8%	76.3%
Share of total before-tax income	100.0	4.5	8.4	9.0	82.6
Share of total spending	100.0	4.3	8.7	9.9	81.5
Share of housing spending	100.0	4.7	9.6	10.9	79.7
SHELTER	100.0	5.4	9.7	11.5	79.0
Owned dwellings*	100.0	5.4	7.3	9.5	83.3
Mortgage interest and charges	100.0	5.8	8.4	11.0	80.8
Mortgage interest	100.0	6.0	8.8	11.4	79.9
Interest paid, home equity loan	100.0	4.9	6.9	9.0	84.1
Interest paid, home equity line of credit	100.0	3.2	2.5	3.6	93.9
Property taxes	100.0	5.7	6.3	8.4	85.4
Maintenance, repairs, insurance, other expenses	100.0	3.9	5.2	6.2	88.8
Homeowner's insurance	100.0	3.2	7.7	6.8	85.7
Ground rent	100.0	–	4.7	8.7	86.7
Maintenance and repair services	100.0	2.5	4.3	5.3	90.8
Painting and papering	100.0	2.9	3.6	2.8	93.6
Plumbing and water heating	100.0	2.1	7.7	8.6	84.0
Heat, air conditioning, electrical work	100.0	3.4	4.8	5.3	90.7
Roofing and gutters	100.0	2.9	3.5	3.4	93.1
Other repair and maintenance services	100.0	2.0	3.5	6.4	90.6
Repair, replacement of hard-surface flooring	100.0	1.7	5.9	5.0	89.0
Repair of built-in appliances	100.0	4.6	7.3	4.8	88.0
Maintenance and repair materials	100.0	1.2	3.2	7.2	89.5
Paints, wallpaper, and supplies	100.0	1.4	4.1	9.7	86.2
Tools, equipment for painting, wallpapering	100.0	1.4	4.1	9.7	86.5
Plumbing supplies and equipment	100.0	3.8	4.4	11.9	83.6
Electrical supplies, heating and cooling equipment	100.0	0.1	1.9	9.1	88.9
Hard-surface flooring, repair and replacement	100.0	2.0	3.5	7.2	89.4
Roofing and gutters	100.0	1.6	0.1	17.7	82.2
Plaster, paneling, siding, windows, doors, screens, awnings	100.0	1.8	2.6	7.8	89.5
Patio, walk, fence, driveway, masonry, brick, stucco materials	100.0	–	16.2	23.5	60.4
Miscellaneous supplies and equipment	100.0	0.1	3.1	2.0	94.9
Property management and security	100.0	6.5	3.9	6.0	90.4
Property management	100.0	6.6	3.8	5.1	91.5
Management and upkeep services for security	100.0	6.0	4.6	10.7	85.1
Parking	100.0	–	6.4	12.3	81.9
Rented dwellings	100.0	5.5	16.9	18.8	64.6
Rent	100.0	5.6	17.1	18.8	64.3
Rent as pay	100.0	5.5	17.4	20.8	62.0
Maintenance, insurance, and other expenses	100.0	0.9	7.1	9.9	83.0
Tenant's insurance	100.0	2.2	10.6	4.9	84.4
Maintenance and repair services	100.0	0.4	6.4	6.4	87.2
Maintenance and repair materials	100.0	0.5	5.2	18.7	76.2
Other lodging	100.0	4.7	5.3	4.1	90.7
Owned vacation homes	100.0	4.3	6.8	3.7	89.6
Mortgage interest and charges	100.0	5.3	10.1	4.4	85.5
Property taxes	100.0	4.7	3.5	4.4	92.2
Maintenance, insurance, and other expenses	100.0	1.5	4.8	1.2	94.0
Housing while attending school	100.0	7.0	8.0	3.2	88.8
Lodging on trips	100.0	4.7	3.6	4.6	91.9

	total consumer units	Asian	black	Hispanic	non-Hispanic white and other
UTILITIES, FUELS, AND PUBLIC SERVICES	**100.0%**	**3.5%**	**12.1%**	**11.1%**	**76.9%**
Natural gas	**100.0**	**4.2**	**11.9**	**9.3**	**79.0**
Electricity	**100.0**	**3.2**	**12.5**	**11.4**	**76.2**
Fuel oil and other fuels	**100.0**	**1.0**	**4.5**	**4.9**	**90.9**
Fuel oil	100.0	1.0	5.8	6.0	88.6
Coal, wood, and other fuels	100.0	–	3.8	3.3	93.1
Bottled gas	100.0	1.2	2.5	3.2	94.2
Telephone services	**100.0**	**3.7**	**12.9**	**12.4**	**74.8**
Residential telephone and pay phones	100.0	3.2	13.8	10.5	75.8
Cellular phone service	100.0	3.9	12.4	13.2	74.6
Phone cards	100.0	10.0	10.2	42.7	47.6
Voice over IP	100.0	7.0	8.0	9.0	83.0
Water and other public services	**100.0**	**3.9**	**11.6**	**11.1**	**77.4**
Water and sewerage maintenance	100.0	4.2	12.8	11.4	75.9
Trash and garbage collection	100.0	3.2	8.1	10.6	81.4
Septic tank cleaning	100.0	–	7.0	2.2	90.7

* See Appendix B for information about mortgage principal reduction.
Note: "Asian" and "black" include Hispanics and non-Hispanics who identify themselves as being of the respective race alone. "Hispanic" includes people of any race who identify themselves as Hispanic. "Other" includes people who identify themselves as non-Hispanic and as Alaska Native, American Indian, Asian (who are also included in the "Asian" column), Native Hawaiian or other Pacific Islander, as well as non-Hispanics reporting more than one race. "–" means sample is too small to make a reliable estimate.
Source: Calculations by New Strategist based on the Bureau of Labor Statistics' 2007 Consumer Expenditure Survey

Spending on Personal Care, Reading, Education, and Tobacco, 2007

The average household spent 13 percent less on personal care products and services in 2007 than in 2000, after adjusting for inflation. Spending on reading material also fell during those years—down a substantial 33 percent as Internet use cut household spending on books, magazines, and newspapers. Not surprisingly, spending on education increased by 24 percent as college tuition soared. The average household spent 16 percent less on tobacco in 2007 than in 2000 as smoking declined in popularity.

Black and Hispanic householders spend slightly less than the average household on personal care products and services, but on a few items their spending is well above average. Blacks spend five times the average on wigs and hairpieces. Because of their large families, Hispanics spend 48 percent more than average on hair care products. Asian householders spend 45 percent more than average on cosmetics, perfume, and bath products.

Asians spend more on education than any other racial or ethnic group, including 74 percent more than average on college tuition and more than twice the average on elementary and high school tuition. Blacks and especially Hispanics spend much less than average on education. Yet Hispanics spend 29 percent above average on books and supplies for elementary and high school.

Spending on reading material is below average for Asians and substantially so for blacks and Hispanics. Minority householders also spend far less than the average household on tobacco products and smoking supplies, a category on which non-Hispanic whites spend 12 percent more.

Table 38. Personal Care, Reading, Education, and Tobacco: Average spending by race and Hispanic origin, 2007

(average annual spending of consumer units on personal care, reading, education, and tobacco products, by race and Hispanic origin of consumer unit reference person, 2007)

	total consumer units	Asian	black	Hispanic	non-Hispanic white and other
Number of consumer units (in 000s)	120,171	4,240	14,422	14,185	91,734
Average number of persons per consumer unit	2.5	2.8	2.6	3.2	2.3
Average before-tax income of consumer units	$63,091.00	$80,487.00	$44,381.00	$48,330.00	$68,285.00
Average spending of consumer units, total	49,637.95	60,402.09	36,067.28	41,501.12	53,002.87
PERSONAL CARE PRODUCTS AND SERVICES	**587.68**	**564.09**	**484.78**	**526.39**	**613.75**
Personal care products	**304.77**	**343.08**	**198.54**	**319.25**	**319.59**
Hair care products	56.10	44.26	31.84	82.97	56.04
Hair accessories	9.33	8.48	8.37	10.59	9.29
Wigs and hairpieces	2.10	0.82	10.45	0.84	0.99
Oral hygiene products	27.64	22.21	19.12	33.35	28.16
Shaving products	14.94	9.92	7.95	13.02	16.27
Cosmetics, perfume, and bath products	152.03	221.19	94.79	140.28	163.04
Deodorants, feminine hygiene, miscellaneous products	30.00	23.56	24.62	29.68	30.85
Electric personal care appliances	12.64	12.64	1.40	8.52	14.95
Personal care services	**282.91**	**221.01**	**286.24**	**207.14**	**294.17**
READING	**117.69**	**98.44**	**46.27**	**37.94**	**141.14**
Newspaper and magazine subscriptions	47.29	37.3	16.99	11.50	57.56
Newspapers and magazines, nonsubscription	14.46	7.26	10.44	7.38	16.17
Books	55.93	53.71	18.84	19.06	67.40
EDUCATION	**945.29**	**1,627.31**	**700.15**	**415.12**	**1,065.01**
College tuition	585.20	1,019.20	433.58	188.20	669.34
Elementary and high school tuition	153.18	334.72	129.01	106.25	165.07
Vocational and technical school tuition	15.42	3.61	1.83	3.61	19.35
Other school tuition	20.13	–	23.97	14.19	20.40
Other school expenses including rentals	42.83	46.81	34.89	20.87	47.39
Books and supplies for college	61.94	90.51	48.24	28.70	69.21
Books and supplies for elementary and high school	16.16	21.39	10.14	20.87	16.36
Books and supplies for vocational and technical schools	0.56	–	0.29	0.21	0.65
Books and supplies for day care and nursery	0.41	0.66	0.08	1.19	0.34
Books and supplies for other schools	2.46	1.59	1.12	1.70	2.79
Miscellaneous school expenses and supplies	47.01	44.75	17.00	29.33	54.11
TOBACCO PRODUCTS AND SMOKING SUPPLIES	**322.98**	**135.35**	**219.21**	**165.25**	**363.31**
Cigarettes	294.95	131.96	201.03	156.78	330.75
Other tobacco products	26.73	3.30	17.07	7.65	31.16
Smoking accessories	1.21	0.09	0.42	0.82	1.39

Note: "Asian" and "black" include Hispanics and non-Hispanics who identify themselves as being of the respective race alone. "Hispanic" includes people of any race who identify themselves as Hispanic. "Other" includes people who identify themselves as non-Hispanic and as Alaska Native, American Indian, Asian (who are also included in the "Asian" column), Native Hawaiian or other Pacific Islander, as well as non-Hispanics reporting more than one race. Subcategories may not add to total because some are not shown.
Source: Bureau of Labor Statistics, unpublished tables from the 2007 Consumer Expenditure Survey

Table 39. Personal Care, Reading, Education, and Tobacco: Indexed spending by race and Hispanic origin, 2007

(indexed average annual spending of consumer units on personal care, reading, education, and tobacco products, by race and Hispanic origin of consumer unit reference person, 2007; index definition: an index of 100 is the average for all consumer units; an index of 132 means that spending by consumer units in that group is 32 percent above the average for all consumer units; an index of 68 indicates spending that is 32 percent below the average for all consumer units)

	total consumer units	Asian	black	Hispanic	non-Hispanic white and other
Average spending of consumer units, total	$49,638	$60,402	$36,067	$41,501	$53,003
Average spending of consumer units, index	100	122	73	84	107
PERSONAL CARE PRODUCTS AND SERVICES	**100**	**96**	**82**	**90**	**104**
Personal care products	**100**	**113**	**65**	**105**	**105**
Hair care products	100	79	57	148	100
Hair accessories	100	91	90	114	100
Wigs and hairpieces	100	39	498	40	47
Oral hygiene products	100	80	69	121	102
Shaving products	100	66	53	87	109
Cosmetics, perfume, and bath products	100	145	62	92	107
Deodorants, feminine hygiene, miscellaneous products	100	79	82	99	103
Electric personal care appliances	100	100	11	67	118
Personal care services	**100**	**78**	**101**	**73**	**104**
READING	**100**	**84**	**39**	**32**	**120**
Newspaper and magazine subscriptions	100	79	36	24	122
Newspapers and magazines, nonsubscription	100	50	72	51	112
Books	100	96	34	34	121
EDUCATION	**100**	**172**	**74**	**44**	**113**
College tuition	100	174	74	32	114
Elementary and high school tuition	100	219	84	69	108
Vocational and technical school tuition	100	23	12	23	125
Other school tuition	100	–	119	70	101
Other school expenses including rentals	100	109	81	49	111
Books and supplies for college	100	146	78	46	112
Books and supplies for elementary and high school	100	132	63	129	101
Books and supplies for vocational and technical schools	100	–	52	38	116
Books and supplies for day care and nursery	100	161	20	290	83
Books and suppliesfor other schools	100	65	46	69	113
Miscellaneous school expenses and supplies	100	95	36	62	115
TOBACCO PRODUCTS AND SMOKING SUPPLIES	**100**	**42**	**68**	**51**	**112**
Cigarettes	100	45	68	53	112
Other tobacco products	100	12	64	29	117
Smoking accessories	100	7	35	68	115

Note: "Asian" and "black" include Hispanics and non-Hispanics who identify themselves as being of the respective race alone. "Hispanic" includes people of any race who identify themselves as Hispanic. "Other" includes people who identify themselves as non-Hispanic and as Alaska Native, American Indian, Asian (who are also included in the "Asian" column), Native Hawaiian or other Pacific Islander, as well as non-Hispanics reporting more than one race.
Source: Calculations by New Strategist based on the Bureau of Labor Statistics' 2007 Consumer Expenditure Survey

Table 40. Personal Care, Reading, Education, and Tobacco: Total spending by race and Hispanic origin, 2007

(total annual spending on personal care, reading, education, and tobacco products, by consumer unit race and Hispanic origin groups, 2007; consumer units and dollars in thousands)

	total consumer units	Asian	black	Hispanic	non-Hispanic white and other
Number of consumer units	120,171	4,240	14,422	14,185	91,734
Total spending of all consumer units	$5,965,042,089	$256,104,862	$520,162,312	$588,693,387	$4,862,165,277
PERSONAL CARE PRODUCTS AND SERVICES	**70,622,093**	**2,391,742**	**6,991,497**	**7,466,842**	**56,301,743**
Personal care products	**36,624,516**	**1,454,659**	**2,863,344**	**4,528,561**	**29,317,269**
Hair care products	6,741,593	187,662	459,196	1,176,929	5,140,773
Hair accessories	1,121,195	35,955	120,712	150,219	852,209
Wigs and hairpieces	252,359	3,477	150,710	11,915	90,817
Oral hygiene products	3,321,526	94,170	275,749	473,070	2,583,229
Shaving products	1,795,355	42,061	114,655	184,689	1,492,512
Cosmetics, perfume, and bath products	18,269,597	937,846	1,367,061	1,989,872	14,956,311
Deodorants, feminine hygiene, miscellaneous products	3,605,130	99,894	355,070	421,011	2,829,994
Electric personal care appliances	1,518,961	53593.6	20,191	120,856	1,371,423
Personal care services	**33,997,578**	**937,082**	**4,128,153**	**2,938,281**	**26,985,391**
READING	**14,142,925**	**417,386**	**667,306**	**538,179**	**12,947,337**
Newspaper and magazine subscriptions	5,682,887	158,152	245,030	163,128	5,280,209
Newspapers and magazines, nonsubscription	1,737,673	30,782	150,566	104,685	1,483,339
Books	6,721,164	227,730	271,710	270,366	6,182,872
EDUCATION	**113,596,445**	**6,899,794**	**10,097,563**	**5,888,477**	**97,697,627**
College tuition	70,324,069	4,321,408	6,253,091	2,669,617	61,401,236
Elementary and high school tuition	18,407,794	1,419,213	1,860,582	1,507,156	15,142,531
Vocational and technical school tuition	1,853,037	15,306	26,392	51,208	1,775,053
Other school tuition	2,419,042	–	345,695	201,285	1,871,374
Other school expenses including rentals	5,146,924	198,474	503,184	296,041	4,347,274
Books and supplies for college	7,443,392	383,762	695,717	407,110	6,348,910
Books and supplies for elementary and high school	1,941,963	90,694	146,239	296,041	1,500,768
Books and supplies for vocational and technical schools	67,296	–	4,182	2,979	59,627
Books and supplies for day care and nursery	49,270	2,798	1,154	16,880	31,190
Books and suppliesfor other schools	295,621	6,742	16,153	24,115	255,938
Miscellaneous school expenses and supplies	5,649,239	189,740	245,174	416,046	4,963,727
TOBACCO PRODUCTS AND SMOKING SUPPLIES	**38,812,830**	**573,884**	**3,161,447**	**2,344,071**	**33,327,880**
Cigarettes	35,444,436	559,510	2,899,255	2,223,924	30,341,021
Other tobacco products	3,212,171	13,992	246,184	108,515	2,858,431
Smoking accessories	145,407	382	6,057	11,632	127,510

Note: "Asian" and "black" include Hispanics and non-Hispanics who identify themselves as being of the respective race alone. "Hispanic" includes people of any race who identify themselves as Hispanic. "Other" includes people who identify themselves as non-Hispanic and as Alaska Native, American Indian, Asian (who are also included in the "Asian" column), Native Hawaiian or other Pacific Islander, as well as non-Hispanics reporting more than one race.
Source: Calculations by New Strategist based on the Bureau of Labor Statistics' 2007 Consumer Expenditure Survey

Table 41. Personal Care, Reading, Education, and Tobacco: Market shares by race and Hispanic origin, 2007

(percentage of total annual spending on personal care, reading, education, and tobacco products accounted for by consumer unit race and Hispanic origin groups, 2007)

	total consumer units	Asian	black	Hispanic	non-Hispanic white and other
Share of total consumer units	100.0%	3.5%	12.0%	11.8%	76.3%
Share of total before-tax income	100.0	4.5	8.4	9.0	82.6
Share of total spending	100.0	4.3	8.7	9.9	81.5
PERSONAL CARE PRODUCTS AND SERVICES	100.0	3.4	9.9	10.6	79.7
Personal care products	100.0	4.0	7.8	12.4	80.0
Hair care products	100.0	2.8	6.8	17.5	76.3
Hair accessories	100.0	3.2	10.8	13.4	76.0
Wigs and hairpieces	100.0	1.4	59.7	4.7	36.0
Oral hygiene products	100.0	2.8	8.3	14.2	77.8
Shaving products	100.0	2.3	6.4	10.3	83.1
Cosmetics, perfume, and bath products	100.0	5.1	7.5	10.9	81.9
Deodorants, feminine hygiene, miscellaneous products	100.0	2.8	9.8	11.7	78.5
Electric personal care appliances	100.0	3.5	1.3	8.0	90.3
Personal care services	100.0	2.8	12.1	8.6	79.4
READING	100.0	3.0	4.7	3.8	91.5
Newspaper and magazine subscriptions	100.0	2.8	4.3	2.9	92.9
Newspapers and magazines, nonsubscription	100.0	1.8	8.7	6.0	85.4
Books	100.0	3.4	4.0	4.0	92.0
EDUCATION	100.0	6.1	8.9	5.2	86.0
College tuition	100.0	6.1	8.9	3.8	87.3
Elementary and high school tuition	100.0	7.7	10.1	8.2	82.3
Vocational and technical school tuition	100.0	0.8	1.4	2.8	95.8
Other school tuition	100.0	–	14.3	8.3	77.4
Other school expenses including rentals	100.0	3.9	9.8	5.8	84.5
Books and supplies for college	100.0	5.2	9.3	5.5	85.3
Books and supplies for elementary and high school	100.0	4.7	7.5	15.2	77.3
Books and supplies for vocational and technical schools	100.0	–	6.2	4.4	88.6
Books and supplies for day care and nursery	100.0	5.7	2.3	34.3	63.3
Books and suppliesfor other schools	100.0	2.3	5.5	8.2	86.6
Miscellaneous school expenses and supplies	100.0	3.4	4.3	7.4	87.9
TOBACCO PRODUCTS AND SMOKING SUPPLIES	100.0	1.5	8.1	6.0	85.9
Cigarettes	100.0	1.6	8.2	6.3	85.6
Other tobacco products	100.0	0.4	7.7	3.4	89.0
Smoking accessories	100.0	0.3	4.2	8.0	87.7

Note: "Asian" and "black" include Hispanics and non-Hispanics who identify themselves as being of the respective race alone. "Hispanic" includes people of any race who identify themselves as Hispanic. "Other" includes people who identify themselves as non-Hispanic and as Alaska Native, American Indian, Asian (who are also included in the "Asian" column), Native Hawaiian or other Pacific Islander, as well as non-Hispanics reporting more than one race.
Source: Calculations by New Strategist based on the Bureau of Labor Statistics' 2007 Consumer Expenditure Survey

Spending on Transportation, 2007

Transportation is the second largest household expenditure category, the average household devoting $8,758 to transportation in 2007—2 percent less than in 2000 after adjusting for inflation. Transportation expenses consume 18 percent of the average household budget.

Spending trends have been mixed in the transportation category during the past seven years. Households devoted less to new cars and trucks (down 19 percent between 2000 and 2007, after adjusting for inflation) and to used cars and trucks (down 26 percent during those years). Spending on rented and leased vehicles fell by 28 percent. Spending on vehicle maintenance and repairs declined by 2 percent, after adjusting for inflation. But gasoline spending by the average household rose a substantial 53 percent between 2000 and 2007 as oil prices climbed. The average household's outlay for vehicle insurance climbed 14 percent in those years. Spending on public transportation, which includes both commuting and travel, increased by 5 percent between 2000 and 2007.

Asians devoted $10,921 to transportation in 2007, or 25 percent more than the average household. Hispanics spent $8,035 on transportation, 8 percent less than the average household. Black householders spent only $6,458 on transportation, 26 percent less than average. Asians spend more than double the average on new cars. Hispanics spend 20 percent more than average on used trucks. Asians spend more than three times the average on airline fares. Asians, blacks, and Hispanics spend much more than the average household on mass transit fares. Together, Asians, blacks, and Hispanics, whose share of all consumer units is 27 percent, account for 46 percent of the spending on mass transit.

Table 42. Transportation: Average spending by race and Hispanic origin, 2007

(average annual spending by consumer units on transportation, by race and Hispanic origin of consumer unit reference person, 2007)

	total consumer units	Asian	black	Hispanic	non-Hispanic white and other
Number of consumer units (in 000s)	120,171	4,240	14,422	14,185	91,734
Average number of persons per consumer unit	2.5	2.8	2.6	3.2	2.3
Average before-tax income of consumer units	$63,091.00	$80,487.00	$44,381.00	$48,330.00	$68,285.00
Average spending of consumer units, total	49,637.95	60,402.09	36,067.28	41,501.12	53,002.87
Transportation, average spending	**8,757.65**	**10,921.22**	**6,457.69**	**8,034.85**	**9,233.51**
VEHICLE PURCHASES	**3,244.00**	**4,006.69**	**2,223.06**	**2,875.57**	**3,462.68**
Cars and trucks, new	**1,571.80**	**2,797.07**	**729.11**	**1,271.14**	**1,752.08**
New cars	712.20	1,646.08	336.18	706.40	775.11
New trucks	859.60	1,150.99	392.93	564.74	976.98
Cars and trucks, used	**1,566.87**	**1,209.62**	**1,459.64**	**1,541.12**	**1,587.81**
Used cars	852.18	641.45	958.24	681.25	863.11
Used trucks	714.69	568.17	501.40	859.88	724.69
Other vehicles	**105.32**	**–**	**34.31**	**63.31**	**122.79**
New motorcycles	63.80	–	16.08	37.96	75.17
Used motorcycles	41.53	–	18.23	25.35	47.62
GASOLINE AND MOTOR OIL	**2,383.67**	**2,391.22**	**1,934.71**	**2,304.38**	**2,465.55**
Gasoline	2,201.60	2,289.16	1,867.28	2,181.49	2,256.55
Diesel fuel	41.26	3.42	6.81	19.17	50.01
Gasoline on trips	130.30	91.04	55.15	91.61	147.94
Motor oil	9.20	6.68	4.91	11.19	9.56
Motor oil on trips	1.32	0.92	0.56	0.93	1.49
OTHER VEHICLE EXPENSES	**2,592.18**	**2,978.03**	**2,000.70**	**2,525.25**	**2,697.17**
Vehicle finance charges	**305.21**	**236.02**	**252.01**	**313.50**	**311.98**
Automobile finance charges	122.03	135.35	145.19	111.98	119.90
Truck finance charges	163.12	100.67	104.96	186.76	168.38
Motorcycle and plane finance charges	6.31	–	1.16	2.93	7.64
Other vehicle finance charges	13.75	–	0.71	11.83	16.07
Maintenance and repairs	**737.62**	**729.27**	**504.94**	**556.57**	**802.23**
Coolant, additives, brake and transmission fluids	3.50	2.57	3.58	4.53	3.32
Tires—purchased, replaced, installed	115.90	91.35	87.00	80.59	125.83
Parts, equipment, and accessories	43.65	59.65	18.01	30.30	49.67
Vehicle audio equipment	5.29	–	5.74	17.96	3.41
Vehicle products and cleaning services	5.17	4.31	1.54	3.93	5.90
Vehicle video equipment	2.48	1.46	1.58	3.17	2.51
Miscellaneous auto repair, servicing	62.03	60.41	36.61	44.83	68.32
Body work and painting	28.03	22.14	16.22	22.12	30.75
Clutch and transmission repair	33.08	13.97	23.69	32.53	34.74
Drive shaft and rear-end repair	6.45	9.67	2.41	3.02	7.61
Brake work	58.44	54.47	49.79	40.29	62.60
Repair to steering or front-end	22.56	7.09	16.59	14.40	24.78
Repair to engine cooling system	22.12	15.78	14.99	24.44	23.53
Motor tune-up	46.08	73.26	35.13	39.72	48.79
Lube, oil change, and oil filters	69.34	69.50	50.26	54.86	74.51
Front-end alignment, wheel balance, rotation	14.63	16.73	9.52	6.48	16.68
Shock absorber replacement	5.26	10.12	1.57	5.27	5.83
Tire repair and other repair work	50.29	57.51	30.48	38.01	55.26
Vehicle air conditioning repair	14.63	3.36	14.19	9.15	15.64
Exhaust system repair	10.20	6.59	6.73	4.01	11.68
Electrical system repair	27.49	19.29	21.97	16.45	30.03
Motor repair, replacement	72.69	99.44	46.09	52.89	79.81
Auto repair service policy	16.14	9.85	11.25	7.62	18.20

	total consumer units	Asian	black	Hispanic	non-Hispanic white and other
Vehicle insurance	**$1,071.37**	**$1,549.55**	**$872.41**	**$1,280.03**	**$1,072.51**
Vehicle rental, leases, licenses, other charges	**477.97**	**463.19**	**371.34**	**375.14**	**510.44**
Leased and rented vehicles	285.01	195.39	247.89	215.50	301.53
Rented vehicles	39.87	39.47	30.64	16.92	44.83
Auto rental	8.33	7.76	10.73	4.56	8.54
Auto rental on trips	24.90	26.22	12.48	9.99	29.12
Truck rental	2.88	0.69	4.48	1.49	2.85
Truck rental on trips	3.21	4.79	2.95	0.88	3.61
Leased vehicles	245.15	155.93	217.24	198.57	256.70
Car lease payments	116.64	67.68	124.53	98.30	118.43
Truck lease payments	111.39	88.25	72.28	92.66	120.23
Vehicle registration, state	85.71	98.94	46.37	76.74	93.16
Vehicle registration, local	8.80	8.22	7.14	5.68	9.55
Driver's license	7.52	7.11	5.88	6.27	7.96
Vehicle inspection	10.70	9.64	6.40	11.65	11.22
Parking fees	35.17	56.64	22.79	19.22	39.59
Parking fees in home city, excluding residence	29.17	47.75	20.03	16.72	32.55
Parking fees on trips	6.00	8.89	2.75	2.50	7.05
Tolls	15.57	49.65	20.13	16.30	14.74
Tolls on trips	4.33	5.97	2.30	3.56	4.78
Towing charges	5.97	6.60	3.26	8.02	6.07
Global positioning services	2.24	6.66	0.46	2.67	2.45
Automobile service clubs	16.94	18.37	8.72	9.54	19.40
PUBLIC TRANSPORTATION	**537.81**	**1,545.29**	**299.22**	**329.65**	**608.12**
Airline fares	359.71	1,192.86	148.81	184.39	420.11
Intercity bus fares	10.49	21.27	6.40	8.92	11.38
Intracity mass transit fares	55.10	138.53	90.50	83.64	45.39
Local transportation on trips	21.39	42.06	10.24	10.38	24.89
Taxi fares and limousine service	16.12	8.88	15.71	19.03	15.75
Intercity train fares	20.75	37.46	13.08	7.42	24.03
Ship fares	53.23	99.84	13.83	14.35	65.57
School bus	1.01	4.38	0.64	1.53	0.99

Note: "Asian" and "black" include Hispanics and non-Hispanics who identify themselves as being of the respective race alone. "Hispanic" includes people of any race who identify themselves as Hispanic. "Other" includes people who identify themselves as non-Hispanic and as Alaska Native, American Indian, Asian (who are also included in the "Asian" column), Native Hawaiian or other Pacific Islander, as well as non-Hispanics reporting more than one race. Subcategories may not add to total because some are not shown. "–" means sample is too small to make a reliable estimate.
Source: Bureau of Labor Statistics, unpublished tables from the 2007 Consumer Expenditure Survey

Table 43. Transportation: Indexed spending by race and Hispanic origin, 2007

(indexed average annual spending of consumer units on transportation, by race and Hispanic origin of consumer unit reference person, 2007; index defini-tion: an index of 100 is the average for all consumer units; an index of 132 means that spending by consumer units in that group is 32 percent above the average for all consumer units; an index of 68 indicates spending that is 32 percent below the average for all consumer units)

	total consumer units	Asian	black	Hispanic	non-Hispanic white and other
Average spending of consumer units, total	$49,638	$60,402	$36,067	$41,501	$53,003
Average spending of consumer units, index	100	122	73	84	107
Transportation, spending index	**100**	**125**	**74**	**92**	**105**
VEHICLE PURCHASES	**100**	**124**	**69**	**89**	**107**
Cars and trucks, new	**100**	**178**	**46**	**81**	**111**
New cars	100	231	47	99	109
New trucks	100	134	46	66	114
Cars and trucks, used	**100**	**77**	**93**	**98**	**101**
Used cars	100	75	112	80	101
Used trucks	100	79	70	120	101
Other vehicles	**100**	**–**	**33**	**60**	**117**
New motorcycles	100	–	25	59	118
Used motorcycles	100	–	44	61	115
GASOLINE AND MOTOR OIL	**100**	**100**	**81**	**97**	**103**
Gasoline	100	104	85	99	102
Diesel fuel	100	8	17	46	121
Gasoline on trips	100	70	42	70	114
Motor oil	100	73	53	122	104
Motor oil on trips	100	70	42	70	113
OTHER VEHICLE EXPENSES	**100**	**115**	**77**	**97**	**104**
Vehicle finance charges	**100**	**77**	**83**	**103**	**102**
Automobile finance charges	100	111	119	92	98
Truck finance charges	100	62	64	114	103
Motorcycle and plane finance charges	100	–	18	46	121
Other vehicle finance charges	100	–	5	86	117
Maintenance and repairs	**100**	**99**	**68**	**75**	**109**
Coolant, additives, brake and transmission fluids	100	73	102	129	95
Tires—purchased, replaced, installed	100	79	75	70	109
Parts, equipment, and accessories	100	137	41	69	114
Vehicle audio equipment	100	–	109	340	64
Vehicle products and cleaning services	100	83	30	76	114
Vehicle video equipment	100	59	64	128	101
Miscellaneous auto repair, servicing	100	97	59	72	110
Body work and painting	100	79	58	79	110
Clutch and transmission repair	100	42	72	98	105
Drive shaft and rear-end repair	100	150	37	47	118
Brake work	100	93	85	69	107
Repair to steering or front-end	100	31	74	64	110
Repair to engine cooling system	100	71	68	110	106
Motor tune-up	100	159	76	86	106
Lube, oil change, and oil filters	100	100	72	79	107
Front-end alignment, wheel balance, rotation	100	114	65	44	114
Shock absorber replacement	100	192	30	100	111
Tire repair and other repair work	100	114	61	76	110
Vehicle air conditioning repair	100	23	97	63	107
Exhaust system repair	100	65	66	39	115
Electrical system repair	100	70	80	60	109
Motor repair, replacement	100	137	63	73	110
Auto repair service policy	100	61	70	47	113

	total consumer units	Asian	black	Hispanic	non-Hispanic white and other
Vehicle insurance	**100**	**145**	**81**	**119**	**100**
Vehicle rental, leases, licenses, other charges	**100**	**97**	**78**	**78**	**107**
Leased and rented vehicles	100	69	87	76	106
Rented vehicles	100	99	77	42	112
Auto rental	100	93	129	55	103
Auto rental on trips	100	105	50	40	117
Truck rental	100	24	156	52	99
Truck rental on trips	100	149	92	27	112
Leased vehicles	100	64	89	81	105
Car lease payments	100	58	107	84	102
Truck lease payments	100	79	65	83	108
Vehicle registration, state	100	115	54	90	109
Vehicle registration, local	100	93	81	65	109
Driver's license	100	95	78	83	106
Vehicle inspection	100	90	60	109	105
Parking fees	100	161	65	55	113
Parking fees in home city, excluding residence	100	164	69	57	112
Parking fees on trips	100	148	46	42	118
Tolls	100	319	129	105	95
Tolls on trips	100	138	53	82	110
Towing charges	100	111	55	134	102
Global positioning services	100	297	21	119	109
Automobile service clubs	100	108	51	56	115
PUBLIC TRANSPORTATION	**100**	**287**	**56**	**61**	**113**
Airline fares	100	332	41	51	117
Intercity bus fares	100	203	61	85	108
Intracity mass transit fares	100	251	164	152	82
Local transportation on trips	100	197	48	49	116
Taxi fares and limousine service	100	55	97	118	98
Intercity train fares	100	181	63	36	116
Ship fares	100	188	26	27	123
School bus	100	434	63	151	98

Note: "Asian" and "black" include Hispanics and non-Hispanics who identify themselves as being of the respective race alone. "Hispanic" includes people of any race who identify themselves as Hispanic. "Other" includes people who identify themselves as non-Hispanic and as Alaska Native, American Indian, Asian (who are also included in the "Asian" column), Native Hawaiian or other Pacific Islander, as well as non-Hispanics reporting more than one race. "–" means sample is too small to make a reliable estimate.
Source: Calculations by New Strategist based on the Bureau of Labor Statistics' 2007 Consumer Expenditure Survey

Table 44. Transportation: Total spending by race and Hispanic origin, 2007

(total annual spending on transportation, by consumer unit race and Hispanic origin groups, 2007; consumer units and dollars in thousands)

	total consumer units	Asian	black	Hispanic	non-Hispanic white and other
Number of consumer units	120,171	4,240	14,422	14,185	91,734
Total spending of all consumer units	$5,965,042,089	$256,104,862	$520,162,312	$588,693,387	$4,862,165,277
Transportation, total spending	1,052,415,558	46,305,973	93,132,805	113,974,347	847,026,806
VEHICLE PURCHASES	389,834,724	16,988,366	32,060,971	40,789,960	317,645,487
Cars and trucks, new	188,884,778	11,859,577	10,515,224	18,031,121	160,725,307
New cars	85,585,786	6,979,379	4,848,388	10,020,284	71,103,941
New trucks	103,298,992	4,880,198	5,666,836	8,010,837	89,622,283
Cars and trucks, used	188,292,335	5,128,789	21,050,928	21,860,787	145,656,163
Used cars	102,407,323	2,719,748	13,819,737	9,663,531	79,176,533
Used trucks	85,885,012	2,409,041	7,231,191	12,197,398	66,478,712
Other vehicles	12,656,410	–	494,819	898,052	11,264,018
New motorcycles	7,666,910	–	231,906	538,463	6,895,645
Used motorcycles	4,990,702	–	262,913	359,590	4,368,373
GASOLINE AND MOTOR OIL	286,448,008	10,138,773	27,902,388	32,687,630	226,174,764
Gasoline	264,568,474	9,706,038	26,929,912	30,944,436	207,002,358
Diesel fuel	4,958,255	14,501	98,214	271,926	4,587,617
Gasoline on trips	15,658,281	386,010	795,373	1,299,488	13,571,128
Motor oil	1,105,573	28,323	70,812	158,730	876,977
Motor oil on trips	158,626	3,901	8,076	13,192	136,684
OTHER VEHICLE EXPENSES	311,504,863	12,626,847	28,854,095	35,820,671	247,422,193
Vehicle finance charges	36,677,391	1,000,725	3,634,488	4,446,998	28,619,173
Automobile finance charges	14,664,467	573,884	2,093,930	1,588,436	10,998,907
Truck finance charges	19,602,294	426,841	1,513,733	2,649,191	15,446,171
Motorcycle and plane finance charges	758,279	–	16,730	41,562	700,848
Other vehicle finance charges	1,652,351	–	10,240	167,809	1,474,165
Maintenance and repairs	88,640,533	3,092,105	7,282,245	7,894,945	73,591,767
Coolant, additives, brake and transmission fluids	420,599	10,897	51,631	64,258	304,557
Tires—purchased, replaced, installed	13,927,819	387,324	1,254,714	1,143,169	11,542,889
Parts, equipment, and accessories	5,245,464	252,916	259,740	429,806	4,556,428
Vehicle audio equipment	635,705	–	82,782	254,763	312,813
Vehicle products and cleaning services	621,284	18,274	22,210	55,747	541,231
Vehicle video equipment	298,024	6,190	22,787	44,966	230,252
Miscellaneous auto repair, servicing	7,454,207	256,138	527,989	635,914	6,267,267
Body work and painting	3,368,393	93,874	233,925	313,772	2,820,821
Clutch and transmission repair	3,975,257	59,233	341,657	461,438	3,186,839
Drive shaft and rear-end repair	775,103	41,001	34,757	42,839	698,096
Brake work	7,022,793	230,953	718,071	571,514	5,742,548
Repair to steering or front-end	2,711,058	30,062	239,261	204,264	2,273,169
Repair to engine cooling system	2,658,183	66,907	216,186	346,681	2,158,501
Motor tune-up	5,537,480	310,622	506,645	563,428	4,475,702
Lube, oil change, and oil filters	8,332,657	294,680	724,850	778,189	6,835,100
Front-end alignment, wheel balance, rotation	1,758,102	70,935	137,297	91,919	1,530,123
Shock absorber replacement	632,099	42,909	22,643	74,755	534,809
Tire repair and other repair work	6,043,400	243,842	439,583	539,172	5,069,221
Vehicle air conditioning repair	1,758,102	14,246	204,648	129,793	1,434,720
Exhaust system repair	1,225,744	27,942	97,060	56,882	1,071,453
Electrical system repair	3,303,501	81,790	316,851	233,343	2,754,772
Motor repair, replacement	8,735,230	421,626	664,710	750,245	7,321,291
Auto repair service policy	1,939,560	41,764	162,248	108,090	1,669,559

	total consumer units	Asian	black	Hispanic	non-Hispanic white and other
Vehicle insurance	$128,747,604	$6,570,092	$12,581,897	$18,157,226	$98,385,632
Vehicle rental, leases, licenses, other charges	57,438,133	1,963,926	5,355,465	5,321,361	46,824,703
Leased and rented vehicles	34,249,937	828,454	3,575,070	3,056,868	27,660,553
Rented vehicles	4,791,218	167,353	441,890	240,010	4,112,435
Auto rental	1,001,024	32,902	154,748	64,684	783,408
Auto rental on trips	2,992,258	111,173	179,987	141,708	2,671,294
Truck rental	346,092	2,926	64,611	21,136	261,442
Truck rental on trips	385,749	20,310	42,545	12,483	331,160
Leased vehicles	29,459,921	661,143	3,133,035	2,816,715	23,548,118
Car lease payments	14,016,745	286,963	1,795,972	1,394,386	10,864,058
Truck lease payments	13,385,848	374,180	1,042,422	1,314,382	11,029,179
Vehicle registration, state	10,299,856	419,506	668,748	1,088,557	8,545,939
Vehicle registration, local	1,057,505	34,853	102,973	80,571	876,060
Driver's license	903,686	30,146	84,801	88,940	730,203
Vehicle inspection	1,285,830	40,874	92,301	165,255	1,029,255
Parking fees	4,226,414	240,154	328,677	272,636	3,631,749
Parking fees in home city, excluding residence	3,505,388	202,460	288,873	237,173	2,985,942
Parking fees on trips	721,026	37,694	39,661	35,463	646,725
Tolls	1,871,062	210,516	290,315	231,216	1,352,159
Tolls on trips	520,340	25,313	33,171	50,499	438,489
Towing charges	717,421	27,984	47,016	113,764	556,825
Global positioning services	269,183	28,238	6,634	37,874	224,748
Automobile service clubs	2,035,697	77,889	125,760	135,325	1,779,640
PUBLIC TRANSPORTATION	64,629,166	6,552,030	4,315,351	4,676,085	55,785,280
Airline fares	43,226,710	5,057,726	2,146,138	2,615,572	38,538,371
Intercity bus fares	1,260,594	90,185	92,301	126,530	1,043,933
Intracity mass transit fares	6,621,422	587,367	1,305,191	1,186,433	4,163,806
Local transportation on trips	2,570,458	178,334	147,681	147,240	2,283,259
Taxi fares and limousine service	1,937,157	37,651	226,570	269,941	1,444,811
Intercity train fares	2,493,548	158,830	188,640	105,253	2,204,368
Ship fares	6,396,702	423,322	199,456	203,555	6,014,998
School bus	121,373	18,571	9,230	21,703	90,817

Note: "Asian" and "black" include Hispanics and non-Hispanics who identify themselves as being of the respective race alone. "Hispanic" includes people of any race who identify themselves as Hispanic. "Other" includes people who identify themselves as non-Hispanic and as Alaska Native, American Indian, Asian (who are also included in the "Asian" column), Native Hawaiian or other Pacific Islander, as well as non-Hispanics reporting more than one race. Numbers may not add to total because of rounding and missing subcategories. "–" means sample is too small to make a reliable estimate.
Source: Calculations by New Strategist based on the Bureau of Labor Statistics' 2007 Consumer Expenditure Survey

Table 45. Transportation: Market shares by race and Hispanic origin, 2007

(percentage of total annual spending on transportation accounted for by consumer unit race and Hispanic origin groups, 2007)

	total consumer units	Asian	black	Hispanic	non-Hispanic white and other
Share of total consumer units	100.0%	3.5%	12.0%	11.8%	76.3%
Share of total before-tax income	100.0	4.5	8.4	9.0	82.6
Share of total spending	100.0	4.3	8.7	9.9	81.5
Share of transportation spending	100.0	4.4	8.8	10.8	80.5
VEHICLE PURCHASES	100.0	4.4	8.2	10.5	81.5
Cars and trucks, new	100.0	6.3	5.6	9.5	85.1
New cars	100.0	8.2	5.7	11.7	83.1
New trucks	100.0	4.7	5.5	7.8	86.8
Cars and trucks, used	100.0	2.7	11.2	11.6	77.4
Used cars	100.0	2.7	13.5	9.4	77.3
Used trucks	100.0	2.8	8.4	14.2	77.4
Other vehicles	100.0	–	3.9	7.1	89.0
New motorcycles	100.0	–	3.0	7.0	89.9
Used motorcycles	100.0	–	5.3	7.2	87.5
GASOLINE AND MOTOR OIL	100.0	3.5	9.7	11.4	79.0
Gasoline	100.0	3.7	10.2	11.7	78.2
Diesel fuel	100.0	0.3	2.0	5.5	92.5
Gasoline on trips	100.0	2.5	5.1	8.3	86.7
Motor oil	100.0	2.6	6.4	14.4	79.3
Motor oil on trips	100.0	2.5	5.1	8.3	86.2
OTHER VEHICLE EXPENSES	100.0	4.1	9.3	11.5	79.4
Vehicle finance charges	100.0	2.7	9.9	12.1	78.0
Automobile finance charges	100.0	3.9	14.3	10.8	75.0
Truck finance charges	100.0	2.2	7.7	13.5	78.8
Motorcycle and plane finance charges	100.0	–	2.2	5.5	92.4
Other vehicle finance charges	100.0	–	0.6	10.2	89.2
Maintenance and repairs	100.0	3.5	8.2	8.9	83.0
Coolant, additives, brake and transmission fluids	100.0	2.6	12.3	15.3	72.4
Tires—purchased, replaced, installed	100.0	2.8	9.0	8.2	82.9
Parts, equipment, and accessories	100.0	4.8	5.0	8.2	86.9
Vehicle audio equipment	100.0	–	13.0	40.1	49.2
Vehicle products and cleaning services	100.0	2.9	3.6	9.0	87.1
Vehicle video equipment	100.0	2.1	7.6	15.1	77.3
Miscellaneous auto repair, servicing	100.0	3.4	7.1	8.5	84.1
Body work and painting	100.0	2.8	6.9	9.3	83.7
Clutch and transmission repair	100.0	1.5	8.6	11.6	80.2
Drive shaft and rear-end repair	100.0	5.3	4.5	5.5	90.1
Brake work	100.0	3.3	10.2	8.1	81.8
Repair to steering or front-end	100.0	1.1	8.8	7.5	83.8
Repair to engine cooling system	100.0	2.5	8.1	13.0	81.2
Motor tune-up	100.0	5.6	9.1	10.2	80.8
Lube, oil change, and oil filters	100.0	3.5	8.7	9.3	82.0
Front-end alignment, wheel balance, rotation	100.0	4.0	7.8	5.2	87.0
Shock absorber replacement	100.0	6.8	3.6	11.8	84.6
Tire repair and other repair work	100.0	4.0	7.3	8.9	83.9
Vehicle air conditioning repair	100.0	0.8	11.6	7.4	81.6
Exhaust system repair	100.0	2.3	7.9	4.6	87.4
Electrical system repair	100.0	2.5	9.6	7.1	83.4
Motor repair, replacement	100.0	4.8	7.6	8.6	83.8
Auto repair service policy	100.0	2.2	8.4	5.6	86.1

	total consumer units	Asian	black	Hispanic	non-Hispanic white and other
Vehicle insurance	**100.0%**	**5.1%**	**9.8%**	**14.1%**	**76.4%**
Vehicle rental, leases, licenses, other charges	**100.0**	**3.4**	**9.3**	**9.3**	**81.5**
Leased and rented vehicles	100.0	2.4	10.4	8.9	80.8
Rented vehicles	100.0	3.5	9.2	5.0	85.8
Auto rental	100.0	3.3	15.5	6.5	78.3
Auto rental on trips	100.0	3.7	6.0	4.7	89.3
Truck rental	100.0	0.8	18.7	6.1	75.5
Truck rental on trips	100.0	5.3	11.0	3.2	85.8
Leased vehicles	100.0	2.2	10.6	9.6	79.9
Car lease payments	100.0	2.0	12.8	9.9	77.5
Truck lease payments	100.0	2.8	7.8	9.8	82.4
Vehicle registration, state	100.0	4.1	6.5	10.6	83.0
Vehicle registration, local	100.0	3.3	9.7	7.6	82.8
Driver's license	100.0	3.3	9.4	9.8	80.8
Vehicle inspection	100.0	3.2	7.2	12.9	80.0
Parking fees	100.0	5.7	7.8	6.5	85.9
Parking fees in home city, excluding residence	100.0	5.8	8.2	6.8	85.2
Parking fees on trips	100.0	5.2	5.5	4.9	89.7
Tolls	100.0	11.3	15.5	12.4	72.3
Tolls on trips	100.0	4.9	6.4	9.7	84.3
Towing charges	100.0	3.9	6.6	15.9	77.6
Global positioning services	100.0	10.5	2.5	14.1	83.5
Automobile service clubs	100.0	3.8	6.2	6.6	87.4
PUBLIC TRANSPORTATION	**100.0**	**10.1**	**6.7**	**7.2**	**86.3**
Airline fares	100.0	11.7	5.0	6.1	89.2
Intercity bus fares	100.0	7.2	7.3	10.0	82.8
Intracity mass transit fares	100.0	8.9	19.7	17.9	62.9
Local transportation on trips	100.0	6.9	5.7	5.7	88.8
Taxi fares and limousine service	100.0	1.9	11.7	13.9	74.6
Intercity train fares	100.0	6.4	7.6	4.2	88.4
Ship fares	100.0	6.6	3.1	3.2	94.0
School bus	100.0	15.3	7.6	17.9	74.8

Note: "Asian" and "black" include Hispanics and non-Hispanics who identify themselves as being of the respective race alone. "Hispanic" includes people of any race who identify themselves as Hispanic. "Other" includes people who identify themselves as non-Hispanic and as Alaska Native, American Indian, Asian (who are also included in the "Asian" column), Native Hawaiian or other Pacific Islander, as well as non-Hispanics reporting more than one race. "–" means sample is too small to make a reliable estimate.
Source: Calculations by New Strategist based on the Bureau of Labor Statistics' 2007 Consumer Expenditure Survey

About the Consumer Expenditure Survey

History

The Consumer Expenditure Survey is an ongoing study of the day-to-day spending of American households. In taking the survey, government interviewers collect spending data on products and services as well as data on the amount and sources of household income, changes in saving and debt, and demographic and economic characteristics of household members. The Bureau of the Census collects data for the survey under contract with the Bureau of Labor Statistics, which is responsible for analysis and release of the data.

Since the late 19th century, the federal government has conducted expenditure surveys about every 10 years. Although the results have been used for a variety of purposes, their primary application is to track consumer prices. Beginning in 1980, the Consumer Expenditure Survey became a continuous survey with annual release of data (and a lag time of about two years between data collection and release). The survey is used to update prices for the market basket of products and services used in calculating the consumer price index.

Description of the Consumer Expenditure Survey

The Consumer Expenditure Survey comprises two components: an interview survey and a diary survey. In the interview portion of the survey, respondents are asked each quarter for five consecutive quarters to report their expenditures for the previous three months. The interview survey records purchases of big-ticket items such as houses, cars, and major appliances, and recurring expenses such as insurance premiums, utility payments, and rent. The interview component covers about 95 percent of all expenditures.

The diary survey records expenditures on small, frequently purchased items during a two-week period. These detailed records include expenses for food and beverages purchased in grocery stores and at restaurants, as well as other items such as tobacco, housekeeping supplies, nonprescription drugs, and personal care products and services. The diary survey is intended to capture expenditures respondents are likely to forget or recall incorrectly over longer periods of time.

Average spending figures shown in this report represent integrated data from both the diary and interview components of the survey. Integrated data provide a more complete accounting of consumer expenditures than either component of the survey is designed to do alone.

Data collection and processing

Interview and diary surveys use two separate, nationally representative samples. For the interview survey, about 7,000 consumer units are interviewed on a rotating panel basis each quarter for five consecutive quarters. Another 7,000 consumer units kept weekly diaries of spending for two consecutive weeks. Data collection is carried out in 91 areas of the country.

The Bureau of Labor Statistics reviews, audits, and cleanses the data, then weights them to reflect the number and characteristics of all U.S. consumer units. Like any sample survey, the Consumer Expenditure Survey is subject to two major types of error. Nonsampling error occurs when respondents misinterpret questions or interviewers are inconsistent in the way they ask questions or record answers. Respondents may forget items, recall expenses incorrectly, or deliberately give wrong answers. A respondent may remember how much he or she spent at the grocery store but forget the items picked up at a local convenience store. Most surveys of alcohol consumption or spending on alcohol suffer from this type of underreporting, for example. Mistakes during the various stages of data processing and refinement can also cause nonsampling error.

Sampling error occurs when a sample does not accurately represent the population it is supposed to represent. This kind of error is present in every sample-based survey and is minimized by using a proper sampling procedure. Standard error tables documenting the extent of sampling error in the Consumer Expenditure Survey are available from the Bureau of Labor Statistics at http://www.bls.gov/cex/csxstnderror.htm.

Although the Consumer Expenditure Survey is the best source of information about the spending behavior of American households, it should be treated with caution because of the above problems. Comparisons with consumption data from other sources show that Consumer Expenditure Survey data tend to underestimate expenditures except for rent, fuel, telephone service, furniture, transportation, and personal care services. Despite these problems, the data reveal important spending patterns by demographic segment that can be used to better understand consumer behavior.

Definition of consumer unit

The Consumer Expenditure Survey uses the consumer unit as the sampling unit instead of the household, the sampling unit used by the Census Bureau. The term household is used interchangeably with the term consumer unit in this book for convenience, although they are not exactly the same. Some households contain more than one consumer unit.

The Bureau of Labor Statistics defines consumer unit as (1) members of a household who are related by blood, marriage, adoption, or other legal arrangements; (2) a person living alone or sharing a household with others or living as a roomer in a private home or lodging house or in permanent living quarters in a hotel or motel, but who is financially independent; or (3) two or more persons living together who pool their income to make joint expenditure decisions. The bureau defines financial independence in terms of the three major expenses categories: housing, food, and other living expenses. To be considered financially independent, at least two of the three major expense categories have to be provided by the respondent.

The Census Bureau uses household as its sampling unit in the decennial census and in the monthly Current Population Survey. The Census Bureau's household consists of all persons who occupy a housing unit. A house, an apartment or other groups of rooms, or a single room is regarded as a housing unit when it is occupied or intended for occupancy as separate living quarters; that is, when the occupants do not live and eat with any other persons in the structure and there is direct access from the outside or through a common hall.

The definition goes on to specify that a household includes the related family members and all the unrelated persons, if any, such as lodgers, foster children, wards, or employees who share the housing unit. A person living alone in a housing unit or a group of unrelated persons sharing a housing unit as partners is also counted as a household. The count of households excludes group quarters.

Because there can be more than one consumer unit in a household, consumer units outnumber households by several million. Young adults under age 25 head most of the additional consumer units.

For more information

To find out more about the Consumer Expenditure Survey, contact the specialists at the Bureau of Labor Statistics at (202) 691-6900, or visit the Consumer Expenditure Survey home page at http://www.bls.gov/cex/. The web site includes news releases, technical documentation, and current and historical summary-level data. The detailed average spending data shown in this report are available from the Bureau of Labor Statistics only by special request.

For a comprehensive look at detailed household spending data for all products and services, see the 14th edition of *Household Spending: Who Spends How Much on What.* New Strategist's books are available in hardcopy or as downloads with links to the Excel version of each table. Find out more by visiting http://www.newstrategist.com or by calling 1-800-848-0842.

Spending on Mortgage Principal and Capital Improvements, 2007

The spending statistics reported by the Consumer Expenditure Survey do not include spending on mortgage principal or capital improvements. Because the survey treats home equity as an asset, principal reduction and capital improvements are regarded as asset accumulation rather than expenditures. The table shows the average amount households spent in 2007 for mortgage principal payments and capital improvements. Adding these figures to expenditures for the category owned dwellings gives a more complete picture of the average amount households devote to housing.

(average annual reduction in mortgage principal and change in capital improvement for owned homes, by race and Hispanic origin of consumer unit reference person, 2007)

	total consumer units	Asian	black	Hispanic	non-Hispanic white and other
Mortgage principal payments	$1,592.17	$2,609.77	$1,123.48	$1,075.13	$1,746.27
Capital improvements	1,039.71	1,268.43	528.94	422.05	1,213.81

Note: "Asian" and "black" include Hispanics and non-Hispanics who identify themselves as being of the respective race alone. "Hispanic" includes people of any race who identify themselves as Hispanic. "Other" includes people who identify themselves as non-Hispanic and as Alaska Native, American Indian, Asian (who are also included in the "Asian" column), Native Hawaiian or other Pacific Islander, as well as non-Hispanics reporting more than one race.
Source: Bureau of Labor Statistics, 2007 Consumer Expenditue Survey

Percent Reporting Expenditure and
Amount Spent, Average Quarter 2007

(percent of consumer units reporting expenditure and amount spent by purchasers during the average quarter, 2007)

	percent reporting expenditure during quarter	average amount spent by purchasers per quarter
FOOD	**99.49%**	**$1,778.38**
Food at home	**98.91**	**1,135.75**
Groceries purchased on trips	10.00	107.50
Food away from home	**83.58**	**772.84**
Meals at restaurants and carryouts	80.48	663.89
Board (including at school)	0.94	630.05
Catered affairs	1.85	1,000.95
Restaurant food on trips	23.51	261.09
School lunches	9.67	183.79
Meals as pay	2.18	369.04
ALCOHOLIC BEVERAGES	**36.75**	**227.01**
At home	**31.31**	**145.20**
Beer, wine, and other alcohol	28.60	144.46
Away from home	**24.18**	**157.01**
Alcoholic beverages at restaurants, taverns	18.35	147.47
Alcoholic beverages purchased on trips	11.57	94.25
HOUSING	**99.56**	**3,973.92**
Shelter	**97.77**	**2,562.82**
• Owned dwellings	**66.90**	**2,515.01**
Mortgage interest and charges	44.73	2,174.17
Mortgage interest	42.40	2,112.93
Interest paid, home equity loan	3.98	593.53
Interest paid, home equity line of credit	5.68	933.10
Property taxes	65.75	649.76
Maintenance, repairs, insurance, other expenses	35.14	804.84
Homeowners insurance	23.63	360.04
Ground rent	1.55	996.29
Maintenance and repair services	11.85	1,212.81
Painting and papering	1.21	1,600.62
Plumbing and water heating	2.98	386.91
Heat, air conditioning, electrical work	3.35	650.22
Roofing and gutters	1.13	2,182.52
Other repair and maintenance services	4.38	1,235.05
Repair/replacement of hard surface flooring	0.42	2,457.14
Repair of built-in appliances	1.04	188.46
Maintenance and repair materials	5.33	423.08
Paints, wallpaper and supplies	2.20	174.89
Tools/equipment for painting, wallpapering	2.20	18.75
Plumbing supplies and equipment	0.58	176.72
Electrical supplies, heating/cooling equipment	0.33	262.12
Hard surface flooring, repair and replacement	0.33	957.58
Roofing and gutters	0.15	996.67
Plaster, paneling, siding, windows, doors, screens, awnings	0.65	584.62
Patio, walk, fence, driveway, masonry, brick, and stucco work	0.29	111.21
Miscellaneous supplies and equipment	1.78	428.23
Insulation, other maintenance/repair	1.78	428.23
Property management and security	5.61	243.54
Property management	5.34	211.70
Management and upkeep services for security	1.43	164.69
Parking	1.67	142.22

	percent reporting expenditure during quarter	average amount spent by purchasers per quarter
• **Rented dwellings**	**31.77%**	**$2,047.42**
Rent	30.71	2,028.26
Rent as pay	1.25	1,392.60
Maintenance, insurance, and other expenses	3.84	265.04
Tenant's insurance	2.68	96.08
Maintenance and repair services	0.44	997.16
Maintenance and repair materials	0.86	373.84
• **Other lodging**	**18.54**	**931.30**
Owned vacation homes	4.86	1,475.36
Mortgage interest and charges	1.67	1,927.84
Property taxes	4.67	510.65
Maintenance, insurance and other expenses	1.73	905.35
Housing while attending school	0.81	1,891.05
Lodging on trips	14.45	592.68
Utilities, fuels, public services	**97.64**	**890.31**
Natural gas	49.04	244.90
Electricity	91.91	354.38
Fueloil and other fuels	8.43	446.68
Fuel oil	3.36	656.10
Coal, wood, and other fuels	0.66	271.97
Bottled gas	4.81	287.16
Telephone services	93.23	297.57
Residential phone service and pay phones	75.26	160.15
Cellular phone service	58.45	259.87
Phone cards	5.99	62.10
Water and other public services	62.43	173.66
Water and sewerage maintenance	56.07	141.45
Trash and garbage collection	37.62	75.31
Septic tank cleaning	0.32	240.63
Household services	**63.84**	**385.15**
Personal services	7.97	1,303.20
Babysitting and child care in your own home	1.80	721.67
Babysitting and child care in someone else's home	1.30	652.88
Care for elderly, invalids, handicapped, etc.	0.48	2,995.83
Adult day care centers	0.07	1,560.71
Day care centers, nursery and preschools	5.39	1,241.47
Other household services	61.99	229.10
Housekeeping services	6.03	490.30
Gardening, lawn care service	13.27	201.47
Water softening service	1.40	80.18
Nonclothing laundry and dry cleaning, sent out	0.66	39.77
Nonclothing laundry and dry cleaning, coin-operated	3.44	23.69
Termite/pest control services	3.19	124.92
Home security system service fee	4.24	117.28
Other home services	1.85	197.84
Termite/pest control products	2.17	29.38
Moving, storage, and freight express	2.00	627.75
Appliance repair, including service center	2.34	170.19
Reupholstering and furniture repair	0.45	266.67
Repairs/rentals of lawn/garden equipment, hand/power tools, etc.	1.01	165.59
Appliance rental	0.23	144.57
Rental of office equipment for nonbusiness use	0.07	157.14
Repair of computer systems for nonbusiness use	0.79	221.20
Computer information services	51.26	94.67
Installation of computer	0.08	128.13
Household furnishings and equipment	**53.41**	**628.30**
Household textiles	19.83	120.41
Bathroom linens	6.62	50.57
Bedroom linens	10.66	106.75

	percent reporting expenditure during quarter	average amount spent by purchasers per quarter
Kitchen and dining room linens	1.87%	$26.60
Curtains and draperies	2.52	188.29
Slipcovers and decorative pillows	1.42	59.68
Sewing materials for household items	3.24	86.50
Other linens	0.45	56.67
Furniture	10.75	1,032.84
Mattress and springs	1.69	821.45
Other bedroom furniture	2.26	850.77
Sofas	2.30	1,224.13
Living room chairs	1.93	593.91
Living room tables	1.45	272.07
Kitchen and dining room furniture	1.39	846.22
Infants' furniture	0.68	334.19
Outdoor furniture	1.30	470.96
Wall units, cabinets, and other furniture	2.89	491.26
Floor coverings	3.14	362.02
Wall-to-wall carpeting, replacement (owner)	0.30	2,012.50
Floor coverings, nonpermanent	2.82	185.82
Major appliances	8.45	667.40
Dishwashers (built-in), garbage disposals, range hoods (owner)	0.89	567.13
Refrigerators and freezers (renter)	0.36	459.03
Refrigerators and freezers (owner)	1.40	975.54
Washing machines (renter)	0.35	390.71
Washing machines (owner)	1.16	691.38
Clothes dryers (renter)	0.30	337.50
Clothes dryers (owner)	1.06	602.59
Cooking stoves, ovens (renter)	0.17	450.00
Cooking stoves, ovens (owner)	0.85	1,027.65
Microwave ovens (renter)	0.66	77.65
Microwave ovens (owner)	0.96	198.18
Window air conditioners (renter)	0.18	222.22
Window air conditioners (owner)	0.28	308.93
Electric floor cleaning equipment	2.24	186.83
Sewing machines	0.29	538.79
Small appliances and miscellaneous housewares	16.64	85.20
Housewares	10.50	75.81
Plastic dinnerware	2.81	22.06
China and other dinnerware	2.60	95.58
Flatware	1.48	68.58
Glassware	2.23	34.98
Silver serving pieces	0.07	71.43
Other serving pieces	0.62	57.26
Nonelectric cookware	3.45	76.96
Small appliances	8.14	76.38
Small electric kitchen appliances	7.02	68.27
Portable heating and cooling equipment	1.38	103.26
Miscellaneous household equipment	36.43	325.22
Window coverings	1.57	510.03
Infants' equipment	0.81	147.84
Outdoor equipment	0.99	254.29
Lamps and lighting fixtures	3.69	127.24
Household decorative items	6.43	164.23
Telephones and accessories	4.51	125.72
Lawn and garden equipment	2.47	431.98
Power tools	2.19	225.00
Office furniture for home use	0.74	361.49
Hand tools	2.01	100.62
Indoor plants and fresh flowers	15.47	94.46

	percent reporting expenditure during quarter	average amount spent by purchasers per quarter
Closet and storage items	1.44%	$57.81
Rental of furniture	0.25	399.00
Luggage	1.39	111.33
Computers and computer hardware, nonbusiness use	5.33	694.56
Computer software and accessories, nonbusiness use	4.23	125.77
Personal digital assistants	0.30	306.67
Internet services away from home	0.85	71.47
Telephone answering devices	0.28	52.68
Business equipment for home use	0.63	89.68
Smoke alarms (owner)	0.67	71.64
Smoke alarms (renter)	0.11	38.64
Other household appliances (owner)	0.95	135.26
Other household appliances (renter)	0.37	75.68
APPAREL AND SERVICES	**75.54**	**421.00**
Men's apparel	**30.44**	**184.19**
Suits	1.57	373.73
Sportcoats and tailored jackets	1.29	212.02
Coats and jackets	3.63	133.82
Underwear	5.37	35.10
Hosiery	4.42	21.27
Nightwear	0.86	41.28
Accessories	3.36	56.25
Sweaters and vests	2.52	87.10
Active sportswear	1.76	61.36
Shirts	17.85	83.47
Pants and shorts	18.58	92.52
Uniforms	0.53	150.94
Costumes	0.24	78.13
Boys' (aged 2 to 15) apparel	**11.12**	**154.38**
Coats and jackets	1.59	84.91
Sweaters	0.82	64.94
Shirts	6.81	67.69
Underwear	2.38	35.29
Nightwear	0.82	34.15
Hosiery	1.69	17.75
Accessories	0.66	37.50
Suits, sportcoats, and vests	0.32	102.34
Pants and shorts	7.86	86.74
Uniforms	0.70	133.21
Active sportswear	1.05	40.00
Costumes	0.61	35.66
Women's apparel	**41.50**	**237.88**
Coats and jackets	5.40	121.81
Dresses	7.38	170.05
Sportcoats and tailored jackets	1.36	122.79
Sweaters and vests	6.72	92.93
Shirts, blouses, and tops	25.23	87.90
Skirts	3.82	68.26
Pants and shorts	23.68	95.57
Active sportswear	3.69	77.64
Sleepwear	4.29	52.68
Undergarments	9.41	55.61
Hosiery	5.88	23.85
Suits	1.95	212.82
Accessories	5.80	87.24
Uniforms	1.20	100.63
Costumes	0.63	102.38

	percent reporting expenditure during quarter	average amount spent by purchasers per quarter
Girls' (aged 2 to 15) apparel	**12.00%**	**$180.75**
Coats and jackets	1.76	77.41
Dresses and suits	2.36	82.31
Shirts, blouses, and sweaters	7.63	84.63
Skirts, pants, and shorts	7.90	88.96
Active sportswear	1.51	47.19
Underwear and sleepwear	3.47	48.41
Hosiery	1.72	18.17
Accessories	1.08	38.66
Uniforms	0.51	149.51
Costumes	0.70	68.57
Children under age two	**14.12**	**133.71**
Coats, jackets, and snowsuits	1.05	58.10
Outerwear including dresses	7.58	82.98
Underwear	7.57	116.02
Nightwear and loungewear	2.59	42.95
Accessories	3.74	55.88
Footwear	**32.86**	**117.36**
Men's	12.72	99.10
Boys'	6.13	75.45
Women's	19.36	87.69
Girls'	6.42	67.83
Other apparel products and services	**38.94**	**171.89**
Material for making clothes	1.30	63.27
Sewing patterns and notions	1.61	29.50
Watches	3.47	147.84
Jewelry	7.92	397.06
Shoe repair and other shoe services	0.93	38.44
Coin-operated apparel laundry and dry cleaning	13.73	74.20
Apparel alteration, repair, and tailoring services	2.99	52.17
Clothing rental	0.39	137.82
Watch and jewelry repair	1.91	47.77
Professional laundry, dry cleaning	16.63	92.15
Clothing storage	0.08	218.75
TRANSPORTATION	**94.38**	**2,253.32**
Vehicle purchases	**5.52**	**14,692.03**
Cars and trucks, new	1.59	24,713.84
New cars	0.84	21,196.43
New trucks	0.76	28,276.32
Cars and trucks, used	3.75	10,445.80
Used cars	2.22	9,596.62
Used trucks	1.58	11,308.39
Other vehicles	0.28	9,403.57
New motorcycles	0.13	12,269.23
Used motorcycles	0.15	6,921.67
Gasoline and motor oil	**90.22**	**660.52**
Gasoline	89.52	614.83
Diesel fuel	1.98	520.96
Gasoline on trips	20.02	162.71
Motor oil	8.00	28.75
Other vehicle expenses	**80.66**	**726.67**
Vehicle finance charges	32.16	237.26
Automobile finance charges	16.34	186.70
Truck finance charges	18.15	224.68
Motorcycle and plane finance charges	1.09	144.72
Other vehicle finance charges	1.24	277.22

	percent reporting expenditure during quarter	average amount spent by purchasers per quarter
Maintenance and repairs	52.63%	$321.92
Coolant, additives, brake, transmission fluids	5.26	16.63
Tires	7.74	374.35
Vehicle products and cleaning services	3.82	41.03
Parts, equipment, and accessories	8.55	127.63
Vechicle audio equipment	0.24	255.21
Vehicle video equipment	0.19	326.32
Body work and painting	1.16	604.09
Clutch, transmission repair	1.26	656.35
Drive shaft and rear-end repair	0.36	447.92
Brake work	4.67	312.85
Repair to steering or front-end	1.22	462.30
Repair to engine cooling system	1.84	300.54
Motor tune-up	4.54	253.74
Lube, oil change, and oil filters	34.05	50.91
Front-end alignment, wheel balance, rotation	2.66	137.50
Shock absorber replacement	0.38	346.05
Repair tires and other repair work	5.64	222.92
Exhaust system repair	0.86	296.51
Electrical system repair	2.14	321.14
Motor repair, replacement	2.76	658.42
Auto repair service policy	0.49	823.47
Vehicle accessories, including labor	0.48	314.58
Vehicle air conditioning repair	1.03	355.10
Vehicle insurance	50.22	437.13
Vehicle rental, leases, licenses, other charges	43.08	280.59
Leased and rented vehicles	6.99	1,019.35
Rented vehicles	3.09	322.57
Auto rental	0.64	325.39
Auto rental, on trips	2.01	309.70
Truck rental	0.27	266.67
Truck rental, on trips	0.20	401.25
Leased vehicles	4.18	1,466.21
Car lease payments	2.32	1,256.90
Truck lease payments	2.14	1,301.29
Vehicle registration, state	16.25	131.86
Vehicle registration, local	1.91	115.18
Driver's license	5.02	37.45
Vehicle inspection	6.16	43.43
Parking fees	11.93	73.70
Parking fees in home city, excluding residence	9.64	75.65
Parking fees, on trips	3.25	46.15
Tolls or electronic toll passes	9.12	57.84
Tolls on trips	6.45	16.78
Towing charges	1.08	138.19
Global positioning services	0.48	116.67
Automobile service clubs	4.87	86.96
Public transportation	**18.53**	**721.18**
Airline fares	10.28	874.78
Intercity bus fares	4.02	65.24
Intracity mass transit fares	6.86	200.80
Local transportation on trips	5.03	67.00
Taxi fares and limousine service	3.20	100.31
Intercity train fares	3.88	133.70
Ship fares	2.06	646.00
School bus	0.08	315.63

	percent reporting expenditure during quarter	average amount spent by purchasers per quarter
HEALTH CARE	**77.57%**	**$869.71**
Health insurance	**62.78**	**615.18**
Commercial health insurance	14.27	512.28
Traditional fee for service health plan (not BCBS)	4.59	482.08
Preferred provider health plan (not BCBS)	9.80	520.13
Blue Cross, Blue Shield	19.93	546.66
Traditional fee for service health plan	3.57	540.34
Preferred provider health plan	8.39	578.96
Health maintenance organization	6.06	516.91
Commercial Medicare supplement	1.71	510.23
Other BCBS health insurance	0.68	152.57
Health maintenance plans (HMOs)	13.29	471.20
Medicare payments	21.82	370.47
Medicare prescription drug premium	7.18	168.38
Commercial Medicare supplements/other health insurance	11.12	285.36
Commercial Medicare supplement (not BCBS)	4.84	467.15
Other health insurance (not BCBS)	6.75	135.15
Long-term care insurance	3.19	528.92
Medical services	**41.27**	**429.14**
Physician's services	26.04	164.27
Dental services	14.24	429.55
Eye care services	6.41	147.74
Service by professionals other than physician	4.84	374.17
Lab tests, x-rays	5.32	183.65
Hospital room and services	4.16	684.68
Care in convalescent or nursing home	0.14	2,789.29
Other medical services	1.69	202.96
Prescription drugs	**41.62**	**215.83**
Medical supplies	**7.54**	**284.95**
Eyeglasses and contact lenses	6.22	245.22
Hearing aids	0.27	1,406.48
Medical equipment for general use	0.49	227.04
Supportive/convalescent medical equipment	0.47	169.15
Rental of medical equipment	0.25	143.00
Rental of supportive, convalescent medical equipment	0.23	73.91
ENTERTAINMENT	**90.66**	**663.46**
Fees and admissions	**46.92**	**330.66**
Recreation expenses, on trips	7.94	87.81
Social, recreation, civic club membership	12.74	242.31
Fees for participant sports	11.41	174.06
Participant sports, on trips	3.62	220.72
Movie, theater, opera, ballet	30.10	96.79
Movie, other admissions, on trips	8.42	127.14
Admission to sports events	6.71	189.08
Admission to sports events, on trips	8.42	42.37
Fees for recreational lessons	6.45	409.15
Other entertainment services, on trips	7.94	87.81
Audio and visual equipment and services	**83.59**	**284.99**
Televisions	3.95	1,026.84
Cable TV or community antenna	72.83	190.56
Satellite radio service	2.63	114.16
Online gaming services	0.94	41.22
VCRs and video disc players	2.29	161.90
Video cassettes, tapes, and discs	16.01	59.84
Video game hardware and software	4.90	214.69
Streaming, downloading video	1.03	25.00
Repair of TV, radio, and sound equipment	0.47	226.60

	percent reporting expenditure during quarter	average amount spent by purchasers per quarter
Rental of televisions	0.06%	$300.00
Radios	0.89	76.97
Tape recorders and players	0.13	94.23
Personal digital audio players	1.91	227.62
Sound components and component systems	0.85	388.53
CDs, records, audio tapes	14.49	47.26
Streaming, downloading audio	2.61	35.25
Rental of VCR, radio, sound equipment	0.05	155.00
Musical instruments and accessories	1.23	304.67
Rental and repair of musical instruments	0.27	119.44
Rental of video cassettes, tapes, discs, films	21.24	36.33
Sound equipment accessories	0.87	181.61
Satellite dishes	0.18	136.11
Installation of televisions	0.12	204.17
Pets, toys, hobbies, and playground equipment	**42.17**	**238.33**
Pets	31.07	221.67
Pet purchase, supplies, and medicines	25.78	134.85
Pet services	5.22	151.72
Veterinary services	9.11	287.46
Toys, games, arts and crafts, and tricycles	17.43	167.97
Stamp and coin collecting	0.83	121.08
Playground equipment	0.40	336.25
Other entertainment supplies, equipment, services	**23.85**	**451.14**
Unmotored recreational vehicles	0.21	8,572.62
Boat without motor and boat trailers	0.11	4,888.64
Trailer and other attachable campers	0.10	12,625.00
Motorized recreational vehicles	0.26	14,207.69
Purchase of motorized camper	0.03	48,816.67
Purchase of other vehicle	0.11	7,068.18
Purchase of boat with motor	0.11	13,202.27
Rental of recreational vehicles	0.54	370.37
Outboard motors	0.03	658.33
Docking and landing fees	0.33	334.85
Sports, recreation, exercise equipment	10.23	257.26
Athletic gear, game tables, exercise equipment	5.93	210.12
Bicycles	1.41	296.45
Camping equipment	0.92	113.04
Hunting and fishing equipment	1.83	226.23
Winter sports equipment	0.27	375.93
Water sports equipment	0.52	215.87
Other sports equipment	0.86	204.36
Rental and repair of miscellaneous sports equipment	0.34	178.68
Photographic equipment and supplies	15.77	116.84
Film	4.93	23.78
Photo processing	10.24	39.01
Repair and rental of photographic equipment	0.11	143.18
Photographic equipment	2.67	301.87
Photographer fees	2.49	202.41
PERSONAL CARE PRODUCTS AND SERVICES	**62.37**	**116.83**
Wigs and hairpieces	0.74	70.95
Electric personal care appliances	3.35	48.21
Personal care services	61.37	115.25
READING	**41.98**	**70.09**
Newspaper and magazine subscriptions	21.20	55.77
Newspapers and magazines, nonsubscription	15.93	22.69
Books purchased through book clubs	1.56	58.01
Books not purchased through book clubs	19.31	67.08

	percent reporting expenditure during quarter	average amount spent by purchasers per quarter
EDUCATION	**13.86%**	**$1,620.27**
College tuition	4.97	2,943.66
Elementary/high school tuition	1.49	2,570.13
Vocational and technical school tuition	0.23	1,676.09
Other schools tuition	0.53	949.53
Other school expenses including rentals	3.41	314.00
Books, supplies for college	3.89	398.07
Books, supplies for elementary, high school	3.36	120.24
Books, supplies for vocational and technical schools	0.07	200.00
Books, supplies for day care, nursery school	0.13	78.85
Books, supplies for other schools	0.32	192.19
TOBACCO PRODUCTS AND SMOKING SUPPLIES	**22.19**	**362.42**
Cigarettes	19.73	373.73
Other tobacco products	3.37	198.29
FINANCIAL PRODUCTS AND SERVICES		
Miscellaneous financial products and services	**39.93**	**464.83**
Lotteries and parimutuel losses	12.04	104.90
Legal fees	2.37	1,651.79
Funeral expenses	0.87	1,674.71
Safe deposit box rental	2.17	39.40
Checking accounts, other bank service charges	12.15	42.74
Cemetery lots, vaults, and maintenance fees	0.62	620.56
Accounting fees	5.02	383.86
Finance charges, except mortgage and vehicles	6.21	674.84
Dating services	0.15	66.67
Vacation clubs	0.26	784.62
Expenses for other properties	5.09	618.86
Expenses for other properties	5.77	212.09
Credit card memberships	0.64	64.84
Shopping club membership fees	3.16	56.09
Cash contributions	**50.12**	**908.56**
Support for college students	2.85	868.95
Alimony expenditures	0.28	2,695.54
Child support expenditures	3.18	1,556.68
Gifts to of stocks, bonds and mutual funds to people in other households	0.25	6,225.00
Cash contributions to charities	17.19	401.31
Cash contributions to religious organizations	28.61	598.36
Cash contributions to educational organizations	2.27	562.78
Cash contributions to political organizations	1.41	185.64
Other cash gifts to people in other households	16.85	607.88
Personal insurance and pensions	**84.50**	**1,578.74**
Life and other personal insurance	28.21	274.26
Life, endowment, annuity, other personal insurance	27.29	273.17
Other nonhealth insurance	2.03	138.92
Pensions and Social Security	**80.64**	**1,558.37**
Deductions for government retirement	2.33	800.11
Deductions for railroad retirement	0.04	1,831.25
Deductions for private pensions	10.67	1,308.79
Nonpayroll deposit to retirement plans	7.79	1,548.97
Deductions for Social Security	80.45	1,214.40
PERSONAL TAXES	**57.08**	**978.22**
Federal income taxes	50.20	781.44
State and local income taxes	34.76	336.64
Other taxes	16.93	289.84

	percent reporting expenditure during quarter	average amount spent by purchasers per quarter
GIFTS FOR PEOPLE IN OTHER HOUSEHOLDS	**28.40%**	**$786.89**
Food	**1.22**	**842.21**
Housing	**9.89**	**389.64**
Household textiles	2.20	75.34
Major appliances	0.32	530.47
Small appliances and miscellaneous housewares	1.52	117.60
Miscellaneous household equipment	4.58	154.15
Other housing	3.06	860.54
Apparel and services	**15.76**	**201.25**
Males aged two or older	3.90	173.85
Females aged two or older	4.99	189.63
Children under age two	9.00	94.50
Other apparel products and services	3.77	184.88
Jewelry and watches	1.84	257.47
All other apparel products and services	2.15	103.84
Transportation	**4.44**	**563.06**
Health care	**1.04**	**505.53**
Entertainment	**8.61**	**238.94**
Toys, games, hobbies, and tricycles	5.35	145.61
Other entertainment	4.05	315.62
Education	**2.12**	**3,282.19**
All other gifts	**4.65**	**484.73**

Source: Calculations by New Strategist based on the 2007 Consumer Expenditure Survey

Spending by Product and Service, Ranked by Amount Spent, 2007

(average annual spending of consumer units on products and services, ranked by amount spent, 2007)

1.	Deductions for Social Security	$3,907.94
2.	Mortgage interest (or rent, $2,491.52)	3,583.53
3.	Groceries (also shown by individual category)	3,465.01
4.	Vehicle purchases (net outlay)	3,244.00
5.	Restaurants (also shown by meal category)	2,467.37
6.	Gasoline and motor oil	2,383.67
7.	Property taxes	1,708.86
8.	Federal income taxes	1,569.13
9.	Health insurance	1,544.83
10.	Electricity	1,302.85
11.	Dinner at restaurants	1,073.51
12.	Vehicle insurance	1,071.37
13.	Lunch at restaurants	761.38
14.	Women's apparel	748.93
15.	Vehicle maintenance and repairs	737.62
16.	Cash contributions to church, religious organizations	684.76
17.	Cellular phone service	607.58
18.	College tuition	585.20
19.	Maintenance and repair services, owner	574.87
20.	Deductions for private pensions	558.59
21.	Cable and satellite television services	555.13
22.	Nonpayroll deposit to retirement plans	482.66
23.	Residential telephone service and pay phones	482.12
24.	Natural gas	480.39
25.	State and local income taxes	468.06
26.	Cash gifts to members of other households	409.71
27.	Airline fares	359.71
28.	Prescription drugs	359.32
29.	Men's apparel	351.05
30.	Lodging on trips	342.57
31.	Homeowner's insurance	340.31
32.	Water and sewerage maintenance	317.25
33.	Life and other personal insurance	309.47
34.	Interest paid, home equity loan/line of credit	306.49
35.	Vehicle finance charges	305.21
36.	Cigarettes	294.95
37.	Owned vacation homes	286.81
38.	Personal care services	282.91
39.	Cash contributions to charities	275.94
40.	Day care centers, nurseries, and preschools	267.66
41.	Restaurant meals on trips	245.53
42.	Leased vehicles	245.15
43.	Dental services	244.67
44.	Beef	216.25
45.	Breakfast at restaurants	215.13
46.	Fresh fruits	201.74
47.	Child support expenditures	198.01
48.	Other taxes	196.28
49.	Computer information services	194.11
50.	Fresh vegetables	190.29
51.	Snacks at restaurants	171.82
52.	Physician's services	171.10
53.	Finance charges, except mortgage and vehicles	167.63
54.	Television sets	162.24
55.	Women's footwear	160.33

56.	Movie, theater, amusement park, and other admissions	$159.35
57.	Legal fees	156.59
58.	Household decorative items	154.92
59.	Elementary and high school tuition	153.18
60.	Cosmetics, perfume, and bath products	152.03
61.	Pork	149.64
62.	Computers and computer hardware for nonbusiness use	148.08
63.	Prepared foods except frozen, salads, and desserts	148.07
64.	Motorized recreational vehicles	147.76
65.	Pet food	146.88
66.	Poultry	141.85
67.	Laundry and cleaning supplies	139.99
68.	Pet purchase, supplies, and medicines	139.06
69.	Fresh milk, all types	138.15
70.	Miscellaneous household products	132.92
71.	Carbonated drinks	131.75
72.	Expenses for other properties	126.00
73.	Jewelry	125.79
74.	Social, recreation, civic club membership	123.48
75.	Fish and seafood	121.93
76.	Girls' (aged 2 to 15) apparel	121.62
77.	Toys, games, hobbies, and tricycles	119.93
78.	Housekeeping services	118.26
79.	Cheese	117.15
80.	Fees for participant sports	116.94
81.	Lawn and garden supplies	115.03
82.	Beer and ale at home	114.93
83.	Lawn and garden equipment	114.63
84.	Hospital room and services	113.93
85.	Trash and garbage collection	113.33
86.	Veterinarian services	113.18
87.	Sofas	112.62
88.	Gardening, lawn care service	106.94
89.	Fees for recreational lessons	105.56
90.	Meats other than pork or beef	104.49
91.	Men's footwear	102.60
92.	Support for college students	99.06
93.	Cleansing and toilet tissue, paper towels, and napkins	98.65
94.	Wine at home	97.21
95.	Potato chips and other snacks	95.81
96.	Vehicle registration	94.51
97.	Children's (under age 2) apparel	93.36
98.	Maintenance and repair materials, owner	90.20
99.	Fuel oil	88.18
100.	Babysitting and child care	85.91
101.	Ready-to-eat and cooked cereals	84.57
102.	Boys' (aged 2 to 15) apparel	84.32
103.	Candy and chewing gum	80.35
104.	Accounting fees	77.08
105.	Bedroom furniture except mattresses and springs	76.91
106.	Lunch meats (cold cuts)	76.14
107.	Nonprescription drugs	75.40
108.	Beer and ale at bars, restaurants	75.29
109.	Stationery, stationery supplies, giftwrap	75.19
110.	Deductions for government retirement	74.57
111.	Postage	74.12
112.	Catered affairs	74.07
113.	Lottery and gambling losses	72.53
114.	Service by professionals other than physician	72.44
115.	Unmotored recreational vehicles	72.01
116.	Frozen meals	71.36
117.	School lunches	71.09

118.	Rent as pay	$69.63
119.	Bedroom linens	67.07
120.	Athletic gear, game tables, exercise equipment	65.55
121.	Frozen prepared foods, except meals	65.38
122.	Admission to sports events	65.02
123.	Video game hardware and software	63.10
124.	Gifts of stocks, bonds, and mutual funds to members of other households	62.25
125.	Books and supplies for college	61.94
126.	Ground rent	61.77
127.	Professional laundry, dry cleaning	61.30
128.	Housing while attending school	61.27
129.	Refrigerators and freezers	61.24
130.	Other alcoholic beverages at bars, restaurants	61.07
131.	Eyeglasses and contact lenses	61.01
132.	Bottled water	60.72
133.	Funeral expenses	58.28
134.	Care for elderly, invalids, handicapped, etc.	57.52
135.	Ice cream and related products	57.37
136.	Wall units, cabinets, and other furniture	56.79
137.	Indoor plants and fresh flowers	56.78
138.	Canned and bottled fruit juice	56.46
139.	Hair care products	56.10
140.	Books	55.93
141.	Mattresses and springs	55.53
142.	Bread, other than white	55.32
143.	Bottled gas	55.25
144.	Intracity mass transit fares	55.10
145.	Ship fares	53.23
146.	Cash contributions to educational institutions	51.10
147.	Coffee	51.07
148.	Moving, storage, and freight express	50.22
149.	Occupational expenses	48.95
150.	Newspaper and magazine subscriptions	47.29
151.	Kitchen and dining room furniture	47.05
152.	Sauces and gravies	46.54
153.	Nonprescription vitamins	46.18
154.	Living room chairs	45.85
155.	Property management, owner	45.22
156.	Cookies	44.89
157.	Biscuits and rolls	44.32
158.	Alcoholic beverages purchased on trips	43.62
159.	Food prepared by consumer unit on trips	43.00
160.	Eggs	42.71
161.	Baby food	42.34
162.	Miscellaneous personal services	41.61
163.	Coin-operated apparel laundry and dry cleaning	40.75
164.	Cakes and cupcakes	40.26
165.	Canned and packaged soups	40.05
166.	Rented vehicles	39.87
167.	Outdoor equipment	39.82
168.	Lab tests, X-rays	39.08
169.	Video cassettes, tapes, and discs	38.32
170.	Cooking stoves, ovens	38.00
171.	Eye care services	37.88
172.	Canned vegetables	37.68
173.	Washing machines	37.55
174.	Wine at bars, restaurants	36.91
175.	Lamps and lighting fixtures	36.69
176.	Nonalcoholic beverages (except carbonated, coffee, fruit-flavored drinks, tea, and bottled water) and ice	36.47
177.	Parking fees	35.17
178.	Girls' footwear	34.18

179. White bread	$33.86
180. Prepared salads	32.63
181. Photographic equipment	32.24
182. Meals as pay	32.18
183. Nuts	32.12
184. Window coverings	32.03
185. Topicals and dressings	31.81
186. Crackers	31.70
187. Pet services	31.68
188. Frozen vegetables	31.34
189. Rental of video cassettes, tapes, discs, films	30.87
190. Fats and oils	30.63
191. Telephones and accessories	30.38
192. Alimony expenditures	30.19
193. Deodorants, feminine hygiene, miscellaneous products	30.00
194. Boys' footwear	29.95
195. Hunting and fishing equipment	29.66
196. Clothes dryers	29.60
197. Tea	28.63
198. Recreation expenses on trips	27.89
199. Oral hygiene products	27.64
200. Compact discs, records, and audio tapes	27.39
201. Salad dressings	27.15
202. Wall-to-wall carpeting	26.87
203. Tobacco products other than cigarettes	26.73
204. Frozen and refrigerated bakery products	26.27
205. Outdoor furniture	26.06
206. Tableware, nonelectric kitchenware	25.66
207. Photographer fees	25.13
208. Bathroom linens	24.80
209. Pasta, cornmeal, and other cereal products	24.77
210. Baking needs	24.60
211. Power tools	24.41
212. Salt, spices, and other seasonings	24.07
213. Noncarbonated fruit-flavored drinks	23.96
214. Board (including at school)	23.69
215. Jams, preserves, other sweets	21.81
216. Local transportation on trips	21.39
217. Computer software and accessories for nonbusiness use	21.28
218. Sweetrolls, coffee cakes, doughnuts	21.18
219. Floor coverings, nonpermanent	20.96
220. Dishwashers (built-in), garbage disposals, range hoods	20.88
221. Checking accounts, other bank service charges	20.77
222. Intercity train fares	20.75
223. Watches	20.55
224. Closet and storage items	20.32
225. School tuition other than college, vocational/technical, elementary, high school	20.13
226. Butter	20.11
227. Tolls	19.90
228. Home security system service fee	19.89
229. Canned fruits	19.47
230. Small electric kitchen appliances	19.17
231. Curtains and draperies	18.98
232. Other alcoholic beverages at home	18.92
233. Frankfurters	18.73
234. Laundry and cleaning equipment	18.62
235. Maintenance and repair services, renter	17.55
236. Personal digital audio players	17.39
237. Fresh fruit juice	17.21
238. Automobile service clubs	16.94
239. Hand tools	16.77
240. Electric floor-cleaning equipment	16.74

241.	Bicycles	$16.72
242.	Rice	16.60
243.	Sugar	16.49
244.	Books and supplies for elementary and high school	16.16
245.	Taxi fares and limousine service	16.12
246.	Photo processing	15.98
247.	Termite and pest control services	15.94
248.	Appliance repair, including at service center	15.93
249.	Living room tables	15.78
250.	Care in convalescent or nursing home	15.62
251.	Vegetable juices	15.56
252.	Cream	15.53
253.	Vocational and technical school tuition	15.42
254.	Cemetery lots, vaults, and maintenance fees	15.39
255.	Hearing aids	15.19
256.	Musical instruments and accessories	14.99
257.	Pies, tarts, turnovers	14.96
258.	Shaving products	14.94
259.	Phone cards	14.88
260.	VCRs and video disc players	14.83
261.	Nonelectric cookware	14.47
262.	Newspapers and magazines, nonsubscription	14.46
263.	Infants' equipment	14.07
264.	Glassware	13.80
265.	Sound equipment accessories	13.79
266.	Nondairy cream and imitation milk	13.56
267.	Sound components and component systems	13.21
268.	Global positioning system devices	13.07
269.	Peanut butter	12.87
270.	Maintenance and repair materials, renter	12.86
271.	Olives, pickles, relishes	12.80
272.	Electric personal care appliances	12.64
273.	Prepared desserts	12.30
274.	Luggage	12.06
275.	Satellite radio service	12.01
276.	Prepared flour mixes	11.60
277.	Portable heating and cooling equipment	11.46
278.	Camping equipment	11.39
279.	Sewing materials for household items	11.21
280.	Dried vegetables	10.94
281.	Office furniture for home use	10.70
282.	Vehicle inspection	10.70
283.	Intercity bus fares	10.49
284.	Cash contributions to political organizations	10.47
285.	Tenant's insurance	10.30
286.	Microwave ovens	9.66
287.	Lamb, organ meats, and others	9.62
288.	Parking at owned home	9.50
289.	Security services, owner	9.42
290.	Rental of party supplies for catered affairs	9.36
291.	Hair accessories	9.33
292.	Live entertainment for catered affairs	9.18
293.	Infants' furniture	9.09
294.	Whiskey at home	8.64
295.	China and other dinnerware	8.56
296.	Vacation clubs	8.16
297.	Dried fruits	8.08
298.	Rental of recreational vehicles	8.00
299.	Driver's license	7.52
300.	Coal, wood, and other fuels	7.18
301.	Shopping club membership fees	7.09
302.	Margarine	7.04

303.	Repair of computer systems for nonbusiness use	$6.99
304.	Sewing patterns and notions	6.77
305.	Repairs and rentals of lawn and garden equipment, hand and power tools, etc.	6.69
306.	Material for making clothes	6.65
307.	Kitchen and dining room linens	6.63
308.	Sewing machines	6.25
309.	Apparel alteration, repair, and tailoring services	6.24
310.	Frozen fruit juices	6.12
311.	Towing charges	5.97
312.	Artificial sweeteners	5.83
313.	Playground equipment	5.38
314.	Flour	5.14
315.	Voice over IP	5.12
316.	Window air conditioners	5.06
317.	Frozen fruits	4.97
318.	Reupholstering and furniture repair	4.80
319.	Film	4.69
320.	Water-softening service	4.49
321.	Water sports equipment	4.49
322.	Medical equipment for general use	4.45
323.	Docking and landing fees	4.42
324.	Repair of TV, radio, and sound equipment	4.26
325.	Bread and cracker products	4.10
326.	Flatware	4.06
327.	Winter sports equipment	4.06
328.	Stamp and coin collecting	4.02
329.	Rental of furniture	3.99
330.	Personal digital assistants	3.68
331.	Streamed and downloaded audio	3.68
332.	Watch and jewelry repair	3.65
333.	Safe deposit box rental	3.42
334.	Slipcovers and decorative pillows	3.39
335.	Tape recorders and players	3.38
336.	Nonclothing laundry and dry cleaning, coin-operated	3.26
337.	Supportive and convalescent medical equipment	3.18
338.	Septic tank cleaning	3.08
339.	Deductions for railroad retirement	2.93
340.	Delivery services	2.88
341.	Radios	2.74
342.	Termite and pest control products	2.55
343.	Miscellaneous sound equipment	2.54
344.	Plastic dinnerware	2.48
345.	Fireworks	2.44
346.	Internet services away from home	2.43
347.	Rental and repair of miscellaneous sports equipment	2.43
348.	Business equipment for home use	2.26
349.	Global positioning services	2.24
350.	Clothing rental	2.15
351.	Wigs and hairpieces	2.10
352.	Smoke alarms	2.09
353.	Credit card memberships	1.66
354.	Online gaming services	1.55
355.	Shoe repair and other shoe services	1.43
356.	Rental of medical equipment	1.43
357.	Other serving pieces	1.42
358.	Appliance rental	1.33
359.	Rental and repair of musical instruments	1.29
360.	Smoking accessories	1.21
361.	Nonclothing laundry and dry cleaning, sent out	1.05
362.	Pinball, electronic video games	1.04
363.	Streamed and downloaded video	1.03
364.	School bus	1.01

365.	Satellite dishes	$0.98
366.	Installation of television sets	0.98
367.	Rental of television sets	0.72
368.	Clothing storage	0.70
369.	Rental of supportive and convalescent medical equipment	0.68
370.	Repair and rental of photographic equipment	0.63
371.	Telephone answering devices	0.59
372.	Portable dishwashers	0.57
373.	Books and supplies for vocational and technical schools	0.56
374.	Rental of office equipment for nonbusiness use	0.44
375.	Installation of computer	0.41
376.	Books and supplies for day care and nursery	0.41
377.	Dating services	0.40
378.	Rental of VCR, radio, and sound equipment	0.31
379.	Rental of computer and video game hardware and software	0.05

Source: Calculations by New Strategist based on the 2007 Consumer Expenditure Survey

Glossary

age The age of the reference person.

alcoholic beverages Includes beer and ale, wine, whiskey, gin, vodka, rum, and other alcoholic beverages.

annual spending The annual amount spent per household. The Bureau of Labor Statistics calculates the annual average for all households in a segment, not just for those that purchased an item. The averages are calculated by integrating the results of the diary (weekly) and interview (quarterly) portions of the Consumer Expenditure Survey. For items purchased by most households—such as bread—average annual spending figures are a fairly accurate account of actual spending. For products and services purchased by few households during a year's time—such as cars—the average annual amount spent is much less than what purchasers spend.

apparel, accessories, and related services Includes the following:

• *men's and boys' apparel* Includes coats, jackets, sweaters, vests, sport coats, tailored jackets, slacks, shorts and short sets, sportswear, shirts, underwear, nightwear, hosiery, uniforms, and other accessories.

• *women's and girls' apparel* Includes coats, jackets, furs, sport coats, tailored jackets, sweaters, vests, blouses, shirts, dresses, dungarees, culottes, slacks, shorts, sportswear, underwear, nightwear, uniforms, hosiery, and other accessories.

• *infants' apparel* Includes coats, jackets, snowsuits, underwear, diapers, dresses, crawlers, sleeping garments, hosiery, footwear, and other accessories for children.

• *footwear* Includes articles such as shoes, slippers, boots, and other similar items. It excludes footwear for babies and footwear used for sports such as bowling or golf shoes.

• *other apparel products and services* Includes material for making clothes, shoe repair, alterations and sewing patterns and notions, clothing rental, clothing storage, dry cleaning, sent-out laundry, watches, jewelry, and repairs to watches and jewelry.

baby boom Americans born between 1946 and 1964.

cash contributions Includes cash contributed to persons or organizations outside the consumer unit including court-ordered alimony, child support payments, and support for college students, and contributions to religious, educational, charitable, or political organizations.

consumer unit (1) All members of a household who are related by blood, marriage, adoption, or other legal arrangements; (2) a person living alone or sharing a household with others or living as a roomer in a private home or lodging house or in permanent living quarters in a hotel or motel, but who is financially independent; or (3) two or more persons living together who pool their income to make joint expenditure decisions. Financial independence is determined by the three major expense categories: housing, food, and other living expenses. To be considered financially independent, at least two of the three major expense categories have to be provided by the respondent. For convenience, called household in the text of this report.

consumer unit, composition of The classification of interview households by type according to (1) relationship of other household members to the reference person; (2) age of the children of the reference person; and (3) combination of relationship to the reference person and age of the children. Stepchildren and adopted children are included with the reference person's own children.

earner A consumer unit member aged 14 or older who worked at least one week during the twelve months prior to the interview date.

education Includes tuition, fees, books, supplies, and equipment for public and private nursery schools, elementary and high schools, colleges and universities, and other schools.

entertainment Includes the following:

• *fees and admissions* Includes fees for participant sports; admissions to sporting events, movies, concerts, plays; health, swimming, tennis, and country club memberships, and other social recreational and fraternal organizations; recreational lessons or instructions; and recreational expenses on trips.

• *audio and visual equipment and services* Includes television sets; radios; cable TV; tape recorders and players; video cassettes, tapes, and discs; video cassette recorders and video disc players; video game hardware and software; personal digital audio players; streaming and downloading audio and video; sound components; CDs, records, and tapes; musical instruments; and rental and repair of TV and sound equipment.

• *pets, toys, hobbies, and playground equipment* Includes pet food, pet services, veterinary expenses, toys, games, hobbies, and playground equipment.

• *other entertainment equipment and services* Includes indoor exercise equipment, athletic shoes, bicycles, trailers, campers, camping equipment, rental of cameras and trailers, hunting and fishing equipment, sports equipment, winter sports equipment, water sports equipment, boats, boat motors and boat trailers, rental of boats, landing and docking fees, rental and repair of sports equipment, photographic equipment, film, photo processing, photographer fees, repair and rental of photo equipment, fireworks, pinball and electronic video games.

expenditure The transaction cost including excise and sales taxes of goods and services acquired during the survey period. The full cost of each purchase is recorded even though full payment may not have been made at the date of purchase. Expenditure estimates include gifts. Excluded from expenditures are purchases or portions of purchases directly assignable to business purposes and periodic credit or installment payments on goods and services already acquired.

federal income tax Includes federal income tax withheld in the survey year to pay for income earned in survey year plus additional tax paid in survey year to cover any underpayment or underwithholding of tax in the year prior to the survey.

financial products and services Includes accounting fees, legal fees, union dues, professional dues and fees, other occupational expenses, funerals, cemetery lots, dating services, shopping club memberships, and unclassified fees and personal services.

food Includes the following:

• *food at home* Refers to the total expenditures for food at grocery stores or other food stores during the interview period. It is calculated by multiplying the number of visits to a grocery or other food store by the average amount spent per visit. It excludes the purchase of nonfood items.

• *food away from home* Includes all meals (breakfast, lunch, brunch, and dinner) at restaurants, carry-outs, and vending machines, including tips, plus meals as pay, special catered affairs such as weddings, bar mitzvahs, and confirmations, and meals away from home on trips.

generation X Americans born between 1965 and 1976; also known as the baby-bust generation.

gifts for people in other households Includes gift expenditures for people living in other consumer units. The amount spent on gifts is also included in individual product and service categories.

health care Includes the following:

• *health insurance* Includes health maintenance plans (HMOs), Blue Cross/Blue Shield, commercial health insurance, Medicare, Medicare supplemental insurance, long-term care insurance, and other health insurance.

• *medical services* Includes hospital room and services, physicians' services, services of a practitioner other than a physician, eye and dental care, lab tests, X-rays, nursing, therapy services, care in convalescent or nursing home, and other medical care.

• *drugs* Includes prescription and nonprescription drugs, internal and respiratory over-the-counter drugs.

• *medical supplies* Includes eyeglasses and contact lenses, topicals and dressings, antiseptics, bandages, cotton, first aid kits, contraceptives; medical equipment for general use such as syringes, ice bags, thermometers, vaporizers, heating pads; supportive or convalescent medical equipment such as hearing aids, braces, canes, crutches, and walkers.

Hispanic origin The self-identified Hispanic origin of the consumer unit reference person. All consumer units are included in one of two Hispanic origin groups based on the reference person's Hispanic origin: Hispanic or non-Hispanic. Hispanics may be of any race.

household According to the Census Bureau, all the people who occupy a household. A group of unrelated people who share a housing unit as roommates or unmarried partners is also counted as a household. Households do not include group quarters such as college dormitories, prisons, or nursing homes. A household may contain more than one consumer unit. The terms household and consumer unit are used interchangeably in this report.

household furnishings and equipment Includes the following:

• *household textiles* Includes bathroom, kitchen, dining room, and other linens, curtains and drapes, slipcovers and decorative pillows, and sewing materials.

• *furniture* Includes living room, dining room, kitchen, bedroom, nursery, porch, lawn, and other outdoor furniture.

• *carpet, rugs, and other floor coverings* Includes installation and replacement of wall-to-wall carpets, room-size rugs, and other soft floor coverings.

• *major appliances* Includes refrigerators, freezers, dishwashers, stoves, ovens, garbage disposals, vacuum cleaners, microwave ovens, air-conditioners, sewing machines, washing machines, clothes dryers, and floor-cleaning equipment.

• *small appliances and miscellaneous housewares* Includes small electrical kitchen appliances, portable heating and cooling equipment, china and other dinnerware, flatware, glassware, silver and other serving pieces, nonelectric cookware, and plastic dinnerware. Excludes personal care appliances.

• *miscellaneous household equipment* Includes computer hardware and software, luggage, lamps and other lighting fixtures, window coverings, clocks, lawn mowers and gardening equipment, hand and power tools, telephone answering devices, personal digital assistants, Internet services away from home, office equipment for home use, fresh flowers and house plants, rental of furniture, closet and storage items, household decorative items, infants' equipment, outdoor equipment, smoke alarms, other household appliances, and small miscellaneous furnishing.

household services Includes the following:

• *personal services* Includes baby sitting, day care, and care of elderly and handicapped persons.

• *other household services* Includes computer information services; housekeeping services; gardening and lawn care services; coin-operated laundry and dry-cleaning of household textiles; termite and pest control products; moving, storage, and freight expenses; repair of household appliances and other household equipment; reupholstering and furniture repair; rental and repair of lawn and gardening tools; and rental of other household equipment.

housekeeping supplies Includes soaps, detergents, other laundry cleaning products, cleansing and toilet tissue, paper towels, napkins, and miscellaneous household products; lawn and garden supplies, postage, stationery, stationery supplies, and gift wrap.

housing tenure Owner includes households living in their own homes, cooperatives, condominiums, or townhouses. Renter includes households paying rent as well as families living rent free in lieu of wages.

income before taxes The total money earnings and selected money receipts accruing to a consumer unit during the 12 months prior to the interview date. Income includes the following components:

• *wages and salaries* Includes total money earnings for all members of the consumer unit aged 14 or older from all jobs, including civilian wages and salaries, Armed Forces pay and allowances, piece-rate payments, commissions, tips, National Guard or Reserve pay (received for training periods), and cash bonuses before deductions for taxes, pensions, union dues, etc.

• *self-employment income* Includes net business and farm income, which consists of net income (gross receipts minus operating expenses) from a profession or unincorporated business or from the operation of a farm by an owner, tenant, or sharecropper. If the business or farm is a partnership, only an appropriate share of net income is recorded. Losses are also recorded.

• *Social Security, private and government retirement* Includes payments by the federal government made under retirement, survivor, and disability insurance programs to retired persons, dependents of deceased insured workers, or to disabled workers; and private pensions or retirement benefits received by retired persons or their survivors, either directly or through an insurance company.

• *interest, dividends, rental income, and other property income* Includes interest income on savings or bonds; payments made by a corporation to its stockholders, periodic receipts from estates or trust funds; net income or loss from the rental of property, real estate, or farms, and net income or loss from roomers or boarders.

• *unemployment and workers' compensation and veterans' benefits* Includes income from unemployment compensation and workers' compensation, and veterans' payments including educational benefits, but excluding military retirement.

• *public assistance, supplemental security income, and food stamps* Includes public assistance or welfare, including money received from job training grants; supplemental security income paid by federal, state, and local welfare agencies to low-income persons who are aged 65 or older, blind, or disabled; and the value of food stamps obtained.

• *regular contributions for support* Includes alimony and child support as well as any regular contributions from persons outside the consumer unit.

• *other income* Includes money income from care of foster children, cash scholarships, fellowships, or stipends not based on working; and meals and rent as pay.

indexed spending Indexed spending figures compare the spending of particular demographic segments with that of the average household. To compute an index, the amount spent on an item by a demographic segment is divided by the amount spent on the item by the average household. That figure is then multiplied by 100. An index of 100 is the average for all households. An index of 132 means average spending by households in a segment is 32 percent above average (100 plus 32). An index of 75 means average spending by households in a segment is 25 percent below average (100 minus 25). Indexed spending figures identify the consumer units that spend the most on a product or service.

life and other personal insurance Includes premiums from whole life and term insurance; endowments; income and other life insurance; mortgage guarantee insurance; mortgage life insurance; premiums for personal life liability, accident and disability; and other non–health insurance other than homes and vehicles.

market share The market share is the percentage of total household spending on an item that is accounted for by a demographic segment. Market shares are calculated by dividing a demographic segment's total spending on an item by the total spending of all households on the item. Total spending on an item for all households is calculated by multiplying average spending by the total number of households. Total spending on an item for each demographic segment is calculated by multiplying the segment's average spending by the number of households in the segment. Market shares reveal the demographic segments that account for the largest share of spending on a product or service.

millennial generation Americans born between 1977 and 1994.

occupation The occupation in which the reference person received the most earnings during the survey period. The occupational categories follow those of the Census of Population. Categories shown in the tables include the following:

• *self-employed* Includes all occupational categories; the reference person is self-employed in own business, professional practice, or farm.

• *wage and salary earners, managers and professionals* Includes executives, administrators, managers, and professional specialties such as architects, engineers, natural and social scientists, lawyers, teachers, writers, health diagnosis and treatment workers, entertainers, and athletes.

• *wage and salary earners, technical, sales, and clerical workers* Includes technicians and related support workers; sales representatives, sales workers, cashiers, and sales-related occupations; and administrative support, including clerical.

• *retired* People who did not work either full- or part-time during the survey period.

owner *See* housing tenure.

pensions and Social Security Includes all Social Security contributions paid by employees; employees' contributions to railroad retirement, government retirement and private pensions programs; retirement programs for self-employed.

personal care Includes products for the hair, oral hygiene products, shaving needs, cosmetics, bath products, suntan lotions, hand creams, electric personal care appliances, incontinence products, other personal care products, personal care services such as hair care services (haircuts, bleaching, tinting, coloring, conditioning treatments, permanents, press, and curls), styling and other services for wigs and hairpieces, body massages or slenderizing treatments, facials, manicures, pedicures, shaves, electrolysis.

quarterly spending Quarterly spending data are collected in the interview portion of the Consumer Expenditure Survey. The quarterly spending tables show the percentage of households that purchased an item during an average quarter, and the amount spent during the quarter on the item by purchasers. Not all items are included in the interview portion of the Consumer Expenditure Survey.

reading Includes subscriptions for newspapers, magazines, and books through book clubs; purchase of single-copy newspapers and magazines, books, and encyclopedias and other reference books.

reference person The first member mentioned by the respondent when asked to Start with the name of the person or one of the persons who owns or rents the home. It is with respect to this person that the relationship of other consumer unit members is determined. Also called the householder or head of household.

region Consumer units are classified according to their address at the time of their participation in the survey. The four major census regions of the United States are the following state groupings:

• *Northeast* Connecticut, Maine, Massachusetts, New Hampshire, New Jersey, New York, Pennsylvania, Rhode Island, and Vermont.

• *Midwest* Illinois, Indiana, Iowa, Kansas, Michigan, Minnesota, Mississippi, Nebraska, North Dakota, Ohio, South Dakota, and Wisconsin.

• *South* Alabama, Arkansas, Delaware, District of Columbia, Florida, Georgia, Kentucky, Louisiana, Maryland, Mississippi, North Carolina, Oklahoma, South Carolina, Tennessee, Texas, Virginia, and West Virginia.

• *West* Alaska, Arizona, California, Colorado, Hawaii, Idaho, Minnesota, Nevada, New Mexico, Oregon, Utah, Washington, and Wyoming.

renter *See* housing tenure.

shelter Includes the following:

• *owned dwellings* Includes interest on mortgages, property taxes and insurance, refinancing and prepayment charges, ground rent, expenses for property management and security, homeowner's insurance, fire insurance and extended coverage, landscaping expenses for repairs and maintenance contracted out (including periodic maintenance and service contracts), and expenses of materials for owner-performed repairs and maintenance for dwellings used or maintained by the consumer unit, but not dwellings maintained for business or rent.

• *rented dwellings* Includes rent paid for dwellings, rent received as pay, parking fees, maintenance, and other expenses.

• *other lodging* Includes all expenses for vacation homes, school, college, hotels, motels, cottages, trailer camps, and other lodging while out of town.

• *utilities, fuels, and public services* Includes natural gas, electricity, fuel oil, coal, bottled gas, wood, other fuels; residential telephone service, cell phone service, phone cards; water, garbage, trash collection; sewerage maintenance, septic tank cleaning; and other public services.

size of consumer unit The number of people whose usual place of residence at the time of the interview is in the consumer unit.

state and local income taxes Includes state and local income taxes withheld in the survey year to pay for income earned in survey year plus additional taxes paid in the survey year to cover any underpayment or underwithholding of taxes in the year prior to the survey.

tobacco and smoking supplies Includes cigarettes, cigars, snuff, loose smoking tobacco, chewing tobacco, and smoking accessories such as cigarette or cigar holders, pipes, flints, lighters, pipe cleaners, and other smoking products and accessories.

transportation Includes the following:

• *vehicle purchases (net outlay)* Includes the net outlay (purchase price minus trade-in value) on new and used domestic and imported cars and trucks and other vehicles, including motorcycles and private planes.

• *gasoline and motor oil* Includes gasoline, diesel fuel, and motor oil.

• *other vehicle expenses* Includes vehicle finance charges, maintenance and repairs, vehicle insurance, and vehicle rental licenses and other charges.

• *vehicle finance charges* Includes the dollar amount of interest paid for a loan contracted for the purchase of vehicles described above.

• *maintenance and repairs* Includes tires, batteries, tubes, lubrication, filters, coolant, additives, brake and transmission fluids, oil change, brake adjustment and repair, front-end alignment, wheel balancing, steering repair, shock absorber replacement, clutch and transmission repair, electrical system repair, repair to cooling system, drive train repair, drive shaft and rear-end repair, tire repair, vehicle video equipment, other maintenance and services, and auto repair policies.

• *vehicle insurance* Includes the premium paid for insuring cars, trucks, and other vehicles.

• *vehicle rental, licenses, and other charges* Includes leased and rented cars, trucks, motorcycles, and aircraft, inspection fees, state and local registration, drivers' license fees, parking fees, towing charges, tolls on trips, and global positioning services.

• *public transportation* Includes fares for mass transit, buses, trains, airlines, taxis, private school buses, and fares paid on trips for trains, boats, taxis, buses, and trains.

weekly spending Weekly spending data are collected in the diary portion of the Consumer Expenditure Survey. The data show the percentage of households that purchased an item during the average week, and the amount spent per week on the item by purchasers. Not all items are included in the diary portion of the Consumer Expenditure Survey.